D0779925

# Korean

## PHRASEBOOK & DICTIONARY

## Acknowledgments

**Editors** Joanne Newell, Jodie Martire, Kristin Odijk, Branislava Vladisavljevi
**Series Designer** Mark Adams
**Layout Designers** Carol Jackson, Joseph Spanti
**Language Writers** Minkyoung Kim, Jonathan Hilts-Park

## Thanks

Grace Dobell, Chris Love

## Published by Lonely Planet Publications Pty Ltd

ABN 36 005 607 983

6th Edition – May 2016
ISBN 978 1 74321 4466
Text © Lonely Planet 2016
**Cover Image** The Lotus Lantern Festival in Seoul, South Korea
Jane Sweeney/AWL ©

Printed in China   10 9 8 7 6 5 4 3 2

## Contact lonelyplanet.com/contact

**HOW TO USE THIS BOOK**

## Look out for the following icons throughout the book:

 **'Shortcut' Phrase**
Easy to remember alternative to the full phrase

 **Q&A Pair**
'Question-and-answer' pair – we suggest a response to the question asked

 **Look For**
Phrases you may see on signs, menus etc

 **Listen For**
Phrases you may hear from officials, locals etc

 **Language Tip**
An insight into the foreign language

 **Culture Tip**
An insight into the local culture

---

#### How to read the phrases:
- Coloured words and phrases throughout the book are phonetic guides to help you pronounce the foreign language.
- Lists of phrases with tinted background are options you can choose to complete the phrase above them.

---

#### These abbreviations will help you choose the right words and phrases in this book:

| | | | | | |
|---|---|---|---|---|---|
| **a** | adjective | **n** | noun | **pron** | pronoun |
| **adv** | adverb | **pl** | plural | **sg** | singular |
| **inf** | informal | **pol** | polite | **v** | verb |
| **lit** | literal | **prep** | preposition | | |

# Contents

    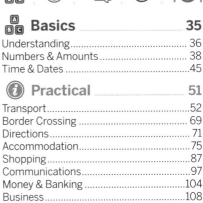

**PAGE 212**

## Menu Decoder
Dishes and ingredients explained –
order with confidence and try new foods.

**PAGE 221**

## Two-Way Dictionary
Quick reference vocabulary guide –
3500 words to help you communicate.

# Korean

한국어 han·gu·gŏ

## Who Speaks Korean?

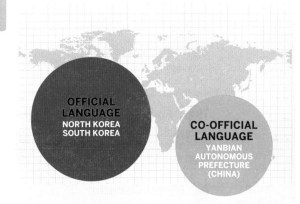

**OFFICIAL LANGUAGE**
NORTH KOREA
SOUTH KOREA

**CO-OFFICIAL LANGUAGE**
YANBIAN AUTONOMOUS PREFECTURE (CHINA)

### Why Bother

To understand what makes Koreans tick, you should know something about harmony and hierarchy, highly valued principles that draw on Confucian ideals. Start with the language: the Korean greeting an·nyŏng ha·se·yo 안녕하세요? (How are you?) is literally translated as 'Are you peaceful?'.

### Distinctive Sounds

Korean distinguishes between 'aspirated' consonants (pronounced with a puff of air) and 'unaspirated' ones.

**70 MILLION**
speak Korean as their
first language

**10 MILLION**
speak Korean as their
second language

## Korean Script

Korean script, Hangul, is simple and accessible. Each character represents a sound of its own. The emphasis is on the formation of syllables: eg 한 (the syllable han) is formed by an h (ㅎ), an a (ㅏ) and an n (ㄴ) in a syllabic 'box'. These 'boxes' are strung together to form words.

## Korean Lexicon

Two sets of numbers are used: 'pure' Korean and 'Sino-Korean' (Korean pronunciation of words of Chinese origin). Each system has cardinal and ordinal numbers, but each is used for counting different types of things. Koreans will be forgiving if you mix them up!

## Borrowings from English

Korean has borrowed many words from English, often combining them in a way that makes sense to Korean ears – eg won-num 원룸, from 'one room', is a studio apartment.

## Language Family

Ural-Altaic – Manchu and Mongolian are listed as close relatives, though many scholars consider Korean a 'language isolate'.

## Must-Know Grammar

Pronouns are generally not used in Korean. Instead, people are referred to by their name, title or relationship to the speaker. This book uses the so-called 'familiar polite form', a practical middle ground suitable for most situations.

## Donations to English

Not many – you may recognise *kimchi* or *taekwondo*.

## 5 Phrases to Learn Before You Go

 **Do you have a Western-style room?**
서양식 방 있나요? sŏ·yang·shik pang in·na·yo

Smaller lodgings may only have Korean-style rooms (with floor mattresses). If you want a 'proper' bed, check ahead.

 **Please bring a fork/knife.**
포크/나이프 가져다 주세요. p'o·k'ŭ/na·i·p'ŭ ka·jŏ·da ju·se·yo

In Korean restaurants the spoon is meant for rice and soup, and chopsticks are for everything else; ask if you need other utensils.

 **Can you make it less spicy?**
덜 맵게 해 주시겠어요? tŏl maep·ké hae·ju·shi·gess·ŏ·yo

Korean food is an enthusiastic assault on the senses, often spicy enough to trigger off sweat or tears – you may want to play it safe.

 **Where can I find a steam-room?**
찜질방 어디에 있나요? jjim·jil·bang ŏ·di·é in·na·yo

Generally open 24 hours, these facilities at public baths are perfect when you need some down time – whether to watch TV, read, just relax or even sleep overnight.

 **Please call the tourist interpreting service.**
통역 서비스에 전화해 주세요.
t'ong·yŏk sŏ·bi·sŭ·é chŏn·hwa·hae·ju·se·yo

To ensure that you get to the right place, Korean taxi drivers have a number to call to hook you up with someone who will translate directions for you.

# **10 Phrases** to Sound Like a Local

| **Hey!** | 여기요! | yŏ·gi·yo |
| **Great!** | 좋아요! | cho·a·yo |
| **Sure!** | 물론이죠! | mul·lo·ni·jo |
| **Maybe.** | 아마도요. | a·ma·do·yo |
| **No way!** | 안 돼요! | an·dwae·yo |
| **Just a minute.** | 잠시만요. | cham·shi·man·nyo |
| **Just joking.** | 농담이에요. | nong·da·mi·e·yo |
| **Never mind.** | 괜찮아요. | kwaen·cha·na·yo |
| **No problem.** | 문제 없어요. | mun·jé ŏp·sŏ·yo |
| **OK!** | 그렇게 해요. | kŭ·rŏ·k'é hae·yo |

**ABOUT** KOREAN

# Pronunciation

Korean pronunciation should be pretty straightforward for English speakers, as most sounds are also found in English or have a close approximation. If you follow the coloured pronunciation guides we provide, you'll be able to produce the correct sounds, or at least come very close.

There are a number of competing Romanisation systems in use today for Hangul (the Korean script), and opinions differ greatly on which system is best suited to represent it. One of the most widely used is the McCune-Reischauer system (M–R), developed in the 1930s by two academics in Korea – George McCune and Edwin Reischauer.

In late 2000, however, a South Korean government agency unilaterally decreed that M–R would henceforth be scrapped in favour of a 'new' system (which is actually based on an older system) – the Revised Romanisation. The government has been changing road signs to reflect the 'new' Romanisation system, so you may encounter signs, maps and tourist literature with at least two different Romanisation systems. North Korea, however, officially tends to use a form of M–R.

In this book we've used a Romanisation system closely modelled on the South Korean government's pre-2000 version of M–R. It's been our experience that this system is easy for Korean-language newbies to use for pronouncing Korean words.

## Vowel Sounds

Korean has six basic vowels, all of which are found in English. The difference between the two 'combination vowels' (ae and e) is very subtle, and younger Koreans often don't make the distinction in their speech.

| LETTER | SYMBOL | ENGLISH SOUND | KOREAN EXAMPLE | TRANSLITERATION |
|--------|--------|---------------|----------------|-----------------|
| ㅏ | a | father | 가수 | ka·su |
| ㅐ | ae | bag | 배우 | pae·u |
| ㅔ | e/é | net | 게시판 | ke·shi·p'an |
| ㅣ | i | keen | 시작 | shi·jak |
| ㅗ | o | go | 오빠 | op·pa |
| ㅓ | ŏ | son | 서울 | sŏ·ul |
| ㅚ | oé | as in 'no entry' | 외삼촌 | oé·sam·ch'on |
| ㅜ | u | nude | 우리 | u·ri |
| ㅡ | ŭ | put | 그림 | kŭ·rim |
| ㅢ | ŭi | as in 'chop suey' | 의사 | ŭi·sa |
| ㅘ | wa | wander | 과일 | kwa·il |
| ㅙ | wae | wag | 쾌락 | k'wae·rak |
| ㅞ | we | wet | 궤도 | kwe·do |
| ㅟ | wi | week | 귀신 | kwi·shin |
| ㅝ | wŏ | wonder | 원숭이 | wŏn·sung·i |
| ㅑ | ya | yahoo | 야구 | ya·gu |
| ㅒ | yae | yank | 얘기 | yae·gi |
| ㅖ | ye | yet | 예절 | ye·jŏl |
| ㅛ | yo | yogurt | 효도 | hyo·do |
| ㅕ | yŏ | young | 여행 | yŏ·haeng |
| ㅠ | yu | you | 유학 | yu·hak |

Note that when e appears at the end of a syllable we've used the symbol é to avoid mispronunciation.

The two other 'combination vowels' (oé and ŭi) are usually pronounced as two separate syllables. The first part is briefer than when it's an independent simple vowel, so that it almost sounds like a 'w'. When ŭi is preceded by a consonant, the ŭ is dropped, and only i is pronounced – eg 희망 hi·mang, not hŭi·mang (hope/desire).

Note also that when certain vowels are preceded by o or u, they're pronounced with a w sound (like the 'w' in 'water') and that a y sound (like the 'y' in 'yellow') can be added to some vowels. In the Hangul script, this is represented by a second hash mark.

## Word Stress

Syllables are pronounced with fairly even emphasis in Korean, so we haven't indicated stressed syllables in this book.

## Consonant Sounds

Most Korean consonant sounds are pretty close to their English counterparts. However, many consonants are pronounced differently depending on their position within a word, or on the letters adjacent to them. You don't have to worry about these rules, though, as our pronunciation guides throughout this book give the correct pronunciation in the context of each phrase. If you'd like to learn more about forming syllables and sound changes in Korean, see **making syllables** and **consonant sound changes** (p14).

Korean distinguishes between aspirated consonants (formed by making a puff of air as they're pronounced) and unaspirated ones (pronounced without a puff of air). When Romanised, aspirated consonants (except for s and h) are immediately followed by an apostrophe. Note, as shown in the following table, that s is pronounced sh when followed by the vowel i.

| LETTER | SYMBOL | ENGLISH SOUND | KOREAN EXAMPLE | TRANSLITERATION |
|--------|--------|---------------|----------------|-----------------|
| ㅂ | h | hed | 바부 | pa·bo |
| ㅈ | ch | change | 지도 | chi·do |
| ㅊ | ch' | change (aspirated) | 치마 | ch'i·ma |
| ㄷ | d | dog | 어디 | ŏ·di |
| ㄱ | g | go | 고구마 | ko·gu·ma |
| ㅎ | h | happy (aspirated) | 학교 | hak·kyo |
| ㅈ | j | joke | 자전거 | cha·jŏn·gŏ |
| ㄱ | k | king | 감자 | kam·ja |
| ㅋ | k' | king (aspirated) | 콩나물 | k'ong·na·mul |
| ㄹ | l | lot | 몰라요 | mol·la·yo |
| ㅁ | m | marry | 마음 | ma·ŭm |
| ㄴ | n | nature | 나눔 | na·num |
| ㅇ | ng | ring | 은행 | ŭn·haeng |
| ㅂ | p | petal | 바다 | pa·da |
| ㅍ | p' | petal (aspirated) | 포도 | p'o·do |
| ㄹ | r | red | 알아요 | a·ra·yo |
| ㅅ | s | sad (aspirated) | 선생님 | sŏn·saeng·nim |
| ㅅ | sh | shot | 심리학 | shim·ni·hak |
| ㄷ | t | talk | 다리 | ta·ri |
| ㅌ | t' | talk (aspirated) | 탈춤 | t'al·ch'um |
| * | w | win | 위치 | wi·ch'i |
| * | y | yes | 예약 | ye·yak |

\* See the alphabet table on page 17 for all the vowels making up w and y.

Making Syllables

In Korean, a syllable always consists of at least one vowel preceded by a consonant. Some syllables also have a consonant following the vowel. All basic vowels are either vertical ( ㅏ, ㅑ, ㅓ, ㅕ and ㅣ) or horizontal (ㅗ, ㅛ, ㅜ, ㅠ and ㅡ). Combination vowels are vertical or horizontal, depending on the leftmost vowel of the combination. Vertical combination vowels are ㅐ ae, ㅔ e/é, ㅒ yae and ㅖ ye, and horizontal combination vowels are ㅚ oé, ㅢ ŭi, ㅘ wa, ㅙ wae, ㅞ we, ㅟ wi and ㅝ wŏ.

The initial position of a consonant is always to the left of a vertical vowel or above a horizontal vowel, as in ㅁ m, 마 ma, 모 mo, 미 mi, 무 mu, 매 mae or 뭐 mwŏ. Consonants following the vowel always go below the vowel, whether it's vertical or horizontal – eg 몸 mom and 맘 mam. Consonants preceding or following vertical or horizontal combination vowels follow the same positioning rules.

You might notice that the spaces between words in our coloured pronunciation guides don't always match the spacing in the Korean script. That's because the official rules for writing Korean are sometimes quite different from how words are coupled or divided in speech. Our pronunciation guides show you how to say the words in order to sound as natural as possible and be understood.

Consonant Sound Changes

**Aspirated & Unaspirated Consonants**

The unaspirated consonants are pronounced differently depending on their position within a word, as shown below:

| LETTER | INITIAL SOUND | MIDDLE SOUND | FINAL SOUND |
|---|---|---|---|
| ㄱ | k- | -g- | -k |
| ㄷ | t- | -d- | -t |
| ㅂ | p- | -b- | -p |
| ㅈ | ch- | -j- | -t |
| ㄹ | r/l- | -r- | -l |

The -l at the end of a syllable or word sounds like a cross between an English 'l' and 'rl' in 'girl' or 'curl'. An unaspirated consonant, when preceded by h ㅎ as the final consonant of the previous syllable, becomes aspirated – compare 안다 an·da (to hug/embrace) and 않다 an·t'a (to not do something).

## Double Consonants

Four unaspirated consonants (ㄱ, ㄷ, ㅂ, ㅈ) can be used to make double consonants. At the start of a word, they're pronounced more quickly and forcefully than their corresponding letters in English. As a general rule, in the middle of a word they're pronounced twice and are separated with a dot (eg k·k, p·p, t·t) in our pronunciation guides to indicate this.

The sound s (ㅅ) is the fifth consonant that can be turned into a double consonant, but represents a 'stronger' sound, rather than a sound pronounced twice. Therefore it's usually not separated with a dot (ie ss) in our pronunciation guides – with some exceptions, when it should actually be said twice (ie s·s). Similarly, two r (ㄹ) sounds representing the final consonant of one syllable and the first consonant of the following syllable are pronounced as l, eg mo·rae 모래 (sand), with one ㄹ, and mol·lae 몰래 (secretly), with two ㄹ. The double consonants are also pronounced differently depending on their position within a word:

| LETTER | INITIAL SOUND | MIDDLE SOUND | FINAL SOUND |
|--------|---------------|--------------|-------------|
| ㄲ | gg- | -kk- | -k |
| ㄸ | dd- | -tt- | – |
| ㅃ | bb- | -pp- | – |
| ㅆ | ss- | -ss- | -t |
| ㅉ | jj- | -tch- | – |

## The 'Vowel Consonant'

The 'vowel consonant' ㅇ can be silent or pronounced, depending on its position within a syllable. At the beginning of a syllable it's silent (it serves as a place holder for a consonant in syllables that begin with a vowel sound). However, at the end of a syllable it's pronounced ng. Thus the two ㅇ characters found in the syllable 앙 ang, as in chung-ang 중앙 (central), sound completely different: the first one is silent, but the second one is pronounced ng.

If the 'vowel consonant' is immediately preceded by a consonant, the pronunciation of that consonant sound is 'moved' to the position of the 'vowel consonant'. For example, 작아요 (it's small), looks like it should be pronounced chag-a-yo, but it is actually pronounced cha-ga-yo.

### Final Sound Changes

Five consonants are pronounced like a t sound when they're at the end of a word: ㅊ ch', ㅈ ch/j, ㅅ s, ㅌ t' and ㄷ t/d.

### Complex Consonants

There are 11 complex consonants, composed of two regular consonants. These are always at the end of a syllable. Their pronunciation depends on whether the following syllable starts with a vowel or not. Most of these complex consonants aren't common, so we won't go into them here.

### Other Consonant Changes

While the pronunciation of a consonant changes according to its position within a word, it can also change depending on the consonant that immediately precedes or follows it. These sound changes are mostly the result of the tongue's position in the mouth. They occur especially when k/g ㄱ, p/b ㅂ and t/d ㄷ are followed by r/l ㄹ, n ㄴ or m ㅁ.

For example, if it's hard to pronounce the sound k followed by the sound m, the k will change to a sound that's closer to the m and easier to pronounce in conjunction with the m, eg 중국말 chung-guk + mal ('Chinese language', lit: China + talk). The k/g ㄱ followed by m ㅁ changes into ng + m, with the result being chung-gung-mal. Here are some more examples:

| WORD | APPARENT PRONUNCIATION | ACTUAL PRONUNCIATION |
|---|---|---|
| 입니다 (am/is/are pol) | ib-ni-da | im-ni-da |
| 있는 (being/having) | it-nŭn | in-nŭn |

# The Hangul Alphabet

Each of the letters of Hangul (the Korean alphabet) represents a
distinct sound. Ten of the letters represent vowel sounds and 14
represent consonant sounds. As the vowel sounds table on page
11 shows, there are also 11 symbols representing the combination
vowels formed from the original basic vowels. Add to that the
symbols for the five double consonants, and you have an alphabet of 40 characters which is quite simple to learn. There are a
further 11 letters for combined consonant sounds, but they follow
the simple rules of the basic 14 consonants. The alphabet is given
below, with the name of each letter.

~ KOREAN ALPHABET ~

| | CONSONANTS | | | | |
|---|---|---|---|---|---|
| ㄱ | ki·yŏk | ㅂ | pi·ŭp | ㅊ | ch'i·ŭt |
| ㄲ | ssang·gi·yŏk | ㅃ | ssang·bi·ŭp | ㅋ | k'i·ŭk |
| ㄴ | ni·ŭn | ㅅ | shi·ot | ㅌ | t'i·ŭt |
| ㄷ | ti·gŭt | ㅆ | ssang·shi·ot | ㅍ | p'i·ŭp |
| ㄸ | ssang·di·gŭt | ㅇ | i·ŭng | ㅎ | hi·ŭt |
| ㄹ | ri·ŭl | ㅈ | chi·ŭt | | |
| ㅁ | mi·ŭm | ㅉ | ssang·ji·ŭt | | |

| | VOWELS | | | | |
|---|---|---|---|---|---|
| ㅏ | a | ㅖ | yé | ㅝ | wŏ |
| ㅐ | ae | ㅗ | o | ㅞ | wé |
| ㅑ | ya | ㅘ | wa | ㅟ | wi |
| ㅒ | yae | ㅙ | wae | ㅠ | yu |
| ㅓ | ŏ | ㅚ | oé | ㅡ | ŭ |
| ㅔ | e/é | ㅛ | yo | ㅢ | ŭi |
| ㅕ | yŏ | ㅜ | u | ㅣ | i |

ABOUT KOREAN

# Grammar

This chapter is designed to explain the main grammatical structures you need in order to make your own sentences. Look under each heading – listed in alphabetical order – for information on functions which these grammatical categories express in a sentence. For example, demonstratives are used for giving instructions, so you'll need them to tell the taxi driver where your hotel is, and so on.

## Adjectives & Adverbs

Describing People/Things • Doing Things

Adjectives in Korean are very similar to verbs (see **verbs**): they change following the same rules that depend on the final vowel of the stem and usually come at the end of a sentence. When translated into English, they include the word 'be'.

| | |
|---|---|
| **(be) high** | 높~<br>nop'~ (last vowel is o) |
| **The mountain is high.** | 산이 높아요.<br>(lit: mountain-i be-high)<br>sa·ni no·p'a·yo (nop' + a·yo) |
| **(be) big** | 크~<br>k'ŭ~ (last vowel is ŭ) |

| **The park is big.** | 공원이 커요. |
| | (lit: park-i be-big) |
| | kong·wŏ·ni k'ŏ·yo |
| | (k'ŭ – ŭ + ŏ·yo) |

When an adjective comes before the noun, the ending ~ŭn ~은 (if the adjective ends in a consonant) or ~n ~ㄴ (if the adjective ends in a vowel) is added.

| **(be) high** | 높~ | |
| | nop'~ (ends in a consonant) | |
| **This is a high mountain.** | 높은 산이에요. | |
| | (lit: high mountain-be) | |
| | no·p'ŭn sa·ni·e·yo | |
| **(be) big** | 크~ | |
| | k'ŭ~ (ends in a vowel) | |
| **It's a big park.** | 큰 공원이에요. | |
| | (lit: big park-be) | |
| | k'ŭn kong·wo·ni·e·yo | |

Adverbs come before the verb they modify (see **verbs**). They're usually made by adding ~gé/~ké ~게 to the adjective stem.

| **(be) safe** | 안전하~ | an·jŏn·ha~ |
| **safely** | 안전하게 | an·jŏn·ha·gé |
| **drive safely** | 안전하게 운전 해요 | an·jŏn·ha·gé un·jŏn |
| | (lit: safely drive) | hae·yo |

# Articles

Naming People/Things

Korean doesn't have an equivalent for 'a' and 'the'. The context will tell you whether something indefinite (corresponding to English 'a') or definite (corresponding to English 'the') is being referred to. A definite thing can be specified by the use of the demonstratives 'this' and 'that' (see **demonstratives**).

# Be

Describing People/Things • Making Statements

In Korean there are several verbs that translate as 'be'. To say that something or someone exists somewhere, iss·ŏ·yo 있어요 (there is/are) or ŏp·sŏ·yo 없어요 (there isn't/aren't) are used:

| | |
|---|---|
| **There's a book.** | 책이 있어요. (lit: book-i exist) ch'ae·gi iss·ŏ·yo |
| **There aren't any books.** | 책이 없어요. (lit: book-i not-exist) ch'ae·gi ŏp·sŏ·yo |

When 'be' combines with adjectives, the various forms of 'be' are built into the adjective itself (see **adjectives**), but when you're talking about who you are, what you do or what something is, the verb to use is i·da 이다. Its polite familiar form is ~i·e·yo ~이에요 (if the preceding word ends in a consonant) or ~ye·yo ~예요 (if the preceding word ends in a vowel):

| | |
|---|---|
| **We're Australians.** | 우리는 호주사람이에요. (lit: we-nŭn Australia-people-be) u·ri·nŭn ho·ju·sa·ra·mi·e·yo |
| **This is a university.** | 대학교예요. (lit: university-be) tae·hak·kyo·ye·yo |

The negative of 'be' is a·ni·e·yo 아니에요, regardless of whether the previous word ends in a vowel or consonant.

| | |
|---|---|
| **This isn't our hotel.** | 우리 호텔이 아니에요. (lit: we hotel-i be-not) u·ri ho·t'e·ri a·ni·e·yo |

The past tense of ~i·e·yo/~ye·yo is ~이었어요 ~i·ŏss·ŏ·yo, and the past tense of a·ni·e·yo is 아니었어요 a·ni·ŏss·ŏ·yo.

## Counters/Classifiers

*Counting People/Things • Describing People/Things • Naming People/Things*

When describing how many there are of an item, you use the 'pure Korean' number (see **numbers & amounts**, p38) and a specific marker (called a 'counter' or 'classifier') for that type of thing. The word order is: noun–number–classifier. Note that the 'pure Korean' words for one, two, three and four (ha·na, tul, set, net), and higher numbers ending in one, two, three or four, are shortened when followed by another word: they become 한~ han~, 두~ tu~, 세~ se~, 네~ ne~.

For example, any flat pieces of paper, including tickets, are counted using the classifier ~jang ~장: han·jang (one ticket), tu·jang (two tickets), se·jang (three tickets) etc. When in doubt, it's acceptable for a foreigner to simply use the classifier ~gae/~kae ~개 for things in general, except for counting people. Here are other useful classifiers:

### ~ COMMON CLASSIFIERS ~

| | | |
|---|---|---|
| **people** pol | ~ 분 | ~ bun |
| **people** pol & inf | ~ 명 | ~ myŏng |
| **animals** | ~ 마리 | ~ ma·ri |
| **things in general** | ~ 개 | ~ gae/~ kae |
| **flat pieces of paper** | ~ 장 | ~ jang |
| **books/notebooks** | ~ 권 | ~ gwŏn |
| **cups/glasses** | ~ 잔 | ~ jan |
| **bottles** | ~ 병 | ~ byŏng |
| **vehicles** | ~ 대 | ~ dae |

## Demonstratives

Giving Instructions • Indicating Location • Pointing Things Out

Three prefixes are used to indicate 'this' and 'that' in Korean: i~ 이~, kŭ~ 그~ and chŏ~ 저~. The prefix i~ (this) indicates something or someone close to the speaker:

| **this photo** | 이 사진 | i·sa·jin |

The prefix kŭ~ (that) is used to indicate something or someone close to the listener, or something previously mentioned:

| **that mobile phone** | 그 핸드폰 | kŭ·haen·dŭ·p'on |

The prefix chŏ~ (that over there) indicates someone or something away from both the speaker and the listener, but still visible:

| **that restaurant over there** | 저 식당 | chŏ·shik·tang |

## Have

Possessing

To express possession in Korean, use the word iss·ŏ·yo (there is/are) for positive statements and ŏp·sŏ·yo (there isn't/aren't) for negative statements. The thing possessed is the subject of the sentence, while the possessor is the topic of the sentence (see **particles** for an explanation of these terms).

| **I have a car.** | 저는 차가 있어요. |
| | (lit: I-nŭn car-ga there-is) |
| | chŏ·nŭn ch'a·ga iss·ŏ·yo |

| | |
|---|---|
| **I don't have a house.** | 저는 집이 없어요.<br>(lit: I-nŭn house-i there-isn't)<br>chŏ nŭn chi bi ŏp ŏ yo |

See also **be** and **possessives**.

## Negatives

Negating

There are two simple ways to make a negative sentence in Korean. The difference between them is primarily a matter of preference. The first way is to precede the verb or adjective with an~ 안~, which functions as 'not':

| | | |
|---|---|---|
| **It's not spicy.** | 안 매워요.<br>(lit: not-spicy) | an·mae·wŏ·yo |
| **I'm not going.** | 안 가요.<br>(lit: not-go) | an·ga·yo |

The second way of making a negative is by adding ~ji a·na·yo to the verb stem (see **verbs**).

| | | |
|---|---|---|
| **go** | 가~ | ka~ |
| **I'm not going.** | 가지 않아요.<br>(lit: go-ji a·na·yo) | ka·ji a·na·yo |

See also **be** and **have** for the negative forms of these verbs.

## Particles

Doing Things • Giving Instructions • Indicating Location • Naming People/Things • Possessing

Korean nouns and pronouns are usually followed by a particle which shows the function of that noun or pronoun in the sentence (eg subject, direct object etc). Other particles act as prepositions (corresponding to the English 'at', 'to' etc), designating time, location, direction, destination and so on. In conversational speech, subject and direct object particles are often omitted, especially when the subject or object is clear.

Since particles are attached to the noun, they become part of the pronunciation of the noun itself. Which form of the particle is used often depends on whether the noun ends in a vowel or a consonant. In this book, for particles which have different forms, we give the form used if the noun ends in a consonant first, followed by the form used if the noun ends in a vowel.

Adding a particle may alter the pronunciation of the consonant that precedes it. (For more on consonant changes, see **pronunciation**.) Below are the most common Korean particles.

## Subject Particle

The subject particle ~i/~ga ~이/~가 (after a consonant/vowel respectively) is attached to the noun that functions as the subject of the sentence.

| **mountain(s)** | 산<br>san |
| **The mountains are beautiful.** | 산이 아름다워요.<br>(lit: mountain-i be-beautiful)<br>sa·ni a·rŭm·da·wŏ·yo |
| **I (as subject)** | 제<br>che |
| **I will do it.** | 제가 하겠어요.<br>(lit: I-ga do-will)<br>che·ga ha·gess·ŏ·yo |

## Topic Particle

The topic particle ~ŭn/~nŭn ~은/~는 (after a consonant/vowel respectively) is used to show the subject of the sentence when you want to emphasise another part of the sentence besides the subject. A topic particle can be used to mention what the sentence is about. Topic particles tend to replace subject particles, and there's a subtle difference between the two, which may be difficult for an English speaker to catch.

| **Busan** | 부산 |
| | pu·san |
| **Busan isn't cold.** | 부산은 춥지 않아요. |
| | (lit: Busan-ŭn cold-not – the emphasis is on 'not cold') |
| | pu·sa·nŭn ch'up·ji a·na·yo |
| **I** | 저 |
| | chŏ |
| **I'm a student.** | 저는 학생이에요. |
| | (lit: I-nŭn student-am – the emphasis is on 'student') |
| | chŏ·nŭn hak·saeng·i·e·yo |

**Direct Object Particle**

The direct object particle ~ŭl/~rŭl ~을/~를 (after a consonant/vowel respectively) indicates the noun or pronoun that's affected by the verb.

| **book** | 책 |
| | ch'aek |
| **My friend wants to buy a book.** | 제 친구가 책을 사고 싶어해요. |
| | (lit: my friend-ga book-ŭl buy want) |
| | ché ch'in·gu·ga ch'ae·gŭl sa·go shi·p'ŏ·hae·yo |
| **bus** | 버스 |
| | bŏ·sŭ |
| **I'm riding the bus.** | 버스를 타요. (lit: bus-rŭl ride) |
| | bŏ·sŭ·rŭl t'a·yo |

**Indirect Object Particle**

The indirect object particles ~han·t'é ~한테 and ~e·gé ~에게 are used to show to whom something is given. There's no real difference between these two particles – the choice is one of personal preference.

| | | |
|---|---|---|
| **that woman** | 그 여자 | kŭ·yŏ·ja |
| **I gave my ticket to that woman.** | 그 여자한테 표를 주었어요. (lit: that-woman-han·t'é ticket-rŭl gave) kŭ·yŏ·ja·han·t'é p'yo·rŭl ju·ŏss·ŏ·yo | |
| **child** | 어린이 | ŏ·ri·ni |
| **I gave the child a cookie.** | 어린이에게 과자를 주었어요. (lit: child-e·gé cookie-rŭl gave) ŏ·ri·ni·e·gé kwa·ja·rŭl ju·ŏss·ŏ·yo | |

## Possessive Particle

The possessive particle in Korean is spelled ~ŭi ~의, but it's almost always pronounced ~é. It's used to indicate the possessor in the sentence, while the word following it shows what's possessed.

| | | |
|---|---|---|
| **Mr Kim** | 미스터 김 | mi·sŭ·t'ŏ kim |
| **Mr Kim's car** | 미스터 김의 차 (lit: Mr Kim-é car) | mi·sŭ·t'ŏ ki·mé ch'a |
| **Japan** | 일본 | il·bon |
| **the Japanese economy** | 일본의 경제 (lit: Japan-é economy) | il·bo·né kyŏng·jé |

When the possession is clear, however, the possessive particle is often dropped. In a series of nouns, the subsequent noun (or nouns) is assumed to belong to the preceding noun. See also **possessives**.

| **our school's carpark** | 우리 학교 주차장 (lit: we school carpark) | u·ri hak·kyo chu·ch'a·jang |

Location Particle

The location particle ~é ~에 is used to indicate time, location or destination. Because of the context there's rarely any confusion about the meaning of this particle.

| **Wednesday** | 수요일 | su·yo·il |
| **on Wednesday** | 수요일에 | su·yo·i·ré (su·yo·il + é) |
| **four o'clock** | 네 시 | ne·shi |
| **at four o'clock** | 네 시에 | ne·shi·é |
| **Korea** | 한국 | han·guk |
| **in Korea** | 한국에 | han·gu·gé (han·guk + é) |
| **Seoul** | 서울 | sŏ·ul |
| **to Seoul** | 서울에 | sŏ·u·ré (sŏ·ul + é) |

# Personal Pronouns

Doing Things • Making Statements

Pronouns are generally not used in Korean, especially in the third person ('he/him', 'she/her' and 'they/them'). Instead, people are referred to by their name, their title, or especially their relationship to the speaker or listener, expressed in the form of speech. For more on this, see **meeting people** (p123).

This book presents the so-called 'familiar polite form', a practical middle ground between the high form (characterised by the verb endings ~m·ni·da ~ㅂ니다 and ~m·nik·ka ~ㅂ니까) and lower forms of speech (characterised by reduced verb endings or no verb endings at all). The high form is appropriate on first meeting someone, but would sound awkward in everyday situations. On the other hand, using the low form for people you don't know could offend them. Some commonly used pronouns are shown in the table below. They can be used for both men and women.

| ~ SINGULAR ~ | | | ~ PLURAL ~ | | |
|---|---|---|---|---|---|
| **I** inf/pol | 내/제 | nae/che | **we/us** | 우리 | u·ri |
| **me** inf/pol | 나/저 | na/chŏ | | | |
| **you** inf | 너 | nŏ | **you** inf | 너희들 | nŏ·hi·dŭl |
| **you** pol | 당신 | tang·shin | **you** pol | 여러분 | yŏ·rŏ·bun |
| **she/her** inf | 그녀 | kŭ·nyŏ | | | |
| **he/him** inf | 그 | kŭ | **they/ them** | 그들 | kŭ·dŭl |
| **she/her/ he/him** pol | 그분 | kŭ·bun | | | |

Note that the third person is usually expressed by combining the words for 'this' and 'that' with the noun (see **demonstratives**). The pronoun 'you' is often replaced by a third-person reference (ie a person's title or their name), especially when speaking to someone in a higher position.

## Plurals

Naming People/Things

Korean has a simple way of turning singular nouns into plurals by adding ~dŭl ~들, but this is usually omitted.

| **person/people** | 사람 | sa·ram |
|---|---|---|
| **people** | 사람들 | sa·ram·dŭl |

# Possessives

Possessing

Possession is generally indicated through the use of the possessive particle (see **particles**). However, special possessive adjectives for 'my' and 'your' have developed based on the possessive particle ~é.

– POSSESSIVES –

| | | | |
|---|---|---|---|
| **my** inf | 내 | nae | from:<br>na 나 (me inf) + é |
| **my** pol | 제 | ché | from:<br>chŏ 저 (me pol) + é |
| **your** inf | 네 | né | from:<br>nŏ 너 (you inf sg) + é |
| **your** pol | 당신의 | tang·shi·né | from:<br>tang·shin 당신 (you pol sg) + é |

In the case of 'your', nŏ·é 너의 (from nŏ + é) can also be used for clarity, since the pronunciation of nae (my inf) and né (your inf) are so similar. See also **have** and **personal pronouns**.

# Questions

Asking Questions

To ask about specific information, add one of the question words shown in the table on the next page just before the verb (usually towards the end of a sentence).

| | |
|---|---|
| **Where's the train station?** | 기차역이 어디예요?<br>(lit: train-station-i where-is)<br>ki·ch'a·yŏ·gi ŏ·di·ye·yo |

– QUESTION WORDS –

| | | |
|---|---|---|
| **how** | 어떻게 | ŏt·tŏ·k'é |
| **what** (as subject) inf | 뭐 | mwŏ |
| **what** (as subject) pol | 뭐가 | mwŏ·ga |
| **what** (as direct object) inf | 뭘 | mwŏl |
| **what** (as direct object) pol | 무엇을 | mu·ŏ·sŭl |
| **when** | 언제 | ŏn·jé |
| **where** | 어디 | ŏ·di |
| **which** | 어느 | ŏ·nŭ |
| **who** (as subject) | 누가 | nu·ga |
| **who** (as direct object) | 누구를 | nu·gu·rŭl |
| **why** | 왜 | wae |

In the familiar polite form of speech, there's no difference in the word order or verb ending for statements and questions – a rising tone at the end indicates a question, as it can in English.

Answering questions in Korean and in English can be somewhat different. A Korean may answer 'yes' or 'no' depending on agreement or disagreement with the question. This can be confusing when the question is negative. For example, an English speaker might answer the question 'You're not a student?' with 'no' (ie 'No, I'm not') but a Korean might answer 'yes' (ie 'Yes, that's right'). The examples of these answers are given below.

| | | |
|---|---|---|
| **yes** | 네 | né |
| **Yes, that's right.** | 네, 맞아요. (lit: yes be-right) | né ma·ja·yo |
| **Yes, it is.** | 네, 그래요. (lit: yes be-like-that) | né kŭ·rae·yo |

| **no** | 아니요 | a·ni·yo |
| **No, it's not.** | 아니요, 안 그래요. (lit. no be·like· that) | a·ni·yo an·gŭ·rae·yo |

## Verbs

*Doing Things • Making Statements*

In Korean, verbs go at the end of the sentence and don't change according to the subject. There are three basic tenses – past, present and future. In a Korean dictionary, verbs are always listed in their basic form, which is the verb stem plus the ending ~da/~ta ~다. You need to know the verb stem in order to use a verb in its past, present or future tense.

Verb endings are not used only to refer to past, present or future, but also to express the relationship between the speaker and the listener, or the speaker and the subject (see also **personal pronouns**). In this phrasebook, including the dictionary, verbs are given in the 'familiar polite' form of speech (verb stem plus the ending ~yo ~요), which is appropriate for most situations you're likely to encounter.

Note that the pronunciation of consonants may change when endings are added. (See **pronunciation** for more on consonant changes.) In the following section, we have only presented regular verbs. An asterisk (*) indicates that the personal pronoun 'I' can be replaced by 'you', 'she', 'he', 'it', 'we' or 'they'.

### Present

The present tense is usually formed by adding a 아 or o 오 to the verb stem. To make the sentence polite, ~yo ~요 is added as a final ending.

If the last vowel of the verb stem is a 아 or o 오, followed by a consonant, the verb ending for the present tense is ~a·yo:

| look for | 찾~ | ch'aj~ (last vowel a) |
| I* look for | 찾아요 | ch'a·ja·yo (ch'aj + a·yo) |
| melt | 녹~ | nok~ (last vowel o) |
| it melts | 녹아요 | no·ga·yo (nok + a·yo) |

If a verb stem ends in a 아 without a consonant following it, ~yo is added instead of ~a·yo:

| go | 가~ | ka~ |
| I* go | 가요 | ka·yo (not ka·a·yo) |

If a verb stem ends in o 오 without a consonant following it, ~o·a·yo at the end (the verb stem's o + a·yo) can be changed to ~wa·yo:

| see | 보~ | po~ |
| I* see | 봐요 | pwa·yo (or po·a·yo 보아요) |

If the verb stem ends in ŭ 으, the ŭ is replaced with ~ŏ·yo:

| use | 쓰~ | ssŭ~ |
| I* use | 써요 | ssŏ·yo (ssŭ – ŭ + ŏ·yo) |

If the last vowel of the verb stem is ŏ, u, i or a combination vowel, ~ŏ·yo is added to the stem:

| learn | 배우~ | pae·u~ |
| I* learn | 배워요 | pae·wŏ·yo (pae·u + ŏ·yo) |

## Past

Forming the past tense is simple – the same rules apply as for the present, depending on the last vowel of the verb stem.

If the last vowel is a 아 or o 오, add ~ass·ŏ·yo or ~ssŏ·yo to the verb stem.

| **I* looked for** | 찾았어요 | ch'a·jass·ŏ·yo (ch'aj + ass·ŏ·yo) |
| **it melted** | 녹았어요 | no·gass·ŏ·yo (nok + ass·ŏ·yo) |
| **I* went** | 갔어요 | kass·ŏ·yo (ka + ssŏ·yo) |
| **I* saw** | 봤어요 | pwass·ŏ·yo (po + ass·ŏ·yo) |

If the last vowel of the verb stem is ŭ 으, drop ŭ and add ~ŏss·ŏ·yo:

| **I* used** | 썼어요 | ssŏss·ŏ·yo (ssŭ – ŭ + ŏss·ŏ·yo) |

If the last vowel is ŏ, u, i or one of the combination vowels, the past tense ending will be ~ŏss·ŏ·yo:

| **I* learned** | 배웠어요 | pae·wŏss·o·yo (pae·u + ŏss·ŏ·yo) |

## Future

If the verb stem ends with a consonant, just add ~ŭl kŏ·ye·yo ~을 거예요 to form the future tense. If the verb stem ends with a vowel, add ~l kŏ·ye·yo ~ㄹ 거예요. These can also appear as ~ŭlk·ke·yo ~을게요 and ~lk·ke·yo ~ㄹ게요, respectively.

| **look for** | 찾~ | ch'aj~ |
| **I\* will look for** | 찾을 거예요 | ch'a·jŭl kŏ·ye·yo |
| | | (ch'aj + ŭl kŏ·ye·yo) |
| **go** | 가~ | ka~ |
| **I\* will go** | 갈 거예요 | kal kŏ·ye·yo |
| | | (ka + l kŏ·ye·yo) |

Alternatively, regardless of whether the verb stem ends with a consonant or a vowel, ~gess·ŏ·yo ~겠어요 can be added in order to make future tense.

## Word Order

### Making Statements

Korean word order differs from that of English: the typical order is subject–object–verb, rather than subject–verb–object. The subject is not always necessary.

| **I came from Australia.** | (저는) 호주에서 왔어요. (lit: |
| | (I-nŭn) Australia-from came) |
| | (chŏ·nŭn) ho·ju·e·sŏ wass·ŏ·yo |

See also **negatives** and **questions**.

---

**LANGUAGE TIP** — **Vowels & Consonants**

Throughout this book, when two options are given to complete words in a follow-on list, the first one is for a word ending with a consonant, and the second one for a word ending with a vowel:

...이/가 ...i/·ga     ...과/와 ...kwa/·wa
...은/는 ...ŭn/·nŭn     ...이에요/예요 ...i·e·yo/·ye·yo
...을/를 ...ŭl/·rŭl     ...이요/요 ...i·yo/·yo

In case of ...으로/로 ...ŭ·ro/·ro, if the noun ends with the consonant l ㄹ, 로 (pronounced ·lo) should be added.

# Basics

# Understanding

## KEY PHRASES

| | | |
|---|---|---|
| **Do you speak English?** | 영어 하실 줄 아시나요? | yŏng·ŏ ha·shil·jul a·shi·na·yo |
| **I don't understand.** | 못 알아 들었어요. | mo·da·ra· dŭ·rŏss·ŏ·yo |
| **What does ... mean?** | ... 무슨 뜻이에요? | ... mu·sŭn· ttŭ·shi·e·yo |

| | | |
|---|---|---|
| **Q Do you speak (English)?** | (영어) 하실 줄 아시나요? | (yŏng·ŏ) ha·shil·jul a·shi·na·yo |
| **Q Does anyone speak (English)?** | (영어) 하시는 분 계시나요? | (yŏng·ŏ) ha·shi·nŭn·bun kye·shi·na·yo |
| **A I speak (English).** | 전 (영어) 해요. | chŏn (yŏng·ŏ) hae·yo |
| **A I don't speak (Korean).** | 전 (한국말) 못 해요. | chŏn (han·gung·mal) mo·t'ae·yo |
| **A I speak a little.** | 조금 할 줄 알아요. | cho·gŭm hal·jul a·ra·yo |
| **Q Do you understand?** | 알아 들으셨나요? | a·ra·dŭ·rŭ·shŏn·na·yo |
| **A I understand.** | 알아 들었어요. | a·ra·dŭ·rŏss·ŏ·yo |
| **A I don't understand.** | 못 알아 들었어요. | mo·da·ra·dŭ·rŏss·ŏ·yo |
| **I'd like to learn some Korean.** | 한국말 좀 배우고 싶어요. | han·gung·mal chom pae·u·go shi·p'ŏ·yo |

**LANGUAGE TIP**

**Konglish**

Koreans have borrowed many words from English. These 'Konglish' terms are often shorter versions of English words (eg a·p'a·t'ŭ 아파트 is 'apartment'), though some are made by combining English words (eg haen·dŭ·p'on 핸드폰 is 'cell phone', lit: 'hand phone'). However, the meanings of the English words and the Konglish terms don't always add up. A hat·to·gŭ 핫도그 (from 'hot dog'), for example, usually refers to a 'corn dog', and a k'on·do 콘도 (from 'condo') means 'time-share'.

| | |
|---|---|
| **What does ... mean?** | ... 무슨 뜻이에요?<br>... mu·sŭn·ttŭ·shi·e·yo |
| **What's this called in Korean?** | 한국말로 이걸<br>뭐라고 하나요?<br>han·gung·mal·lo i·gŏl<br>mwŏ·ra·go ha·na·yo |
| **How do you say ... in Korean?** | ...이/가 한국말로 뭐예요?<br>...·i/·ga han·gung·mal·lo<br>mwŏ·ye·yo |
| **How do you pronounce this?** | 이걸 어떻게 발음하나요?<br>i·gŏl ŏt·tŏ·k'é pa·rŭm·ha·na·yo |
| **How do you write ...?** | ... 어떻게 쓰나요?<br>... ŏt·tŏ·k'é ssŭ·na·yo |
| **Could you please repeat that?** | 다시 말씀해 주시겠어요?<br>ta·shi mal·ssŭm·hae<br>ju·shi·gess·ŏ·yo |
| **Could you please write it down?** | 적어 주시겠어요?<br>chŏ·gŏ ju·shi·gess·ŏ·yo |
| **Could you please speak more slowly?** | 천천히 말씀해 주시겠어요?<br>ch'ŏn·ch'ŏn·hi mal·ssŭm·hae<br>ju·shi·gess·ŏ·yo |
| ✂ **Slowly, please!** | 천천히요!    ch'ŏn·ch'ŏn·hi·yo |

# Numbers & Amounts

## KEY PHRASES

| | | |
|---|---|---|
| **How much?** | 얼만큼요? | ŏl·man·k'ŭm·myo |
| **How many?** | 몇 개나요? | myŏk·kae·na·yo |
| **a little/some** | 조금 | cho·gŭm |
| **a lot/many** | 많이 | ma·ni |

## Pure Korean Cardinal Numbers

Pure Korean numbers are used for expressing the hour when telling the time, for counting objects and people, and for expressing your age. They can only be written in Hangul or as digits, not in Chinese characters. From 100 on, however, Sino-Korean numbers take over (p40). Note also that there's no pure Korean word for 'zero'.

| | | |
|---|---|---|
| **1** | 하나 | ha·na |
| **2** | 둘 | tul |
| **3** | 셋 | set |
| **4** | 넷 | net |
| **5** | 다섯 | ta·sŏt |
| **6** | 여섯 | yŏ·sŏt |
| **7** | 일곱 | il·gop |
| **8** | 여덟 | yŏ·dŏl |
| **9** | 아홉 | a·hop |
| **10** | 열 | yŏl |
| **11** | 열하나 | yŏl·ha·na |
| **12** | 열둘 | yŏl·dul |

| 13 | 열셋 | yŏl·set |
| 14 | 열넷 | yŏl·let |
| 15 | 열다섯 | yŏl·da·sŏt |
| 16 | 열여섯 | yŏl·yŏ·sŏt |
| 17 | 열일곱 | yŏl·il·gop |
| 18 | 열여덟 | yŏl·yŏ·dŏl |
| 19 | 열아홉 | yŏ·ra·hop |
| 20 | 스물 | sŭ·mul |
| 21 | 스물하나 | sŭ·mul·ha·na |
| 22 | 스물둘 | sŭ·mul·dul |
| 30 | 서른 | sŏ·rŭn |
| 40 | 마흔 | ma·hŭn |
| 50 | 쉰 | shwin |
| 60 | 예순 | ye·sun |
| 70 | 일흔 | il·hŭn |
| 80 | 여든 | yŏ·dŭn |
| 90 | 아흔 | a·hŭn |

**BASICS**    **NUMBERS & AMOUNTS**

**LANGUAGE TIP**

### 'Pure' & Sino-Korean Numbers

Two numbering systems are used in Korea: the 'pure Korean' words for numbers and those with 'Sino-Korean' pronunciation (the Korean pronunciation of numbers of Chinese origin).

Each system has both cardinal and ordinal numbers. Both pure Korean and Sino-Korean numbers are used to state quantities of things. Pure Korean numbers are also used as counters or classifiers (see **grammar**, p21). There's a clear separation between the types of things counted with each system, but Korean speakers will be forgiving if you mix up the two.

# Sino-Korean Cardinal Numbers

Sino-Korean numbers are used to express minutes when telling the time, as well as dates and months of the year. They're also used for addresses, phone numbers, amounts of money and floors of a building. From 100 on, they take over from pure Korean numbers. They may be written in Hangul, as digits, or in Chinese characters.

| 0 | 영/공 | yŏng/kong |
| 1 | 일 | il |
| 2 | 이 | i |
| 3 | 삼 | sam |
| 4 | 사 | sa |
| 5 | 오 | o |
| 6 | 육 | yuk |
| 7 | 칠 | ch'il |
| 8 | 팔 | p'al |
| 9 | 구 | ku |
| 10 | 십 | ship |
| 11 | 십일 | shi·bil |
| 12 | 십이 | shi·bi |
| 13 | 십삼 | ship·sam |
| 14 | 십사 | ship·sa |
| 15 | 십오 | shi·bo |
| 16 | 십육 | shim·nyuk |
| 17 | 십칠 | ship·ch'il |
| 18 | 십팔 | ship·p'al |
| 19 | 십구 | ship·ku |
| 20 | 이십 | i·ship |
| 21 | 이십일 | i·shi·bil |
| 22 | 이십이 | i·shi·bi |
| 30 | 삼십 | sam·ship |

| 40 | 사십 | sa·ship |
| 50 | 오십 | o·ship |
| 60 | 육십 | yuk·ship |
| 70 | 칠십 | ch'il·ship |
| 80 | 팔십 | p'al·ship |
| 90 | 구십 | ku·ship |
| 100 | 백 | paek |
| 200 | 이백 | i·baek |
| 1000 | 천 | ch'ŏn |
| 2000 | 이천 | i·ch'ŏn |
| 10,000 | 만 | man |
| 50,000 | 오만 | o·man |
| 100,000 | 십만 | shim·man |
| 800,000 | 팔십만 | p'al·shim·man |
| 1,000,000 | 백만 | paeng·man |
| 3,000,000 | 삼백만 | sam·baeng·man |

## Ordinal Numbers

Add the suffix ·tchae 째 to pure Korean cardinal numbers to create ordinals. Note that here, ha·na 하나 (one) has been replaced by a new word, ch'ŏt 첫. For two-digit ordinal numbers ending in 1 or 2, abbreviated forms are used (han 한 and tu 두).

| 1st | 첫째 | ch'ŏt·tchae |
| 2nd | 둘째 | tul·tchae |
| 3rd | 셋째 | set·tchae |
| 4th | 넷째 | net·tchae |
| 5th | 다섯째 | ta·sŏt·chae |

Unlike the cardinal numbers, pure Korean and Sino-Korean ordinal numbers are more easily interchangeable. The Sino-Korean method is to simply add the prefix che· before the Sino-Korean cardinal number.

| 1st | 제일/제1 | che·il |
|-----|---------|--------|
| 2nd | 제이/제2 | che·i |
| 3rd | 제삼/제3 | che·sam |

## Fractions & Decimals

Fractions use Sino-Korean numbers, but they're in reverse order from the words in English. Note that 'half' has its own Sino-Korean word, ban 반. When counting objects, 'half' comes after the counting marker (see the literal translations below).

| a half | 이분의 일/반 | i·bu·ne·il/ban |
|--------|-------------|----------------|
| two and a half (things) | 두 개 반 (lit: two-gae-half) | tu·gae·ban |
| a quarter | 사분의 일 | sa·bu·ne·il |
| a third | 삼분의 일 | sam·bu·ne·il |
| three-quarters | 사분의 삼 (lit: four-divide-é-three) | sa·bu·ne·sam |
| all | 다 | ta |

Decimals are read using Sino-Korean numbers. The word for the decimal point itself is tchŏm 점.

| 3.14 | 삼 점 일 사 | sam·tchŏ·mil·sa |
|------|------------|-----------------|
| 4.2 | 사 점 이 | sa·tchŏ·mi |

**LANGUAGE TIP**

### Counters/Classifiers

When describing how many there are of an item, you use the pure Korean number followed by a specific marker used to count that type of thing – a bit like saying 'three pairs of shoes' in English. For examples of counters (or 'classifiers') and how to use them, see **grammar** (p21).

## Useful Amounts

| How much? | 얼만큼요? ŏl·man·k'ŭm·myo |
|---|---|
| How many? | 몇 개나요? myŏk·kae·na·yo |
| Please give me ... | ... 주세요. ... ju·se·yo |

| | | |
|---|---|---|
| double | 두 배 | tu·bae |
| triple | 세 배 | se·bae |
| 10 times as much | 열 배 | yŏl·bae |
| enough ... | ... 충분히 | ... ch'ung·bun·hi |
| a few | 몇 개 | myŏk·kae |
| less ... | ... 덜 | ... tŏl |
| a little | 조금 | cho·gŭm |
| a lot | 많이 | ma·ni |
| many | 많이 | ma·ni |
| more ... | ... 더 | ... tŏ |
| much | 많이 | ma·ni |
| some ... | ... 조금 | ... cho·gŭm |

**BASICS**

**NUMBERS & AMOUNTS**

**CULTURE TIP** **Weights & Measures**

Korea generally employs the metric system. However, there are still some traditional measures for food (kŭn 근 and ton 돈) and area (p'yŏng 평, most commonly used to measure floor space). In addition, Koreans still use the imperial system in some sports such as golf.

In 2006 the government set out to officially convert all nonmetric measurements in both the public and corporate sectors to metric, with threats of fines to back up the move. In particular, they're targeting traditional measures, but it's still not clear how well the new rules will be applied by Mr Cho hawking vegetables in the local market or Ms Park trying to sell that 30-*pyong* apartment.

Note that certain measures use pure Korean numbers, while others use Sino-Korean numbers:

### Pure Korean numbers

| | | |
|---|---|---|
| 한 돈 | han·don | *ton* (3.75g) |
| 한 근 | han·gŭn | *kun* (600g) |
| ... 한 병 | ... han·byŏng | a bottle of ... |
| 한 쌍 | han·ssang | pair |
| 한 조각 | han·jo·gak | slice |
| 한 캔 | han·k'aen | tin (can) |

### Sino-Korean numbers

| | | |
|---|---|---|
| 일 그램 | il·kŭ·raem | gram |
| 일 킬로그램 | il·k'il·lo·kŭ·raem | kilogram |
| 오백 시시 | o·baek·shi·shi | half a litre (500 mL) |
| 일 리터 | il·li·tŏ | litre |
| 일 평 | il·p'yŏng | *pyong* (3.3 sq metres) |
| (만 원)어치 ... | (ma·nwŏn)·ŏ·ch'i ... | (10,000 won) worth of ... |

# Time & Dates

### KEY PHRASES

| | | |
|---|---|---|
| What time is it? | 몇 시예요? | myŏs·shi·ye·yo |
| At what time ...? | 몇 시에 ...? | myŏs·shi·é ... |
| What date is it today? | 오늘이 며칠이에요? | o·nŭ·ri myŏ·chi·ri·e·yo |

## Telling the Time

In Korean, time is usually told using a 12-hour clock, but schedules for trains, buses, movies and so on typically use a 24-hour clock. Both the pure Korean and the Sino-Korean numbering systems are used (see **numbers & amounts**, p38). The hour is expressed with pure Korean cardinal numbers followed by ·shi 시 (hour), and the minutes are expressed with Sino-Korean cardinal numbers followed by ·pun/·bun 분 (minutes). The suffix ·ban 반 (half) can be used to indicate half past the hour. To describe a time before the hour, add ·jŏn 전 (before) to the number of minutes (in Sino-Korean cardinal numbers) before the hour.

| | | |
|---|---|---|
| **Q** What time is it? | 몇 시예요?<br>myŏs·shi·ye·yo | |
| **A** It's (one) o'clock. | (한) 시요.<br>(han)·shi·yo | |
| **A** It's (two) o'clock. | (두) 시요.<br>(tu)·shi·yo | |
| **A** Five past (two). | (두) 시 오 분이요.<br>(tu)·shi o·bu·ni·yo | |
| **A** Quarter past (two). | (두) 시 십오 분이요.<br>(tu)·shi shi·bo·bu·ni·yo | |

| | | |
|---|---|---|
| 🅐 **Half past (two).** | (두) 시 삼십 분이요.<br>(tu)·shi ba·ni·yo<br>(두) 시 반이요.<br>(tu)·shi sam·ship·pu·ni·yo | |
| 🅐 **Quarter to (three).** | (세) 시 십오 분 전이요.<br>(se)·shi shi·bo·bun jŏ·ni·yo | |
| 🅐 **Twenty to (three).** | (세) 시 이십 분 전이요.<br>(se)·shi i·ship·pun jŏ·ni·yo | |
| **(9)am** | 오전 (아홉 시)<br>o·jŏn (a·hop·shi) | |
| **(3)pm** | 오후 (세 시)<br>o·hu (se·shi) | |
| 🅠 **At what time ...?** | 몇 시에 ...?<br>myŏs·shi·é ... | |
| 🅐 **At (five) o'clock.** | (다섯) 시에요.<br>(ta·sŏs)·shi·é·yo | |
| 🅐 **At (7.57pm).** | (오후 일곱 시 오십칠 분)에요.<br>(o·hu il·gop·shi o·ship·ch'il·bun)·é·yo | |
| **dawn** | 새벽 | sae·byŏk |
| **sunrise** | 해돋이/일출 | hae·do·ji/il·ch'ul |
| **morning** | 아침 | a·ch'im |
| **day** | 낮 | nat |
| **noon** | 정오 | chŏng·o |
| **afternoon** | 오후 | o·hu |
| **evening** | 저녁 | chŏ·nyŏk |
| **night** | 밤 | pam |
| **sunset** | 해넘이/일몰 | hae·nŏ·mi/il·mol |
| **midnight** | 자정 | cha·jŏng |

## The Calendar

Like their English counterparts, the Korean words which represent the days of the week have a special meaning. Starting with Sunday, the names represent the sun, the moon, fire, water, trees, gold and land.

| Monday | 월요일 | wŏ·ryo·il |
|---|---|---|
| Tuesday | 화요일 | hwa·yo·il |
| Wednesday | 수요일 | su·yo·il |
| Thursday | 목요일 | mo·gyo·il |
| Friday | 금요일 | kŭ·myo·il |
| Saturday | 토요일 | t'o·yo·il |
| Sunday | 일요일 | i·ryo·il |

The word for each month is simply its corresponding Sino-Korean cardinal number followed by ·wŏl 월 (the Sino-Korean word for 'moon/month'). The only exceptions are that yuk 육 (six) becomes yu 유 and ship 십 (10) becomes shi 시. Lunar calendar dates use the same terminology, so Koreans may differentiate between the two by referring to yang·nyŏk 양력 (Western calendar) or ŭm·nyŏk 음력 (lunar calendar).

| January | 일월 | i·rwŏl |
|---|---|---|
| February | 이월 | i·wŏl |
| March | 삼월 | sa·mwŏl |
| April | 사월 | sa·wŏl |
| May | 오월 | o·wŏl |
| June | 유월 | yu·wŏl |
| July | 칠월 | ch'i·rwŏl |
| August | 팔월 | p'a·rwŏl |
| September | 구월 | ku·wŏl |
| October | 시월 | shi·wŏl |
| November | 십일월 | shi·bi·rwŏl |
| December | 십이월 | shi·bi·wŏl |

Dates are given from larger to smaller (ie year–month–date) using Sino-Korean cardinal numbers followed by ·nyŏn 년, ·wŏl 월 and ·il 일 to express the year, month and date respectively. For counting the actual number of days, see the box on page 49.

**CULTURE TIP** **The Lunar Calendar**
The Western (Gregorian) calendar is used in Korea, but traditional holidays such as Chusok (which falls on the 15th day of the eighth lunar month), Buddha's Birthday and, of course, Lunar New Year (the first day of the first lunar month) are calculated according to the lunar calendar. Korean calendars often have lunar dates printed in small numbers at the bottom of each day. The lunar year starts in late January or in early February. Like the Gregorian calendar, the lunar calendar has 12 months. Most Koreans know their birth date in both calendars.

**What date is it today?**
오늘이 며칠이에요?
o·nŭ·ri myŏ·chi·ri·e·yo

**It's (13 October 2012).**
(이천십이년 시월 십삼일)이에요.
(i·ch'ŏn·shi·bi·nyŏn shi·wŏl ship·sa·mir)·i·e·yo

The Korean calendar is divided into four seasons, each starting a few weeks earlier than its Western counterpart. Korean seasons are further divided into four periods corresponding roughly to that season starting, rising, falling and ending.

| spring | 봄 | pom |
| summer | 여름 | yŏ·rŭm |
| autumn/fall | 가을 | ka·ŭl |
| winter | 겨울 | kyŏ·ul |
| summer solstice | 하지 | ha·ji |
| winter solstice | 동지 | tong·ji |
| rainy season | 장마 | chang·ma |

## Present

| (right) now | (바로) 지금 | (pa·ro) chi·gŭm |
| today | 오늘 | o·nŭl |

| tonight | 오늘 밤 | o·nŭl·bam |
|---|---|---|
| for (two days) | (이틀) 동안 | (i·t'ŭl)·dong·an |
| this morning | 오늘 아침 | o·nŭl a·ch'im |
| this afternoon | 오늘 오후 | o·nŭl o·hu |
| this week | 이번 주 | i·bŏn·ju |
| this month | 이번 달 | i·bŏn·dal |
| this year | 올해 | ol·hae |

## Past

| yesterday | 어제 | ŏ·jé |
|---|---|---|
| the day before yesterday | 그저께 | kŭ·jŏk·ké |
| since (May) | (오월)부터 | (o·wŏl)·bu·t'ŏ |
| half an hour ago | 삼십 분 전에 | sam·ship·pun·jŏ·né |
| three days ago | 사흘 전에 | sa·hŭl·jŏ·né |

**LANGUAGE TIP** — **Counting Days**

Korean uses both a Sino-Korean and a pure Korean system of counting days. The first one is easy: you just combine Sino-Korean numbers with il 일, the Sino-Korean word for 'day':

| one day | 일일 | i·ril |
|---|---|---|
| two days | 이일 | i·il |
| three days | 삼일 | sa·mil |
| four days | 사일 | sa·il |
| five days | 오일 | o·il |
| six days | 육일 | yu·gil |

Pure Korean, however, has special words for 'one day' (ha·ru 하루), 'two days' (i·t'ŭl 이틀), 'three days' (sa·hŭl 사흘) and so on.

| five years ago | 오 년 전에 | o·nyŏn·jŏ·né |
| a while ago | 얼마 전에 | ŏl·ma·jŏ·né |
| yesterday morning | 어제 아침 | ŏ·jé a·ch'im |
| yesterday afternoon | 어제 오후 | ŏ·jé o·hu |
| yesterday evening | 어제 저녁 | ŏ·jé jŏ·nyŏk |
| last night | 어젯밤 | ŏ·jép·pam |
| last week | 지난주 | chi·nan·ju |
| last month | 지난달 | chi·nan·dal |
| last year | 작년 | chang·nyŏn |

## Future

| tomorrow | 내일 | nae·il |
| the day after tomorrow | 모레 | mo·ré |
| until (June) | (유월)까지 | (yu·wŏl)k·ka·ji |
| in five minutes | 오 분 안에 | o·bun a·né |
| in an hour | 한 시간 안에 | han·shi·gan a·né |
| in six days | 엿새 안에 | yŏs·sae a·né |
| in a month | 한 달 안에 | han·dal a·né |
| tomorrow morning | 내일 아침 | nae·il a·ch'im |
| tomorrow afternoon | 내일 오후 | nae·il o·hu |
| tomorrow evening | 내일 저녁 | nae·il chŏ·nyŏk |
| next week | 다음 주 | ta·ŭm·ju |
| next month | 다음 달 | ta·ŭm·dal |
| next year | 내년 | nae·nyŏn |

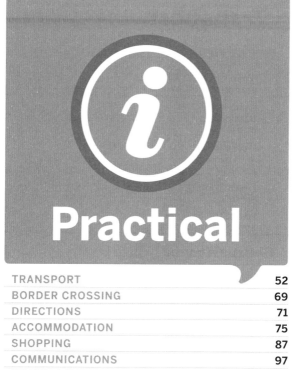
# Practical

# Transport

## KEY PHRASES

| | | |
|---|---|---|
| **When's the next bus?** | 다음 버스 언제 있나요? | ta·ŭm bŏ·sŭ ŏn·jé in·na·yo |
| **A one-way ticket to ..., please.** | ... 편도 표 주세요. | ... p'yŏn·do p'yo chu·se·yo |
| **Please tell me when we get to ...** | ...에 도착하면 좀 알려주세요. | ...é to·ch'a·k'a·myŏn chom al·lyŏ·ju·se·yo |
| **Please take me to ...** | ...으로 가 주세요. | ...ŭ·ro ka·ju·se·yo |
| **I'd like to hire a car.** | 차 빌리고 싶어요. | ch'a pil·li·go shi·p'ŏ·yo |

## Getting Around

| | | |
|---|---|---|
| **Does this ... go to (Cheonan)?** | 이 ... (천안)에 가나요? | i ... (ch'ŏ·nan)·é ka·na·yo |
| **Which ... goes to (Myeongdong)?** | 어느 ...이/가 (명동)에 가나요? | ŏ·nŭ ...·i/·ga (myŏng·dong)·é ka·na·yo |
| **boat** | 배 | pae |
| **bus** | 버스 | bŏ·sŭ |
| **metro line** | 지하철 노선 | chi·ha·ch'ŏl no·sŏn |
| **train** | 기차 | ki·ch'a |

| | |
|---|---|
| **When's the first (bus)?** | 첫 (버스) 언제 있나요?<br>ch'ŏt (bŏ·sŭ) ŏn·jé in·na·yo |
| **When's the last (bus)?** | 마지막 (버스) 언제<br>있나요?<br>ma·ji·mak (bŏ·sŭ) ŏn·jé<br>in·na·yo |
| **When's the next (bus)?** | 다음 (버스) 언제 있나요?<br>ta·ŭm (bŏ·sŭ) ŏn·jé in·na·yo |
| **What time does it leave?** | 언제 떠나요?<br>ŏn·jé ttŏ·na·yo |
| **What time does it get to (Busan)?** | (부산)에 언제<br>도착하나요?<br>(pu·san)·é ŏn·jé<br>to·ch'a·k'a·na·yo |
| **How long will it be delayed?** | 얼마나 연착되나요?<br>ŏl·ma·na yŏn·ch'ak·toé·na·yo |
| **Is this seat available?** | 여기 자리 있나요?<br>yŏ·gi cha·ri in·na·yo |

| | | | |
|---|---|---|---|
| ✂ | **Is it free?** | 빈 자리예요? | pin cha·ri·ye·yo |

| | |
|---|---|
| **That's my seat.** | 제 자리예요.<br>ché cha·ri·ye·yo |
| **Please tell me when we get to (Daejeon).** | (대전)에 도착하면<br>좀 알려주세요.<br>(tae·jŏn)·é to·ch'a·k'a·myŏn<br>chom al·lyŏ·ju·se·yo |
| **How long do we stop here?** | 여기서 얼마 동안 서나요?<br>yŏ·gi·sŏ ŏl·ma dong·an<br>sŏ·na·yo |
| **Can we get there by public transport?** | 대중교통으로 갈 수 있나요?<br>tae·jung·gyo·t'ong·ŭ·ro kal·su<br>in·na·yo |
| **Let's walk there.** | 우리 걸어 가요.<br>u·ri kŏ·rŏ·ga·yo |

## Buying Tickets

| | | |
|---|---|---|
| **Where do I buy a ticket?** | 표 어디에서 사나요? | p'yo ŏ·di·e·sŏ sa·na·yo |
| **Do I need to book?** | 예약해야 하나요? | ye·ya·k'ae·ya ha·na·yo |
| **A ... ticket (to Daegu), please.** | (대구 가는) ... 표 주세요. | (tae·gu ka·nŭn) ... p'yo chu·se·yo |

| | | |
|---|---|---|
| **1st-class** | 일등석 | il·dŭng·sŏk |
| **child's** | 어린이 | ŏ·ri·ni |
| **one-way** | 편도 | p'yŏn·do |
| **return** | 왕복 | wang·bok |
| **standard class** | 일반석 | il·ban·sŏk |
| **standing room** | 입석 | ip·sŏk |
| **student** | 학생 | hak·saeng |

| | | |
|---|---|---|
| **I'd like a/an ... seat.** | ... 주세요. | ... chu·se·yo |

| | | |
|---|---|---|
| **aisle** | 내측 좌석 | nae·ch'ŭk chwa·sŏk |
| **nonsmoking** | 금연석 | kŭ·myŏn·sŏk |
| **smoking** | 흡연석 | hŭ·byŏn·sŏk |
| **window** | 창측 좌석 | ch'ang·ch'ŭk chwa·sŏk |

| | | |
|---|---|---|
| **Is there a couchette/ sleeper?** | 침대차 있나요? | ch'im·dae·ch'a in·na·yo |
| **Is there a toilet?** | 화장실 있나요? | hwa·jang·shil in·na·yo |
| **How long does the trip take?** | 얼마나 걸리나요? | ŏl·ma·na kŏl·li·na·yo |

# Buying a Ticket

## What time is the next ...?
다음 ... 언제 있나요?
ta·ŭm ... ŏn·jé in·na·yo

**boat**
배
pae

**bus**
버스
bŏ·sŭ

**train**
기차
ki·ch'a

## One ... ticket, please.
... 표 주세요.
... p'yo chu·se·yo

**one-way**
편도
p'yŏn·do

**return**
왕복
wang·bok

## I'd like a/an ... seat.
... 주세요.
... chu·se·yo

**aisle**
내측 좌석
nae·ch'ŭk
chwa·sŏk

**window**
창측 좌석
ch'ang·ch'ŭk
chwa·sŏk

## Which platform does it depart from?
어느 승강장에서 출발하나요?
ŏ·nŭ sŭng·gang·jang·e·sŏ ch'ul·bal ha·na·yo

| Is it a direct route? | 직행 노선인가요?<br>chi·k'aeng no·sŏ·nin·ga·yo |
| Can I get a stand-by ticket? | 대기표를 살 수 있나요?<br>tae·gi·p'yo·rŭl sal·su in·na·yo |
| What time should I check in? | 체크인 몇 시예요?<br>ch'e·k'ŭ·in myŏs·shi·ye·yo |
| I'd like to cancel my ticket. | 표를 취소해 주세요.<br>p'yo·rŭl ch'wi·so·hae ju·se·yo |
| I'd like to change my ticket. | 표를 바꿔 주세요.<br>p'yo·rŭl pak·kwŏ ju·se·yo |
| I'd like to collect my ticket. | 표를 받으려고요.<br>p'yo·rŭl pa·dŭ·ryŏ·go·yo |
| I'd like to confirm my ticket. | 표 예약 확인<br>해 주세요.<br>p'yo yc yak hwa gin<br>hae·ju·se·yo |

## Luggage

| My luggage is damaged. | 제 짐이 망가졌어요.<br>ché chi·mi mang·ga·jŏss·ŏ·yo |
| My luggage is lost. | 제 짐이 없어졌어요.<br>ché chi·mi ŏp·sŏ·jŏss·ŏ·yo |

◀)) **LISTEN FOR**

| 갈아타는 곳 | ka·ra·t'a·nŭn·got | transfer point |
| 종점 | chong·tchŏm | final stop |
| 만석 | man·sŏk | full |
| 승강장 | sŭng·gang·jang | platform |
| 지연/연착 | chi·yŏn/yŏn·ch'ak | delayed |
| 취소/결항 | ch'wi·so/kyŏl·hang | cancelled |

## 🔊 LISTEN FOR

| | | |
|---|---|---|
| 기내 반입<br>수하물 | ki·nae pa·nip<br>su·ha·mul | carry-on baggage |
| 초과 수하물 | ch'o·gwa su·ha·mul | excess baggage |
| 탑승권 | t'ap·sǔng·gwǒn | boarding pass |
| 환승 | hwan·sǔng | transit |

**PRACTICAL TRANSPORT**

| | | |
|---|---|---|
| **My luggage has been stolen.** | 제 짐을<br>도둑 맞았어요. | ché chi·mǔl<br>to·dung·ma·jass·ǒ·yo |
| **Where can I find a/the ...?** | ... 어디에 있나요? | ... ǒ·di·é in·na·yo |
| **baggage claim** | 수하물<br>수취대 | su·ha·mul<br>su·ch'wi·dae |
| **left-luggage office** | 분실 수하물<br>보관소 | pun·shil su·ha·mul<br>po·gwan·so |
| **luggage locker** | 짐 보관소 | chim po·gwan·so |
| **trolley/cart** | 짐 카트 | chim k'a·t'ǔ |

## Plane

| | | |
|---|---|---|
| **Where does flight (OZ 603) arrive/depart?** | (OZ603)편<br>언제 도착하나요/<br>출발하나요? | (o·ji yuk·kong·sam)·p'yǒn<br>ǒn·jé to·ch'a·k'a·na·yo/<br>ch'ul·bal·ha·na·yo |

PRACTICAL TRANSPORT

| Where's (the) ...? | | ... 어디 있나요?<br>... ŏ·di in·na·yo |
|---|---|---|
| airport shuttle<br>bus | 공항 리무진<br>버스 | kong·hang ri·mu·jin<br>bŏ·sŭ |
| arrivals hall | 입국장 | ip·kuk·chang |
| departures hall | 출국장 | ch'ul·guk·chang |
| duty-free shop | 면세점 | myŏn·se·jŏm |
| gate (20) | (이십)번<br>게이트 | (i·ship)·pŏn<br>ge·i·t'ŭ |

## Bus

| Where's the bus stop? | 버스 정류장이<br>어디예요?<br>bŏ·sŭ chŏng·nyu·jang·i<br>ŏ·di·ye·yo |
|---|---|
| How often do buses come? | 버스가 얼마나 자주 오나요?<br>bŏ·sŭ·ga ŏl·ma·na cha·ju<br>o·na·yo |
| What's the next stop? | 다음 정류장이 어디예요?<br>ta·ŭm chŏng·nyu·jang·i<br>ŏ·di·ye·yo |
| I'd like to get off at<br>(Nadaemun). | (남대문)에서 내려요.<br>(nam·dae·mun)·e·sŏ<br>nae·ryŏ·yo |

---

###  LOOK FOR

| 노약자, 장애인,<br>임산부 좌석 | no·yak·cha chang·ae·in<br>im·san·bu chwa·sŏk | seats for seniors,<br>the disabled, and<br>pregnant women |
|---|---|---|

| ... bus | ... 버스 | |
| | ... bŏ·sŭ | |

| **1st-class city** | 좌석 | chwa·sŏk |
| **city** | 시내 | shi·nae |
| **city tour** | 시티투어 | shi·t'i·t'u·ŏ |
| **express** | 고속 | ko·sok |
| **intercity** | 광역 | kwang·yŏk |
| **local** | 마을/지선 | ma·ŭl/chi·sŏn |
| **rural** | 직행 | chi·k'aeng |
| **shuttle** | 순환 | sun·hwan |
| **tourist** | 관광 | kwan·gwang |

## Metro/Subway

There's no difference in meaning between the terms chŏn·ch'ŏl 전 철 (metro) and chi·ha·ch'ŏl 지하철 (subway) in Korean. The signs in all of the subway systems are bilingual (Korean and English) or even trilingual (with Chinese characters) and are colour-coordinated, so it's easy to get around.

| **Does this train go to (Incheon)?** | 이 기차 (인천) 가나요?<br>i·gi·ch'a (in·ch'ŏn) ka·na·yo |
| **Where's exit (1)?** | (1)번 출구가<br>어디예요?<br>(il)·bŏn ch'ul·gu·ga<br>ŏ·di·ye·yo |
| **Where do I go to transfer to ...?** | ...으로/로 갈아타려면<br>어디로 가야 해요?<br>...·ŭ·ro/·ro ka·ra·t'a·ryŏ·myŏn<br>ŏ·di·ro ka·ya hae·yo |

## Train

| | | |
|---|---|---|
| **What's the next station?** | 다음 역이 어디예요? | ta·ŭm yŏ·gi ŏ·di·ye·yo |
| **Does it stop at (Gyeongju)?** | (경주) 가나요? | (kyŏng·ju) ka·na·yo |
| **Do I need to change?** | 갈아타야 하나요? | ka·ra·t'a·ya ha·na·yo |
| **Is it direct?** | 직행 노선이에요? | chi·k'aeng no·sŏ·ni·e·yo |
| **I'd like (the) ...** | ... 주세요. | ... chu·se·yo |

| | | |
|---|---|---|
| **1st class** | 특실 | t'ŭk·shil |
| **dining section** | 식당칸 | shik·tang·k'an |
| **KTX (bullet train) regular class** | 케이티엑스 일반실 | k'e·i·t'i·ek·sŭ il·ban·shil |
| **sleeping section** | 침대칸 | ch'im·dae·k'an |

---

**CULTURE TIP** · **Train Types**

Train service in Korea varies according to the type of train you're on.

The sae·ma·ŭl 새마을 *(Saemaeul)* are comfortable express trains that hit only a few cities on their cross-country journey. These are cheaper than the KTX (bullet train), but take about twice as long to make the journey.

One notch lower still is the mu·gung·hwa 무궁화 *(Mugunghwa)*, which is cheaper and stops at even more stations.

## 🔊 LISTEN FOR

| | |
|---|---|
| 교통카드 충전소 | kyo·t'ung k'a·dŭ ch'ung jŏn so<br>place to add money to prepaid transit card |
| 노선도 | no·sŏn·do<br>subway/railway line information |
| ... 방면 | ... bang·myŏn<br>(trains going) in the direction of ... |
| 안내도 | an·nae·do<br>map with information about facilities |
| 운임표 | u·nim·p'yo<br>list of fares |
| 첫 차/막 차 | ch'ŏt·ch'a/mak·ch'a<br>first/last train (of the day) |
| 현 위치 | hyŏn wi·ch'i<br>You are here. |

## Boat

| | |
|---|---|
| **Where does the boat leave from?** | 배가 어디서 출발하나요?<br>pae·ga ŏ·di·sŏ ch'ul·bal ha·na·yo |
| **Is this a sightseeing boat?** | 이게 유람선인가요?<br>i·gé yu·ram·sŏn·in·ga·yo |
| **Can I take my car on the boat?** | 차를 배에 실을 수 있나요?<br>ch'a·rŭl pae·é shi·rŭl·su in·na·yo |
| **cabin** | 선실<br>sŏn·shil |
| **deck** | 갑판<br>kap·p'an |
| **high-speed ferry** | 쾌속선<br>k'wae·sok·sŏn |
| **lifeboat** | 구명선<br>ku·myŏng·sŏn |
| **life jacket** | 구명조끼<br>ku·myŏng·jok·ki |

# Taxi

To make communication easier between drivers and overseas visitors, taxi drivers who don't speak English have a number to call to hook you up with someone who will translate for you.

| | | |
|---|---|---|
| **Where's the taxi rank?** | 택시 정류장이 어디예요? | t'aek·shi chŏng·nyu·jang·i ŏ·di·ye·yo |
| **bullet (fast) taxi** | 총알 택시 | ch'ong·al t'aek·shi |
| **deluxe taxi** | 모범 택시 | mo·bŏm t'aek·shi |
| **regular taxi** | 일반 택시 | il·ban t'aek·shi |
| **Is this taxi available?** | 이 택시 타도 되나요? | i t'aek·shi t'a·do doé·na·yo |
| ✂ **Is it free?** | 빈 차예요? | pin ch'a·ye·yo |
| **I'd like a taxi at (9am).** | (오전 아홉시)에 택시 타려고요. | (o·jŏn a·hop·shi)·é t'aek·shi t'a·ryŏ·go·yo |
| **I'd like a taxi tomorrow.** | 내일 택시 타려고요. | nae·il t'aek·shi t'a·ryŏ·go·yo |

**CULTURE TIP**

### Sharing a Ride

To make some extra money and to ease demand during busy times (especially after the subways and most buses stop running), regular taxis may double up on passengers, a practice called hap·sŭng 합승. Although technically illegal, hap·sŭng still happens. It offers no savings benefit for the passengers, but it can dramatically increase the likelihood of getting a taxi at busy times and is generally safe.

| | | |
|---|---|---|
| **I'd like a taxi at (9am).** | (오전 아홉시)에 택시 타려고요. | (o·jŏn a·hop·shi)·é t'aek·shi t'a·ryŏ·gu·yo |
| **How much is the ...?** | ... 얼마예요? | ... ŏl·ma·ye·yo |
| call-out fee | 호출료 | ho·ch'ul·lyo |
| fare to (Gangnam station) | (강남역)까지 가는 요금 | (kang·nam·nyŏk)·kka·ji ka·nŭn yo·gŭm |
| flag fall/hiring charge | 기본 요금 | ki·bon yo·gŭm |
| late-night surcharge | 할증 | hal·tchŭng |
| **Please put the meter on.** | 미터기 켜 주세요. | mi·t'ŏ·gi k'yŏ·ju·se·yo |
| **Please don't pick up another passenger.** | 합승하지 마세요. | hap·sŭng ha·ji ma·se·yo |
| **Please take me to (Insa-dong).** | (인사동)으로 가 주세요. | (in·sa·dong)·ŭ·ro ka·ju·se·yo |
| ✄ **To ...** | ···이요/요. | ...·i·yo/·yo |
| **Please slow down.** | 천천히 가 주세요. | ch'ŏn·ch'ŏn·hi ka·ju·se·yo |
| **Please stop here.** | 여기 내릴게요. | yŏ·gi nae·rilk·ke·yo |
| **Please wait here.** | 여기서 기다려 주세요. | yŏ·gi·sŏ ki·da·ryŏ·ju·se·yo |

For other useful phrases, see **directions** (p71), and **money & banking** (p104).

## Car

| I'd like to hire a/an ... | | ... 빌리고 싶어요. |
|---|---|---|
| | | ... pil·li·go shi·p'ŏ·yo |

| 4WD | 사륜구동 | sa·ryun·gu·dong |
| automatic | 오토매틱 | o·t'o·mae·t'ik |
| car | 차 | ch'a |
| manual | 수동 | su·dong |

| with air conditioning/ a driver | 에어컨/기사 있는 e·ŏ·k'ŏn/ki·sa in·nŭn |
|---|---|
| How much for daily/ weekly hire? | 하루/한 주 렌트에 얼마예요? ha·ru/han·ju ren·t'ŭ·é ŏl·ma·ye·yo |
| Do you have a road map/ atlas? | 지도 있나요? chi·do in·na·yo |

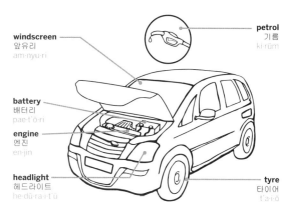

**windscreen**
앞유리
am·nyu·ri

**petrol**
기름
ki·rŭm

**battery**
배터리
pae·t'ŏ·ri

**engine**
엔진
en·jin

**headlight**
헤드라이트
he·dŭ·ra·i·t'ŭ

**tyre**
타이어
t'a·i·ŏ

| | |
|---|---|
| **What's the speed limit?** | 제한 속도가 얼마예요?<br>che·han·sok·to·ga ŏl·ma·ye·yo |
| **Is this the road to (Donghae)?** | 이게 (동해) 가는<br>길인가요?<br>i·gé (tong·hae) ka·nŭn<br>ki·rin·ga·yo |
| **Do you have a guide to the road rules (in English)?** | (영어로 된)<br>교통법규 책자 있나요?<br>(yŏng·ŏ·ro·doén)<br>kyo·t'ong·bŏp·kyu ch'aek·cha<br>in·na·yo |
| **Where's a petrol/gas station?** | 주유소가 어디있나요?<br>chu·yu·so·ga ŏ·di in·na·yo |
| **Where's the LPG filling station?** | 엘피지 충전소가 어디있나요?<br>el·p'i·ji ch'ung·jŏn·so·ga ŏ·di<br>in·na·yo |
| **What kind of fuel does this take?** | 어떤 연료를 써요?<br>ŏt·tŏn yŏl·lyo·rŭl ssŏ·yo |
| **Please fill it up.** | 가득 채워주세요.<br>ka·dŭk ch'ae·wŏ·ju·se·yo |
| **I'd like (30,000) won worth of fuel, please.** | (삼만) 원어치 넣어주세요.<br>(sam·man)·wŏ·nŏ·ch'i<br>nŏ·ŏ·ju·se·yo |

 **LOOK FOR**

| | | |
|---|---|---|
| 경유 | kyŏng·yu | diesel |
| 디젤 | di·jel | diesel |
| 엘피지 | el·p'i·ji | LPG |
| (무연)<br>휘발유 | (mu·yŏn)<br>hwi·bal·lyu | (unleaded)<br>petrol/gas |

**PRACTICAL TRANSPORT**

## 🔊 LISTEN FOR

| 고속도로 요금 | ko·sok·to·ro yo·gŭm | expressway toll |
| 과속 카메라 | kwa·sok k'a·me·ra | speed camera |
| 무료 | mu·ryo | free |
| 벌금 | pŏl·gŭm | fine |
| 안전벨트 | an·jŏn·bel·t'ŭ | seat belt |
| 운전면허증 | un·jŏn·myŏn·hŏ·tchŭng | drivers licence |
| 터널 요금 | t'ŏ·nŏl yo·gŭm | tunnel toll |

| | |
|---|---|
| **(How long) Can I park here?** | (얼마 동안) 여기 주차해도 되나요? (ŏl·ma·dong·an) yŏ·gi chu·ch'a·hae·do doé·na·yo |
| **Do I have to pay?** | 돈 내야 하나요? ton nae·ya ha·na·yo |
| **Please check the engine oil.** | 엔진오일 체크해 주세요. en·jin o·il ch'e·k'ŭ·hae·ju·se·yo |
| **Please check the tyre pressure.** | 타이어 공기압 체크해 주세요. t'a·i·ŏ kong·gi·ap ch'e·k'ŭ·hae·ju·se·yo |
| **Please check the water.** | 냉각수 체크해 주세요. naeng·gak·su ch'e·k'ŭ·hae·ju·se·yo |
| **I need a mechanic.** | 자동차정비사가 필요해요. cha·dong·ch'a chŏng·bi·sa·ga p'i·ryo·hae·yo |
| **I've had an accident.** | 사고가 났어요. sa·go·ga nass·ŏ·yo |
| **The car has broken down (at Jongno).** | (종로에서) 차가 고장났어요. (chong·no·e·sŏ) ch'a·ga ko·jang·nass·ŏ·yo |

자전거 빌리려고요.
cha·jŏn·gŏ pil·li·ryŏ·go·yo
*I'd like to hire a bicycle.*

## Bicycle

| | |
|---|---|
| **I'd like my bicycle repaired.** | 자전거 고치려고요.<br>cha·jŏn·gŏ ko·ch'i·ryŏ·go·yo |
| **I'd like to buy a bicycle.** | 자전거 사려고요.<br>cha·jŏn·gŏ sa·ryŏ·go·yo |
| **I'd like to hire a bicycle.** | 자전거 빌리려고요.<br>cha·jŏn·gŏ pil·li·ryŏ·go·yo |
| **Do I need a helmet?** | 헬멧 써야 하나요?<br>hel·met ssŏ·ya ha·na·yo |
| **Are there bicycle paths?** | 자전거 도로가 있나요?<br>cha·jŏn·gŏ to·ro·ga in·na·yo |
| **I have a puncture.** | 타이어에 펑크 났어요.<br>t'a·i·ŏ·é p'ŏng·k'ŭ nass·ŏ·yo |
| **How much is it per day/hour?** | 하루에/한 시간에 얼마예요?<br>ha·ru·é/han·shi·ga·né ŏl·ma·ye·yo |

PRACTICAL TRANSPORT

 🔍 **LOOK FOR**

| | | |
|---|---|---|
| 견인지역 | kyŏn·in·ji·yŏk | Tow-away Zone |
| 고속도로 | ko·sok·to·ro | Expressway |
| 낙석 지역 | nak·sŏk chi·yŏk | Falling Rocks |
| 무료주차 | mu·ryo·ju·ch'a | Free Parking |
| 버스전용차로 | bŏ·sŭ·chŏ·nyong·ch'a·ro | Bus-only Lane |
| 보행금지 | po·haeng·gŭm·ji | Pedestrians Prohibited |
| 비보호 | pi·bo·ho | Turn When Safe |
| 안개지역 | an·gae·ji·yŏk | Fog Zone |
| 양보 | yang·bo | Give Way |
| 어린이 보호 구역 | ŏ·ri·ni po·ho ku·yŏk | Beware of Children |
| 요금 | yo·gŭm | Toll |
| 우회 | u·hoé | Detour |
| 유료주차 | yu·ryo·ju·ch'a | Pay Parking |
| 위험 | wi·hŏm | Danger |
| 일방통행 | il·bang·t'ong·haeng | One Way |
| 입구 | ip·ku | Entrance |
| 정지 | chŏng·ji | Stop |
| 좌신호시 | chwa·shin·ho·shi | On Left Turn Arrow Only |
| 주차금지 | chu·ch'a·gŭm·ji | No Parking |
| 진입금지 | chi·nip·kŭm·ji | No Entry |
| 적신호시 | chŏk·shin·ho·shi | On Red Light Only |
| 천천히 | ch'ŏn·ch'ŏn·hi | Slow Down |
| 출구 | ch'ul·gu | Exit |

# Border Crossing

**KEY PHRASES**

| I'm here for ... days. | ...일 동안 있을 거예요. | ...il dong·an iss·ŭl·kŏ·ye·yo |
| I'm staying at ... | ...에 묵어요. | ...é mu·gŏ·yo |
| I have nothing to declare. | 신고할 것이 없습니다. | shin·go·hal gŏ·shi ŏp·sŭm·ni·da |

## Passport Control

| I'm here in transit. | 환승하려고요. | hwan·sŭng ha·ryŏ·go·yo |
| I'm here for a holiday. | 여행하러 왔어요. | yŏ·haeng ha·rŏ wass·ŏ·yo |
| I'm here on business. | 사업차 왔어요. | sa·ŏp·ch'a wass·ŏ·yo |
| I'm here to study. | 공부하러 왔어요. | kong·bu ha·rŏ wass·ŏ·yo |
| I'm here for ... | ... 동안 있을 거예요. | ... dong·an iss·ŭl·kŏ·ye·yo |

| one day | 하루 | ha·ru |
| two days | 이틀 | i·t'ŭl |
| three days | 사흘 | sa·hŭl |
| (10) days | (십) 일 | (shib)·il |
| (three) weeks | (삼) 주 | (sam)·ju |
| (two) months | (두) 달 | (tu)·dal |

| I'm going to (Gwangju). | (광주)에 가요. | (kwang·ju)·é ka·yo |

| | |
|---|---|
| I'm staying at the (Balhae Hotel). | (발해 호텔)에 묵어요.<br>(pal·hae ho·t'er)·é mu·gŏ·yo |

## At Customs

| | |
|---|---|
| I have nothing/something to declare. | 신고할 것이<br>없습니다/있습니다.<br>shin·go·hal gŏ·shi<br>ŏp·sŭm·ni·da/iss·sŭm·ni·da |
| Do I have to declare this? | 이거 신고해야 하나요?<br>i·gŏ shin·go hae·ya ha·na·yo |
| I didn't know I had to declare it. | 신고해야 하는 줄 몰랐습니다.<br>shin·go hae·ya ha·nŭn·jul<br>mol·lass·sŭm·ni·da |
| That's mine. | 그건 제 거예요.<br>kŭ·gŏn chék·kŏ·ye·yo |
| That's not mine. | 그건 제 것이 아닌데요.<br>kŭ·gŏn chek·kŏ·shi a·nin·de·yo |
| I need an (English) interpreter. | (영어) 통역이<br>필요한데요.<br>(yŏng·ŏ) t'ong·yŏ·gi<br>p'i·ryo·han·de·yo |
| Do you have this form in (English)? | (영어)로 된 서류 있나요?<br>(yŏng·ŏ)·ro doén sŏ·ryu<br>in·na·yo |

For payments and receipts, see **money & banking** (p104).

### 🔍 LOOK FOR

| | | |
|---|---|---|
| 검역 심사 | kŏ·myŏk shim·sa | Quarantine |
| 면세점 | myŏn·se·jŏm | Duty-Free Shop |
| 세관 신고 | se·gwan shin·go | Customs |
| 외국인<br>심사대 | oé·gu·gin<br>shim·sa·dae | Inspection for<br>Visitors |
| 입국 심사 | ip·kuk shim·sa | Immigration |

# Directions

**KEY PHRASES**

| Where is ...? | ... 어디 있나요? | ... ŏ·di in·na·yo |
| What's the address? | 주소가 뭐예요? | chu·so·ga mwŏ·ye·yo |
| How far is it? | 얼마나 먼가요? | ŏl·ma·na mŏn·ga·yo |

**Q** Where's a bank?

은행 어디 있나요?
ŭn·haeng ŏ·di in·na·yo

**Q** Where's the market?

시장 어디 있나요?
shi·jang ŏ·di in·na·yo

**A** It's ...

... 에 있어요.
...·é iss·ŏ·yo

**What's the address?**

주소가 뭐예요?
chu·so·ga mwŏ·ye·yo

**How do I get there?**

거기에 어떻게 가나요?
kŏ·gi·é ŏt·tŏ·k'é ka·na·yo

**How far is it?**

얼마나 먼가요?
ŏl·ma·na mŏn·ga·yo

**Please show me (on the map).**

(지도에서) 어디인지 가르쳐 주세요.
(chi·do·e·sŏ) ŏ·di·in·ji ka·rŭ·ch'ŏ ju·se·yo

## 🔊 LISTEN FOR

Koreans often arrange to meet at a local landmark, like a subway exit, a fast-food joint or the entrance to a department store. When you ask for directions, don't be surprised if total strangers go out of their way to take you to exactly where you're going instead of just explaining it. Businesses often give out cards that include not just their address, but also a small map, called yak·to 약도, which indicates their location in relation to a subway station or a well-known structure.

| ... 뒤에 | ... dwi·é | behind ... |
| 여기 | yŏ·gi | here |
| ... 앞에 | ... a·p'é | in front of ... |
| ... 가까이에 | ... kak·ka·i·é | near ... |
| ... 옆에 | ... yŏ·p'é | next to ... |
| 모퉁이에 | mo·t'ung·i·é | on the corner |
| ... 반대편에 | ... pan·dae·p'yŏ·né | opposite ... |
| 저기 | chŏ·gi | over there |
| 정면에 | chŏng·myŏ·né | straight ahead |

| 가까워요. | kak·ka·wŏ·yo<br>It's near. |
| 멀어요. | mŏ·rŏ·yo<br>It's far. |
| 좌회전 하세요. | chwa·hoé·jŏn ha·se·yo<br>Turn left. |
| 우회전 하세요. | u·hoé·jŏn ha·se·yo<br>Turn right. |
| (다음) 모퉁이에서<br>도세요. | (ta·ŭm) mo·t'ung·i·e·sŏ to·se·yo<br>Turn at the (next) corner. |
| 횡단보도에서 도세요. | hoéng·dan·bo·do·e·sŏ to·se·yo<br>Turn at the pedestrian crossing. |

| | |
|---|---|
| **by bus** | 버스로<br>bŏ·sŭ·ro |
| **by subway** | 지아셜노<br>chi·ha·ch'ŏl·lo |
| **by taxi** | 택시로<br>t'aek·shi·ro |
| **by train** | 기차로<br>ki·ch'a·ro |
| **on foot** | 걸어서<br>kŏ·rŏ·sŏ |

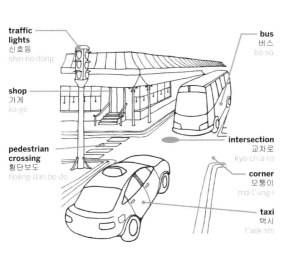

**traffic lights**
신호등
shin·ho·dŭng

**shop**
가게
ka·gé

**pedestrian crossing**
횡단보도
hoëng·dan·bo·do

**bus**
버스
bŏ·sŭ

**intersection**
교차로
kyo·ch'a·ro

**corner**
모퉁이
mo·t'ung·i

**taxi**
택시
t'aek·shi

**CULTURE TIP** **Writing Addresses**

Postal addresses, or chu·so 주소, are written in reverse order from those in the West: they go from the largest to the smallest administrative unit, with the block and house or apartment number last. When writing an address in English, however, it's acceptable to write it as you would in the West, from local to national.

The largest unit is do 도 (lit: province), kwang·yŏk·shi 광역시 (lit: wide-area city, meaning 'metropolitan prefecture') or t'ŭk·pyŏl·shi 특별시 (lit: special city, only used for Seoul). The urban parts of provinces are usually divided into shi 시 (lit: city), which are then divided into ·ku/·gu 구 (urban district) and dong 동 (neighbourhood), or just dong, depending on their size. The rural parts of both provinces and kwang·yŏk·shi are divided into kun 군 (lit: county), which are further divided into townships and villages called ŭp 읍, myŏn 면 or ri 리, depending on how urbanised or rural they are.

In 2006, the Seoul government decided to give every street a name and each building a number. The idea was to make sense of building locations through a logical system; if it works, other cities may follow suit.

In the old system, an address might have looked like this:
서울특별시 도봉구 쌍문동 150번지 1호
sŏ·ul·t'ŭk·pyŏl·shi to·bong·gu ssang·mun·dong
pae·go·ship·pŏn·ji il·ho
**Seoul-shi, Tobong-gu district, Ssangmun-dong neighbourhood, block 150, building 1**

In the new system, the same address would read:
서울특별시 도봉구 정의4길 21번
sŏ·ul·t'ŭk·pyŏl·shi to·bong·gu chŏng·i sa·gil i·shi·bil·bŏn
**Seoul-shi, Tobong-gu district, Chŏngi-4-gil street, number 21**

# Accommodation

## KEY PHRASES

| | | |
|---|---|---|
| **Where's a hotel?** | 호텔 어디있어요? | ho·t'el ŏ·di iss·ŏ·yo |
| **Do you have a double room?** | 더블 룸 있나요? | tŏ·bŭl rum in·na·yo |
| **How much is it per night?** | 하룻밤에 얼마예요? | ha·rup·pa·mé ŏl·ma·ye·yo |
| **Is breakfast included?** | 아침 포함인가요? | a·ch'im p'o·ha·min·ga·yo |
| **What time is checkout?** | 체크아웃 언제예요? | ch'e·k'ŭ·a·ut ŏn·je·ye·yo |

## Finding Accommodation

**Where's a ...?**   ... 어디있어요?
　　　　　　　　　... ŏ·di iss·ŏ·yo

| | | |
|---|---|---|
| **campsite** | 야영장 | ya·yŏng·jang |
| **guesthouse** | 민박집 | min·bak·chip |
| **hotel** | 호텔 | ho·t'el |
| **motel** | 여관/여인숙 | yŏ·gwan/yŏ·in·suk |
| **mountain hut** | 산장 | san·jang |
| **temple to stay at** | 템플 스테이 | t'em·p'ŭl sŭ·t'e·i |
| **traditional house** | 한옥 | ha·nok |
| **youth hostel** | 유스 호스텔 | yu·sŭ ho·sŭ·t'el |

| Can you recommend somewhere ...? | | ... 숙소 추천해 주세요.<br>... suk·so ch'u·ch'ŏn hae·ju·se·yo |
|---|---|---|
| cheap | 싼 | ssan |
| clean | 깨끗한 | ggaek·kŭ·t'an |
| good | 좋은 | cho·ŭn |
| nearby | 가까운 | kak·ka·un |
| safe for women | 여자가 있기에<br>안전한 | yŏ·ja·ga ik·ki·é<br>an·jŏn·han |

| I want something near the ... | | ...에서 가까우면 좋겠어요.<br>...·e·sŏ kak·ka·u·myŏn cho·k'ess·ŏ·yo |
|---|---|---|
| beach | 해변 | hae·byŏn |
| city centre | 시내 | shi·nae |
| mountains | 산 | san |
| metro station | 지하철역 | chi·ha·ch'ŏl·yŏk |
| train station | 기차역 | ki·ch'a·yŏk |

## Booking Ahead & Checking In

| I'd like to book a room, please. | 방 예약하려고 하는데요.<br>pang ye·ya·k'a·ryŏ·go ha·nŭn·de·yo |
|---|---|
| ✂ **Are there rooms?** | 방 있나요?    pang in·na·yo |
| I have a reservation. | 예약했어요.<br>ye·ya·k'aess·ŏ·yo |
| For (three) nights/weeks. | (삼) 박이요/주요.<br>(sam)·ba·gi·yo/·ju·yo |

| From (2 July) to (6 July). | (칠월 이일)부터 (칠월 육일)까지요. (ch'i·rwŏl i·il)·bu·t'ŏ (ch'i·rwŏl yu·gil)k·ka·ji·yo |
|---|---|
| Do you have a single room? | 싱글 룸 있나요? shing·gŭl rum in·na·yo |
| Do you have a double room? | 더블 룸 있나요? tŏ·bŭl rum in·na·yo |
| Do you have a twin room? | 트윈 룸 있나요? t'ŭ·win rum in·na·yo |
| I want a room with (a/an) ... | ... 방으로 할게요. ... bang·ŭ·ro halk·ke·yo |

| bathroom | 욕실 있는 | yok·shi·rin·nŭn |
|---|---|---|
| cable TV | 케이블 나오는 | k'e·i·bŭl na·o·nŭn |
| internet connection | 인터넷 되는 | in·t'ŏ·net toé·nŭn |
| view | 전망 좋은 | chŏn·mang cho·ŭn |

| How much per night? | 하룻밤에 얼마예요? ha·rup·pam·é ŏl·ma·ye·yo |
|---|---|
| How much per person? | 한 명에 얼마예요? han·myŏng·é ŏl·ma·ye·yo |
| Is breakfast included? | 아침 포함인가요? a·ch'im p'o·ha·min·ga·yo |
| Is there anything cheaper? | 더 싼 건 없나요? tŏ·ssan·gŏn ŏm·na·yo |
| Can I see it? | 좀 볼 수 있나요? chom pol·su in·na·yo |
| I'll take it. | 이 방으로 할게요. i·bang·ŭ·ro halk·ke·yo |

For methods of payment, see **money & banking** (p104).

## Requests & Queries

| | | |
|---|---|---|
| When/Where is breakfast served? | 아침은 언제/어디서 먹나요? | a·ch'i·mŭn ŏn·jé/ŏ·di·sŏ mŏng·na·yo |
| Is there hot water all day? | 온수 하루 종일 나오나요? | on·su ha·ru·jong·il na·o·na·yo |
| When is the hot water on? | 온수 언제 나오나요? | on·su ŏn·jé na·o·na·yo |
| Please wake me at (seven). | (일곱) 시에 깨워주세요. | (il·gop)·shi·é kkae·wŏ·ju·se·yo |
| Can I use the internet? | 인터넷 써도 되나요? | in·t'ŏ·net ssŏ·do doé·na·yo |
| Can I use the kitchen? | 주방 써도 되나요? | chu·bang ssŏ·do doé·na·yo |
| Can I use the telephone? | 전화 써도 되나요? | chŏn·hwa ssŏ·do doé·na·yo |
| Is there a/an ...? | ... 있나요? | ... in·na·yo |

| | | |
|---|---|---|
| elevator/lift | 엘리베이터 | el·li·be·i·t'ŏ |
| laundry service | 세탁 서비스 | se·t'ak sŏ·bi·sŭ |
| message board | 메모 남길 알림판 | me·mo·nam·gil al·lim·p'an |
| safe | 금고 | kŭm·go |
| swimming pool | 수영장 | su·yŏng·jang |

| | | |
|---|---|---|
| Can I have an extra blanket, please? | 이불 더 주실 수 있나요? | i·bul tŏ ju·shil·su in·na·yo |
| Can I have my key, please? | 열쇠 주실 수 있나요? | yŏl·soé ju·shil·su in·na·yo |

# Finding a Room

 **Do you have a ... room?**
... 룸 있나요?
... rum in·na·yo

 **double**
더블
tŏ·bŭl

 **single**
싱글
shing·gŭl

 **How much is it per ...?**
...에 얼마예요?
...·é ŏl·ma·ye·yo

 **night**
하룻밤
ha·rup·pam

**person**
한 명
han·myŏng

 **Is breakfast included?**
아침 포함인가요?
a·ch'im p'o·ha·min·ga·yo

 **Can I see the room?**
좀 볼 수 있나요?
chom pol·su in·na·yo

 **'ll take it.**
l 방으로 할게요.
bang·ŭ·ro halk·ke·yo

**I won't take it.**
이 방은 안 할래요.
i·bang·ŭn an·hal·lae·yo

**CULTURE TIP**

### Room Types

Large hotels have 'Western-style' rooms (sŏ·yang·shik 서양식), with beds in every room, but smaller places may only have 'Korean-style' rooms (chŏn·t'ong 전통), offering yo 요 (floor mattresses) instead. These are very comfortable in the winter, when the on·dol 온돌 (floor-heating systems) are turned on.

| | |
|---|---|
| I'm locked out of my room. | 열쇠를 방에 두고<br>나와 버렸어요.<br>yŏl·soé·rŭl bang·é du·go<br>na·wa·bŏ·ryŏss·ŏ·yo |
| Do you arrange tours here? | 여행 주선<br>해주시나요?<br>yŏ·haeng·ju·sŏn<br>hae·ju·shi·na·yo |
| Do you change money here? | 여기서 환전할 수 있나요?<br>yŏ·gi·sŏ hwan·jŏn hal·su<br>in·na·yo |
| Is there a message for me? | 저한테 온 메시지 없나요?<br>chŏ·han·t'é on·me·shi·ji<br>ŏm·na·yo |
| Can I leave a message for someone? | 메시지 남길 수 있나요?<br>me·shi·ji nam·gil·su in·na·yo |

 **LISTEN FOR**

| | | |
|---|---|---|
| 몇 박이요? | myŏp·pa·gi·yo | How many nights? |
| 신분증 | shin·bun·tchŭng | identification |
| 전용 욕실 | chŏ·nyong yok·shil | private bathroom |
| 공용 욕실 | kong·yong yok·shil | shared bathroom |
| 열쇠 | yŏl·soé | key |
| 프런트 | p'u·rŏn·t'ŭ | reception |

# Complaints

It's too ...           너무 ...
                  nŏ·mu ...

| bright | 밝아요 | pal·ga·yo |
| cold | 추워요 | ch'u·wŏ·yo |
| dark | 어두워요 | ŏ·du·wŏ·yo |
| dirty | 지저분해요 | ji·jŏ·bun·hae·yo |
| noisy | 시끄러워요 | shik·kŭ·rŏ·wŏ·yo |
| small | 작아요 | cha·ga·yo |

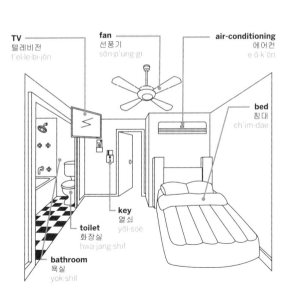

**TV**
텔레비전
t'el·le·bi·jŏn

**fan**
선풍기
sŏn·p'ung·gi

**air-conditioning**
에어컨
e·ŏ·k'ŏn

**bed**
침대
ch'im·dae

**key**
열쇠
yŏl·soé

**toilet**
화장실
hwa·jang·shil

**bathroom**
욕실
yok·shil

| The air-conditioning doesn't work. | 에어컨이 안 돼요.<br>e·ŏ·k'ŏ·ni an·dwae·yo |
| The toilet won't flush. | 변기가 막혔어요.<br>pyŏn·gi·ga ma·k'yŏss·ŏ·yo |
| There's no hot water. | 온수가 안 나와요.<br>on·su·ga an·na·wa·yo |
| This (pillow) isn't clean. | 이 (베개) 깨끗하지 않은데요.<br>i (pe·gae) ggaek·ku·t'a·ji a·nŭn·de·yo |
| Please change the sheets. | 시트 갈아 주세요.<br>shi·t'ŭ ka·ra·ju·se·yo |
| Please clean the room. | 방 청소 해 주세요.<br>pang ch'ŏng·so hae·ju·se·yo |

## Answering the Door

| Who is it? | 누구세요?<br>nu·gu·se·yo |
| Just a moment. | 잠시만요.<br>cham·shi·man·nyo |
| Come in. | 들어오세요.<br>tŭ·rŏ·o·se·yo |
| Come back later, please. | 이따가 오세요.<br>it·ta·ga o·se·yo |

### 🔍 LOOK FOR

| 방 있음 | pang·iss·ŭm | Rooms Available |
| 산장 | san·jang | Mountain Hut |
| 세탁 | se·t'ak | Laundry |
| 식당 | shik·tang | Restaurant |
| 욕실 | yok·shil | Bathroom |

## Checking Out

| | |
|---|---|
| What time is checkout? | 체크아웃 언제예요?<br>ch'e·k'ŭ·a·ut ŏn·je·ye·yo |
| Can I have a late checkout? | 체크아웃 좀 늦게<br>해도 되나요?<br>ch'e·k'ŭ·a·ut chom nŭk·ké<br>hae·do doé·na·yo |
| Can you call a taxi for me (for 11 o'clock)? | (열한 시까지) 택시<br>불러 주시겠어요?<br>(yŏl·han·shik·ka·ji) t'aek·shi<br>pul·lŏ·ju·shi·gess·ŏ·yo |
| Can I leave my (backpack) here? | (배낭) 여기 두고<br>가도 되나요?<br>(pae·nang) yŏ·gi·du·go<br>ka·do·doé·na·yo |
| Can I have my deposit, please? | 보증금 돌려<br>주시겠어요?<br>po·jŭng·gŭm tol·lyŏ<br>ju·shi·gess·ŏ·yo |
| Can I have my passport, please? | 여권 돌려 주시겠어요?<br>yŏk·kwŏn tol·lyŏ ju·shi·gess·ŏ·yo |
| Can I have my valuables, please? | 귀중품 돌려<br>주시겠어요?<br>kwi·jung·p'um tol·lyŏ<br>ju·shi·gess·ŏ·yo |
| I'm leaving now. | 지금 가요.<br>chi·gŭm ka·yo |
| I'll be back in (three) days. | (삼) 일 안에 돌아올게요.<br>(sam)·i·ra·né to·ra·olk·ke·yo |
| I'll be back on (Tuesday). | (화요일)에 돌아올게요.<br>(hwa·yo·ir)·é to·ra·olk·ke·yo |
| Thank you for all your help. | 여러가지로<br>고맙습니다.<br>yŏ·rŏ·ga·ji·ro<br>ko·map·sŭm·ni·da |

## Camping

| | | |
|---|---|---|
| **Is there a campsite nearby?** | 근처에 야영장 있나요? | kŭn·ch'ŏ·é ya·yŏng·jang in·na·yo |
| **Does this temple offer sleeping accommodation?** | 여기서 템플 스테이 할 수 있나요? | yŏ·gi·sŏ t'em·p'ŭl sŭ·t'e·i hal·su in·na·yo |
| **Where can we get permits for camping?** | 야영하려면 어디서 허락 받나요? | ya·yŏng ha·ryŏ·myŏn ŏ·di·sŏ hŏ·rak pan·na·yo |
| **Do you have ...?** | ... 있나요? | ... in·na·yo |

| | | |
|---|---|---|
| electricity | 전기 시설 | chŏn·gi shi·sŏl |
| a laundry | 세탁할 곳 | se·t'a·k'al·got |
| shower facilities | 샤워 시설 | sha·wŏ shi·sŏl |
| tents for hire | 빌릴 텐트 | pil·lil t'en·t'ŭ |

| | | |
|---|---|---|
| **How much per person?** | 일인당 얼마예요? | i·rin·dang ŏl·ma·ye·yo |
| **How much per tent?** | 텐트당 얼마예요? | t'en·t'ŭ·dang ŏl·ma·ye·yo |
| **How much per vehicle?** | 한 차당 얼마예요? | han·ch'a·dang ŏl·ma·ye·yo |
| **Is the water drinkable?** | 마셔도 되는 물인가요? | ma·shŏ·do doé·nŭn mu·rin·ga·yo |
| **Can I camp here?** | 여기서 야영해도 되나요? | yŏ·gi·sŏ ya·yŏng·hae·do doé·na·yo |
| **Could I borrow ...?** | ... 빌릴 수 있나요? | ... pil·lil·su in·na·yo |

예약했어요.
ye·ya·k'aess·ŏ·yo

*I have a reservation.*

安國房
ANGUK GUESTHOUSE

## Renting

Renting apartments or houses for short-term stays is almost unheard of in Korea. Renting rooms in boarding houses, however, is quite common, and can be arranged through pu·dong·san 부동산 (real estate agencies) for a small fee.

| **Do you have a/an ... for rent?** | ... 빌릴 수 있나요? <br> ... pil·lil·su in·na·yo | |
|---|---|---|
| **apartment** | 아파트 | a·p'a·t'ŭ |
| **cabin** | 방갈로 | pang·gal·lo |
| **house** | 집 | chip |
| **room** | 방 | pang |

| I'd like to rent it for (one) month. | (한) 달 동안 빌릴게요.<br>(han)·dal·dong·an pil·lilk·ke·yo |
| Is there a bond? | 보증금 내야 하나요?<br>po·jŭng·gŭm nae·ya ha·na·yo |
| How much is the bond? | 보증금이 얼마예요?<br>po·jŭng·gŭm·i ŏl·ma·ye·yo |
| Are bills extra? | 공공요금은 따로 내나요?<br>kong·gong yo·gŭ·mŭn dda·ro nae·na·yo |

## Staying with Locals

| Can I stay at your place? | 당신 집에서 지내도 될까요?<br>tang·shin chi·be·sŏ ji·nae·do doélk·ka·yo |
| I have my own floor mattress. | 제 요 있어요.<br>ché yo iss·ŏ·yo |
| I have my own sleeping bag. | 제 침낭 있어요.<br>ché ch'im·nang iss·ŏ·yo |
| Is there anything I can do to help? | 뭐 도와드릴 것 없나요?<br>mwŏ to·wa·du·ril·gŏt ŏm·na·yo |
| Can I bring anything for the meal? | 먹을 것 가져갈까요?<br>mŏ·gŭl·gŏt ka·jŏ kalk·ka·yo |
| Can I do the dishes? | 설거지 할까요?<br>sŏl·gŏ·ji halk·ka·yo |
| Can I set/clear the table? | 상을 차릴까요/치울까요?<br>sang·ŭl ch'a·rilk·ka·yo/ch'i·ulk·ka·yo |
| Can I take out the rubbish? | 쓰레기 버릴까요?<br>ssŭ·re·gi pŏ·rilk·ka·yo |
| Thank you for your hospitality. | 환대해 주셔서 고맙습니다.<br>hwan·dae hae·ju·shŏ·sŏ ko·map·sŭm·ni·da |

To compliment your hosts' cooking, see **eating out** (p198).

# Shopping

**KEY PHRASES**

| | | |
|---|---|---|
| **Do you have ...?** | ... 있나요? | ... in·na·yo |
| **Can I look at it?** | 보여 주시겠어요? | po·yŏ ju·shi·gess·ŏ·yo |
| **Can I try it on?** | 입어봐도 되나요? | i·bŏ·bwa·do doé·na·yo |
| **How much is it?** | 얼마예요? | ŏl·ma·ye·yo |
| **That's too expensive.** | 너무 비싸요. | nŏ·mu piss·a·yo |

## Looking For ...

| | |
|---|---|
| **What hours are shops open?** | 영업 시간이 언제예요? yŏng·ŏp shi·ga·ni ŏn·je·ye·yo |
| **Where can I buy (a padlock)?** | (자물쇠) 어디서 살 수 있나요? (cha·mul·soé) ŏ·di·sŏ sal·su in·na·yo |
| **Where's the nearest ...?** | 제일 가까운 ...이/가 어디 있나요? chě·il kak·ka·un ...·i/·ga ŏ·di in·na·yo |

| | | |
|---|---|---|
| **big discount store** | 대형할인점 | tae·hyŏng ha·rin·jŏm |
| **convenience store** | 편의점 | p'yŏ·ni·jŏm |
| **department store** | 백화점 | pae·k'wa·jŏm |
| **supermarket** | 슈퍼마켓 | shu·p'ŏ·ma·k'et |
| **market** | 시장 | shi·jang |

For more items and shopping locations, see the **dictionary**.

## Making a Purchase

| | |
|---|---|
| I'm just looking. | 그냥 구경할게요.<br>kŭ·nyang ku·gyŏng halk·ke·yo |
| Do you have (tissues)? | (휴지) 있나요?<br>(hyu·ji) in·na·yo |
| Can I look at it? | 보여 주시겠어요?<br>po·yŏ ju·shi·gess·ŏ·yo |
| Do you have any others? | 다른 건 없나요?<br>ta·rŭn·gŏn ŏm·na·yo |
| How much is it? | 얼마예요?<br>ŏl·ma·ye·yo |
| I'd like a bag, please. | 봉투 주세요.<br>pong·t'u chu·se·yo |
| Does it have a guarantee? | 품질 보증 되나요?<br>p'um·jil po·jŭng dóe·na·yo |
| Can you order it for me? | 주문해 주실 수 있나요?<br>chu·mun·hae ju·shil·su in·na·yo |
| Can I pick it up later? | 나중에 가져 가도 되나요?<br>na·jung·é ka·jŏ·ga·do dóe·na·yo |

### 🔊 LISTEN FOR

| | | |
|---|---|---|
| 도와 드릴까요? | to·wa dŭ·rilk·ka·yo | Can I help you? |
| 뭐 드릴까요? | mwŏ dŭ·rilk·ka·yo | What would you like? |
| 다른 것 도와<br>드릴 것 없나요? | ta·rŭn·gŏt to·wa dŭ·ril·gŏt ŏm·na·yo | Anything else? |
| 없는데요. | ŏm·nŭn·de·yo | No, we don't have any. |

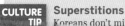

**Superstitions**
Koreans don't mind if you just browse, but be aware that if you're the first customer of the day in a small shop, they'll press you to buy something – superstition dictates you'll set the pace for the rest of the day.

PRACTICAL

SHOPPING

| | | |
|---|---|---|
| **Could I have it wrapped?** | 포장해 주시겠어요?<br>p'o·jang·hae ju·shi·gess·ŏ·yo | |
| **The quality isn't good.** | 품질이 안 좋아요.<br>p'um·ji·ri an·jo·a·yo | |
| **It's faulty.** | 불량이에요.<br>pul·lyang·i·e·yo | |
| **I'd like to return this, please.** | 반품하고<br>싶습니다.<br>pan·p'um ha·go<br>ship·sŭm·ni·da | |
| **I'd like my change, please.** | 잔돈 주세요.<br>chan·don ju·se·yo | |
| **I'd like a refund, please.** | 환불하고 싶습니다.<br>hwan·bul ha·go ship·sŭm·ni·da | |
| **Could I have a receipt, please?** | 영수증 주시겠어요?<br>yŏng·su·jŭng chu·shi·gess·ŏ·yo | |
| ✂ **Receipt, please.** | 영수증<br>주세요. | yŏng·su·jŭng<br>chu·se·yo |

## Bargaining

Bargaining is still done in small shops and with street vendors, but it's gradually falling out of favour. A good rule of thumb is that if something has a price tag on it, that price should be considered non-negotiable.

| **That's too expensive.** | 너무 비싸요.<br>nŏ·mu piss·a·yo |
|---|---|

### 🔊 LISTEN FOR

| 흥정 | hŭng·jŏng | bargain |
|---|---|---|
| 판매 | p'an·mae | for sale |
| 바가지 | pa·ga·ji | rip-off n |
| 세일 | se·il | sale n |
| 매진 | mae·jin | sold out |
| 특가 상품 | t'ŭk·ka sang·p'um | specially priced item |

| Do you have something cheaper? | 더 싼 것 있나요?<br>tŏ·ssan·gŏt in·na·yo |
|---|---|
| Please give me a discount. | 깎아 주세요.<br>ggak·ka·ju·se·yo |
| What's your final price? | 얼마까지 해 주실 수 있나요?<br>ŏl·mak·ka·ji hae·ju·shil·su in·na·yo |
| No more than (20,000 won). | (이만 원) 이상은 안 돼요.<br>(i·man·wŏn) i·sang·ŭn an·dwae·yo |
| I'll give you (90,000 won). | (구만 원) 드릴게요.<br>(ku·man·wŏn) dŭ·rilk·ke·yo |

## Books & Reading

| Is there a/an ...? | ... 있나요?<br>... in·na·yo |
|---|---|

| bookshop | 서점 | sŏ·jŏm |
|---|---|---|
| dictionary | 사전 | sa·jŏn |
| newspaper (in English) | (영자) 신문 | (yŏng·tcha) shin·mun |
| (English-language) section | (영어 책) 코너 | (yŏng·ŏ ch'aek) k'o·nŏ |

# Making a Purchase

## I'd like to buy...
…을/를 사고 싶어요.
…ŭl/·rŭl sa·go shi·p'ŏ·yo

## How much is it?
얼마예요?
ŏl·ma·ye·yo

--- OR ---

## Can you write down the price?
가격을 써 주시겠어요?
ka·gyŏ·gŭl ssŏ ju·shi·gess·ŏ·yo

## Do you accept credit cards?
신용카드 받으시나요?
shi·nyong k'a·dŭ pa·dŭ·shi·na·yo

## Could I have a ..., please?
… 주세요.
… chu·se·yo

**receipt**
영수증
yŏng·su·jŭng

**bag**
봉투
pong·t'u

| | | |
|---|---|---|
| **Can you recommend a book for me?** | | 책 추천해 주시겠어요?<br>ch'aek ch'u·ch'ŏn<br>hae·ju·shi·gess·ŏ·yo |
| **Do you have any books in English by (Hyon Hui)?** | | 영어로 된 (현희)의<br>책 있나요?<br>yŏng·ŏ·ro·doén (hyŏn·hi)·é<br>ch'aek in·na·yo |

## Clothes

| | | |
|---|---|---|
| **My size is ...** | | 제 사이즈는 ...<br>이에요/예요.<br>ché sa·i·jŭ·nŭn<br>...·i·e·yo/·ye·yo |
| **(40)** | (사십) | (sa·ship) |
| **small** | 스몰 | sŭ·mol |
| **medium** | 미디엄 | mi·di·ŏm |
| **large** | 라지 | ra·ji |
| **Can I try it on?** | | 입어봐도 되나요?<br>i·bŏ·bwa·do doé·na·yo |
| **It doesn't fit.** | | 안 맞아요.<br>an·ma·ja·yo |

## Music & DVD

| | | |
|---|---|---|
| **I'd like a ...** | | ... 있나요?<br>... in·na·yo |
| **CD** | 시디 | shi·di |
| **DVD** | 디브이디 | di·bŭ·i·di |
| **mp3 player** | 엠피스리<br>플레이어 | em·p'i·sŭ·ri<br>p'ŭl·le·i·ŏ |
| **video** | 비디오 | bi·di·o |

| I'm looking for a CD by (Sumi Jo). | (조수미) 시디 찾는데요. (cho·su·mi) shi·di ch'an·nŭn·de·yo |
| What's his/her best recording? | 그 사람의 제일 좋은 음반이 뭐예요? kŭ sa·ra·mé che·il cho·ŭn ŭm·ba·ni mwŏ·ye·yo |
| Can I listen to this here? | 이거 들어볼 수 있나요? i·gŏ dŭ·rŏ·bol·su in·na·yo |
| What region is this DVD for? | 이 디브이디 지역코드가 뭐예요? i·di·bŭ·i·di ji·yŏk k'o·dŭ·ga mwŏ·ye·yo |

## Video & Photography

| Can you ...? | ... 수 있나요? ... su in·na·yo |
|---|---|
| develop this film | 이 필름 현상할 i·p'il·lüm hyŏn·sang·hal |
| load my film | 필름 끼울 p'il·lŭm kki·ul |
| print digital photos | 디지털 사진 인쇄할 di·ji·t'ŏl sa·jin in·swae·hal |
| recharge the battery for my digital camera | 디카 배터리 충전할 ti·k'a pae·t'ŏ·ri ch'ung·jŏn·hal |
| transfer photos from my camera to CD | 디카 안의 사진을 시디로 옮길 ti·k'a a·né sa·ji·nŭl shi·di·ro om·gil |

**Do you have (a) ... for this camera?**
이 카메라용 ... 있나요?
i·k'a·me·ra·yong ... in·na·yo

| | | |
|---|---|---|
| batteries | 배터리 | pae·t'ŏ·ri |
| flash | 플래시 | p'ŭl·lae·shi |
| (zoom) lens | (줌) 렌즈 | (chum) ren·jŭ |
| light meter | 조명 | cho·myŏng |
| | 측정기 | ch'ŭk·chŏng·gi |
| memory cards | 메모리 카드 | me·mo·ri k'a·dŭ |

**I need a/an ... film for this camera.**
이 카메라용 ... 필름이
필요해요.
i·k'a·me·ra·yong ... p'il·lŭ·mi
p'i·ryo·hae·yo

| | | |
|---|---|---|
| B&W | 흑백 | hŭk·paek |
| colour | 컬러 | k'ŏl·lŏ |
| slide | 슬라이드 | sŭl·la·i·dŭ |
| (200) speed | 감도 (이백) | kam·do (i·baek) |

**I need a cable to recharge this battery.**
충전용 케이블이 필요해요.
ch'ung·jŏn·nyong k'e·i·bŭ·ri
p'i·ryo·hae·yo

**I need a video cassette for this camera.**
이 카메라용 비디오
카세트가 필요해요.
i·k'a·me·ra·yong bi·di·o
k'a·se·t'ŭ·ga p'i·ryo·hae·yo

**... camera**
... 카메라
... k'a·me·ra

| | | |
|---|---|---|
| digital | 디지털 | di·ji·t'ŏl |
| disposable | 일회용 | il·hoé·yong |
| underwater | 수중 | su·jung |
| video | 비디오 | bi·di·o |

# Repairs

**Can I have my ... repaired here?**
... 고칠 수 있나요?
... ko·ch'il·su in·na·yo

| | | |
|---|---|---|
| **backpack** | 배낭 | pae·nang |
| **bag** | 가방 | ka·bang |
| **(video) camera** | (비디오) 카메라 | (bi·di·o) k'a·me·ra |
| **shoes** | 신발 | shin·bal |
| **sunglasses** | 선글라스 | sŏn·gŭl·la·sŭ |

**When will it be ready?**
언제 다 되나요?
ŏn·je ta·doé·na·yo

얼마예요?
ŏl·ma·ye·yo
*How much is it?*

**CULTURE TIP**  Holidays & Festivals

| | |
|---|---|
| **Cherry Blossom Festivals (April)** | 벚꽃 축제<br>pŏk·kot ch'uk·ché |
| **Chusok (Harvest Moon Festival)** | 추석<br>ch'u·sŏk |
| **Hangul Day (9 October)** | 한글날<br>han·gŭl·lal |
| **Lunar New Year** | 구정/설날<br>ku·jŏng/sŏl·lal |
| **National Foundation Day (3 October)** | 개천절<br>kae·ch'ŏn·jŏl |

## Souvenirs

| | |
|---|---|
| **embroidery** | 자수품<br>cha·su·p'um |
| **lacquerware** | 나전칠기<br>na·jŏn·ch'il·gi |
| **pottery** | 도자기<br>to·ja·gi |
| **traditional Korean clothing** | 한복<br>han·bok |
| **traditional Korean paper** | 한지<br>han·ji |
| **traditional stone figures of Jejudo** | 하르방<br>ha·rŭ·bang |

# Communications

### KEY PHRASES

| | | |
|---|---|---|
| **Is there an internet cafe nearby?** | 주변에 피시방 있나요? | chu·byŏ·né p'i·shi·bang in·na·yo |
| **I'd like to check my email.** | 이메일 확인하려고요. | i·me·il hwa·gin ha·ryŏ·go·yo |
| **I want to send a parcel.** | 소포 부치려고요. | so·p'o pu·ch'i·ryŏ·go·yo |
| **I want to make a call.** | 전화하고 싶어요. | chŏn·hwa·ha·go shi·p'ŏ·yo |
| **I'd like to buy a phonecard.** | 전화카드 사고 싶어요. | chŏn·hwa·k'a·dŭ sa·go shi·p'ŏ·yo |

## The Internet

| | |
|---|---|
| **Is there an internet cafe nearby?** | 주변에 피시방 있나요? chu·byŏ·né p'i·shi·bang in·na·yo |
| **Do you have internet access here?** | 여기 인터넷 연결 되나요? yŏ·gi in·t'ŏ·net yŏn·gyŏl doé·na·yo |
| **Is there wireless internet access here?** | 여기 무선 인터넷 되나요? yŏ·gi mu·sŏn in·t'ŏ·net toé·na·yo |
| **Can I connect my laptop here?** | 여기 노트북 연결해도 되나요? yŏ·gi no·t'ŭ·buk yŏn·gyŏl hae·do doé·na·yo |

**I'd like to ...**

| | | |
|---|---|---|
| **burn a CD** | 시디 구우려고요. | shi·di ku·u·ryŏ·go·yo |
| **check my email** | 이메일 확인하려고요. | i·me·il hwa·gin ha·ryŏ·go·yo |
| **download my photos** | 사진 다운 받으려고요. | sa·jin da·un pa·dŭ·ryŏ·go·yo |
| **get internet access** | 인터넷 연결 하려고요. | in·t'ŏ·net yŏn·gyŏl ha·ryŏ·go·yo |
| **use a printer/ scanner** | 프린터/스캐너 쓰려고요. | p'ŭ·rin·t'ŏ/sŭ·k'ae·nŏ ssŭ·ryŏ·go·yo |
| **use Skype** | 스카이프 쓰고 싶어요. | sŭ·k'a·i·p'ŭ ssŭ·go shi·p'o·yo |

| | |
|---|---|
| **Do you have Macs?** | 매킨토시 있나요? mae·k'in·t'o·shi in·na·yo |
| **Do you have PCs?** | 윈도우 깔린 컴퓨터 있나요? win·do·u kka·rin k'ŏm·p'yu·t'ŏ in·na·yo |
| **Do you have headphones (with a microphone)?** | (마이크 달린) 헤드폰 있나요? (ma·i·k'ŭ dal·lin) he·dŭ·pon in·na·yo |
| **Can I connect my ... to this computer?** | 제 ...을/를 이 컴퓨터에 연결해도 되나요? ché ...·ŭl/·rŭl i k'ŏm·pyu·t'ŏ·é yŏn·gyŏl hae·do doé·na·yo |

| | | |
|---|---|---|
| **camera** | 카메라 | k'a·me·ra |
| **iPod** | 아이팟 | a·i·p'at |
| **MP3 player** | 엠피스리 | em·p'i·sŭ·ri |
| **portable hard drive** | 외장 하드 | oé·jang ha·dŭ |
| **PSP** | 피에스피 | p'i·e·sŭ·p'i |
| **USB flash drive** | 유에스비 | yu·e·sŭ·bi |

**CULTURE TIP**

**PC-Rooms**

In Korea, you can take advantage of cheap high-speed connections at home or in the ubiquitous 24-hour p'i·shi·bang 피시방 (lit: PC-room). These are the Korean equivalent of internet cafes, and can be found even in the most out-of-the-way towns.

| | |
|---|---|
| **How much per hour?** | 시간당 얼마예요?<br>shi·gan dang ŏl·ma·ye·yo |
| **How much per page?** | 페이지당 얼마예요?<br>p'e·i·ji dang ŏl·ma·ye·yo |
| **How do I log in?** | 로그인 어떻게 하나요?<br>ro·gŭ·in ŏt·tŏ·k'é ha·na·yo |
| **What's the password?** | 비밀번호가 뭐예요?<br>pi·mil·bŏn·ho·ga mwŏ·ye·yo |
| **It's crashed.** | 얼었어요.<br>ŏ·rŏss·ŏ·yo |
| **I've finished.** | 다 했어요.<br>ta haess·ŏ·yo |

## Mobile/Cell Phone

| | |
|---|---|
| **I'd like a charger for my phone.** | 휴대폰 충전기 주세요.<br>hyu·dae·p'on ch'ung·jŏn·gi ju·se·yo |
| **I'd like a mobile/cell phone for hire.** | 휴대폰 빌리려고요.<br>hyu·dae·p'on pil·li·ryŏ·go·yo |

 **LISTEN FOR**

| | | |
|---|---|---|
| 일 분당<br>(육십) 원이요. | il·bun·dang<br>(yuk·shib)·wŏ·ni·yo | (60) won per minute. |

| I'd like a prepaid mobile/ cell phone. | 선불 휴대폰 주세요. sŏn·bul hyu·dae·p'on ju·se·yo |

## Phone

| Q What's your phone number? | 전화번호가 뭐예요? chŏn·hwa·bŏn·ho·ga mwŏ·ye·yo |
|---|---|
| A The number is ... | 번호는 ...이에요/예요. pŏn·ho·nŭn ... ·i·e·yo/·ye·yo |
| Where's the nearest telephone office/public phone? | 제일 가까운 전화국/공중전화 어디 있나요? che·il kak·ka·un chŏn·hwa·guk/ kong·jung·jŏn·hwa ŏ·di in·na·yo |
| Can I have some coins? | 동전 좀 주실 수 있나요? tong·jŏn chom ju·shil·su in·na·yo |

### 🔊 LISTEN FOR

| 잘못 거셨습니다. | chal·mot kŏ·shŏss·sŭm·ni·da Wrong number. |
|---|---|
| 누구신데요? | nu·gu·shin·de·yo Who's calling? |
| 누구 바꿔 드릴까요? | nu·gu pak·kwŏ dŭ·rilk·ka·yo Who do you want to speak to? |
| 잠시만요. | cham·shi·man·nyo One moment, please. |
| 지금 없는데요. | chi·gŭm ŏm·nŭn·de·yo He/She isn't here. |

| | |
|---|---|
| **Can I look at a phone book?** | 전화번호부 볼 수 있나요?<br>chŏn·hwa·bŏn·ho·bu pol·su in·na·yo |
| **What's the area/country code for ...?** | ... 지역/국가 번호가 뭐예요?<br>... ji·yŏk/kuk·ka pŏn·ho·ga mwŏ·ye·yo |
| **Does this phone take credit cards?** | 이 전화 신용카드로 걸 수 있나요?<br>i·jŏn·hwa shi·nyong·k'a·dŭ·ro kŏl·su in·na·yo |
| **How much does a (one)-minute call cost?** | (일) 분 통화에 얼마예요?<br>(il)·bun t'ong·hwa·é ŏl·ma·ye·yo |
| **I want to ...** | ... 싶어요.<br>... shi·p'ŏ·yo |

| | | |
|---|---|---|
| **buy a phonecard** | 전화카드 사고 | chŏn·hwa·k'a·dŭ sa·go |
| **call (Singapore)** | (싱가포르)에 전화하고 | (shing·ga·p'o·rŭ)·é chŏn·hwa·ha·go |
| **make a (local) call** | (시내) 전화하고 | (shi·nae) chŏn·hwa·ha·go |
| **reverse the charges** | 수신자 부담 전화하고 | su·shin·ja pu·dam chŏn·hwa·ha·go |
| **speak for (three) minutes** | (삼) 분 동안 통화하고 | (sam)·bun dong·an t'ong·hwa·ha·go |

| | |
|---|---|
| **It's engaged.** | 통화 중이에요.<br>t'ong·hwa·jung·i·e·yo |
| **I've been cut off.** | 전화가 끊겼어요.<br>chŏn·hwa·ga kkŭn·k'yŏss·ŏ·yo |

**PRACTICAL COMMUNICATIONS**

> **LANGUAGE TIP**
>
> **Saying Phone Numbers**
> In Korean, phone numbers are read in the following order: first the area code, followed by é 에, then the three- or four-digit prefix, followed by é, and at the end the last four digits – eg kong·il·gong·é sa·mo·gu·ch'i·ré i·gong·o·gu 공일공에 삼오구칠에 이공오구 (010 3597 2059). Note that in Seoul the 02 area code is often dropped.

| | |
|---|---|
| The connection's bad. | 연결 상태가 나빠요.<br>yŏn·gyŏl sang·t'ae·ga nap·pa·yo |
| Hello. | 여보세요.<br>yŏ·bo·se·yo |
| It's … | …인데요.<br>…in·de·yo |
| Can I speak to (Eunjeong)? (name ends in a consonant) | (은정)이 있어요?<br>(ŭn·jŏng)·i iss·ŏ·yo |
| Can I speak to (Hyemi)? (name ends in a vowel) | (혜미) 있어요?<br>(hye·mi) iss·ŏ·yo |
| Please tell him/her I called. | 제가 전화했다고 전해 주세요.<br>che·ga chŏn·hwa haet·ta·go chŏn·hae ju·se·yo |
| Can I leave a message? | 메시지 남길 수 있나요?<br>me·shi·ji nam·gil·su in·na·yo |
| I don't have a contact number. | 전 연락처가 없어요.<br>chŏn yŏl·lak·ch'ŏ·ga ŏp·sŏ·yo |
| I'll call back later. | 제가 다시 전화할게요.<br>che·ga ta·shi chŏn·hwa halk·ke·yo |
| Is there a mobile phone number I can reach him/her at? | 연락 가능한 휴대폰 번호 알 수 있나요?<br>yŏl·lak ka·nŭng·han hyu·dae·p'on bŏn·ho al·su in·na·yo |

| What time should I call? | 언제 전화하면 돼요? |
| | ŏn·jé chŏn·hwa ha·myŏn dwae·yo |

For telephone numbers, see **numbers & amounts** (p90).

## Post Office

| I want to send a letter. | 편지 부치려고요. |
| | p'yŏn·ji pu·ch'i·ryŏ·go·yo |
| I want to send a parcel. | 소포 부치려고요. |
| | so·p'o pu·ch'i·ryŏ·go·yo |
| I want to send a postcard. | 엽서 부치려고요. |
| | yŏp·sŏ pu·ch'i·ryŏ·go·yo |
| I want to buy an envelope. | 봉투 사려고 하는데요. |
| | pong·t'u sa·ryŏ·go ha·nŭn·de·yo |
| I want to buy a stamp. | 우표 사려고 하는데요. |
| | u·p'yo sa·ryŏ·go ha·nŭn·de·yo |
| Can you send it by express mail? | 빠른 우편으로 보낼 수 있나요? |
| | bba·rŭn u·p'yŏ·nŭ·ro po·nael su in·na·yo |
| Please send it by air/ surface mail to (Australia). | (호주)에 항공편으로/선편으로 보내주세요. |
| | (ho·ju)·é hang·gong·p'yŏ·nŭ·ro/ sŏn·p'yŏ·nŭ·ro po·nae ju·se·yo |

## 🔊 LISTEN FOR

| 항공 우편 | hang·gong u·p'yŏn | airmail |
| 국내 | kung·nae | domestic |
| 빠른 우편 | bba·rŭn u·p'yŏn | express mail |
| 파손주의 | p'a·son·ju·i | fragile |
| 국제 | kuk·che | international |
| 등기우편 | tŭng·gi u·p'yŏn | registered mail |
| 선편 우편 | sŏn·p'yŏn u·p'yŏn | surface (sea) mail |

PRACTICAL

MONEY & BANKING

# Money & Banking

**KEY PHRASES**

| How much is this? | 이거 얼마예요? | i·gŏ ŏl·ma·ye·yo |
| What's the exchange rate? | 환율이 얼마예요? | hwa·nyul·i ŏl·ma·ye·yo |
| Where's an ATM? | 현금 인출기 어디 있어요? | hyŏn·gŭm in·ch'ul·gi ŏ·di iss·ŏ·yo |
| I'd like to change money. | 환전해 주세요. | hwan·jŏn hae·ju·se·yo |
| I'd like to get change for this note. | 작은 돈으로 바꿔주세요. | cha·gŭn to·nŭ·ro pak·kwŏ·ju·se·yo |

## Paying the Bill

| Q How much is this? | 이거 얼마예요?<br>i·gŏ ŏl·ma·ye·yo |
| A It's (1000) won. | (천) 원이에요.<br>(ch'ŏn)·wŏ·ni·e·yo |
| A It's free. | 무료예요.<br>mu·ryo·ye·yo |
| Please write down the price. | 가격을 적어주세요.<br>ka·gyŏ·gŭl chŏ·gŏ·ju·se·yo |
| There's a mistake in the bill. | 계산서가 이상해요.<br>kye·san·sŏ·ga i·sang·hae·yo |
| Do you accept credit cards? | 신용카드 받으시나요?<br>shi·nyong·k'a·dŭ pa·dŭ·shi·na·yo |

| Do you accept debit cards? | 체크카드 받으시나요?<br>ch'e·k'ŭ·k'a·dŭ pa·dŭ·shi·na·yo |
| Do you accept travellers cheques? | 여행자 수표 받으시나요?<br>yŏ·haeng·ja su·p'yo pa·dŭ·shi·na·yo |
| Do you accept dollars/yen? | 달러/엔 받으시나요?<br>dal·lŏ/en pa·dŭ·shi·na·yo |
| I'd like my change, please. | 거스름돈 주세요.<br>kŏ·sŭ·rŭm·don chu·se·yo |
| I'd like a receipt, please. | 영수증 주세요.<br>yŏng·su·jŭng chu·se·yo |
| I'd like a refund, please. | 환불하고 싶습니다.<br>hwan·bul ha·go ship·sŭm·ni·da |

## Banking

| What time does the bank open/close? | 은행 문 언제 여나요/닫나요?<br>ŭn·haeng mun ŏn·jé yŏ·na·yo/tan·na·yo |
| What days is the bank open? | 무슨 요일에 문 여나요?<br>mu·sŭn yo·i·ré mun yŏ·na·yo |

**CULTURE TIP — Korean Currency**

The standard unit of currency in South Korea is the won. It's symbolised by a ₩ and is sometimes written 'KRW'. The largest paper denomination is ₩50,000 (around US$50), but Koreans bypass the need to carry lots of notes by using su·p'yo 수표, a kind of 'cheque' that can come in fixed denominations (especially ₩100,000) or can be made on demand in specific amounts. The su·p'yo aren't made out to individuals, so anyone can cash them in. The government has been under increasing pressure to produce a ₩100,000 note.

**PRACTICAL MONEY & BANKING**

| | |
|---|---|
| **Where's a bank?** | 은행 어디 있어요?<br>ŭn·haeng ŏ·di iss·ŏ·yo |
| **Where's an ATM?** | 현금인출기 어디<br>있어요?<br>hyŏn·gŭm in·ch'ul·gi ŏ·di<br>iss·ŏ·yo |
| **Where's a foreign exchange office?** | 환전소 어디 있어요?<br>hwan·jŏn·so ŏ·di iss·ŏ·yo |
| **I'd like to cash a cheque.** | 수표를 현금으로<br>바꿔주세요.<br>su·p'yo·rŭl hyŏn·gŭ·mŭ·ro<br>pak·kwŏ·ju·se·yo |
| **I'd like to change a travellers cheque.** | 여행자 수표를 현금으로<br>바꿔주세요.<br>yŏ·haeng·ja su·p'yo·rŭl<br>hyŏn·gŭ mŭ·ro<br>pak·kwŏ·ju·se·yo |
| **I'd like to change money.** | 환전해 주세요.<br>hwan·jŏn hae·ju·se·yo |
| **I'd like to get a cash advance.** | 현금서비스<br>받으려고요.<br>hyŏn·gŭm sŏ·bi·sŭ<br>pa·dŭ·ryŏ·go·yo |
| **I'd like to get change for this note.** | 작은 돈으로<br>바꿔주세요.<br>cha·gŭn to·nŭ·ro<br>pak·kwŏ·ju·se·yo |
| **I'd like to withdraw money.** | 현금 인출 하려고요.<br>hyŏn·gŭm in·ch'ul ha·ryŏ·go·yo |
| **What's the charge for that?** | 수수료가 얼마예요?<br>su·su·ryo·ga ŏl·ma·ye·yo |
| **What's the exchange rate?** | 환율이 얼마예요?<br>hwa·nyul·i ŏl·ma·ye·yo |
| **I've forgotten my PIN.** | 핀 넘버를 잊어 버렸어요.<br>p'in nŏm·bŏ·rŭl<br>i·jŏ·bŏ·ryŏss·ŏ·yo |

## 🔊 LISTEN FOR

| | |
|---|---|
| 수수료 | su·su·ryo<br>commission/fee |
| 신분증 | shin·bun·tchŭng<br>identification |
| 문제가 있어요. | mun·je·ga iss·ŏ·yo<br>There's a problem. |
| 잔고가 없어요. | chan·go·ga ŏp·sŏ·yo<br>You have no funds left. |
| 그건 안 되는데요. | kŭ·gŏn an·doé·nŭn·de·yo<br>We can't do that. |
| 여기 서명하세요/<br>사인하세요. | yŏ·gi sŏ·myŏng·ha·se·yo/<br>sa·in·ha·se·yo<br>Sign here. |

| | |
|---|---|
| **The ATM took my card.** | 현금인출기가<br>카드를 먹었어요.<br>hyŏn·gŭm in·ch'ul·gi·ga<br>k'a·dŭ·rŭl mŏ·gŏss·ŏ·yo |
| **Can I use my credit card to withdraw money?** | 신용카드로<br>현금인출 할 수<br>있나요?<br>shi·nyong·k'a·dŭ·ro<br>hyŏn·gŭ·min·ch'ul hal·su<br>in·na·yo |
| **Has my money arrived yet?** | 제 돈이 도착했나요?<br>che to·ni to·ch'a·k'aen·na·yo |
| **Can I transfer money overseas?** | 해외 송금 할 수<br>있나요?<br>hae·oé song·gŭm hal·su<br>in·na·yo |
| **How long will it take to arrive?** | 도착하는 데 얼마나<br>걸리나요?<br>to·ch'a·k'a·nŭn·dé ŏl·ma·na<br>kŏl·li·na·yo |

PRACTICAL BUSINESS

# Business

### KEY PHRASES

| I'm attending a conference. | 회의에 참가하러 왔어요. | hoé·i·é ch'am·ga ha·rŏ wass·ŏ·yo |
| I have an appointment with ... | ...과/와 약속이 있어요. | ...·gwa/·wa yak·so·gi iss·ŏ·yo |
| Can I have your business card? | 명함 좀 부탁드립니다. | myŏng·ham chom pu·t'ak dŭ·rim·ni·da |

| **Where's the business centre?** | 비즈니스 센터 어디있나요? pi·jŭ·ni·sŭ sen·t'ŏ ŏ·di in·na·yo |
|---|---|
| **Where's the conference/meeting?** | 회의장 어디있나요? hoé·i·jang ŏ·di in·na·yo |
| **I'm attending a ...** | ...에 참가하러 왔어요. ...·é ch'am·ga ha·rŏ wass·ŏ·yo |

| conference | 회의 | hoé·i |
| course | 강의 | kang·i |
| meeting | 회의 | hoé·i |
| trade fair | 무역 박람회 | mu·yŏk pang·nam·hoé |

| **I'm with (the UN).** | (유엔) 일 때문에 왔어요. (yu·en)·ilt· tae·mu·né wass·ŏ·yo |
|---|---|
| **I'm with my colleague(s).** | 동료와/동료들과 같이 왔어요. tong·nyo·wa/tong·nyo·dŭl·gwa ka·ch'i wass·ŏ·yo |

| | |
|---|---|
| I'm with (two) others. | 다른 (두) 명과 같이 왔어요. <br> ta·rŭn (tu)·myŏng·gwa ka·ch'i wass·ŏ·yo |
| I'm alone. | 혼자예요. <br> hon·ja·ye·yo |
| I have an appointment with ... | ...과/와 약속이 있어요. <br> ...·gwa/·wa yak·so·gi iss·ŏ·yo |
| Q Can I have your business card? | 명함 좀 부탁드립니다. <br> myŏng·ham chom pu·t'ak dŭ·rim·ni·da |
| A Here's my business card. | 제 명함입니다. <br> ché myŏng·ham im·ni·da |
| I need (a/an) ... | ...이/가 필요해요. <br> ...·i/·ga p'i·ryo·hae·yo |

| | | |
|---|---|---|
| business card | 명함 | myŏng·ham |
| computer | 컴퓨터 | k'ŏm·p'yu·t'ŏ |
| internet connection | 인터넷 접속 | in·t'ŏ·net chŏp·sok |
| interpreter who speaks (English) | (영어) 통역 | (yŏng·ŏ) t'ong·yŏk |

| | |
|---|---|
| That went very well. | 잘 되었어요. <br> chal doé·ŏss·ŏ·yo |
| Thank you for your time. | 시간 내 주셔서 고맙습니다. <br> shi·gan nae·ju·shŏ·sŏ ko·map·sŭm·ni·da |
| Shall we go for a drink? | 술 마시러 갈까요? <br> sul ma·shi·rŏ kalk·ka·yo |
| Shall we go for a meal? | 밥 먹으러 갈까요? <br> pap·mŏ·gŭ·rŏ kalk·ka·yo |

# Sightseeing

**KEY PHRASES**

| | | |
|---|---|---|
| I'd like a guide. | 여행안내서 주세요. | yŏ·haeng an·nae·sŏ ju·se·yo |
| Can I take a photo? | 사진 찍어도 될까요? | sa·jin tchi·gŏ·do doélk·ka·yo |
| When's the museum open? | 박물관 문 언제 여나요? | pang·mul·gwan mun ŏn·jé yŏ·na·yo |
| I'm interested in ... | ...을/를 좋아해요. | ...ŭl/·rŭl cho·a·hae·yo |
| When's the next tour? | 다음 투어 언제예요? | ta·ŭm t'u·ŏ ŏn·je·ye·yo |

## Requests & Queries

I'd like a/an ...      ... 주세요.
     ... ju·se·yo

| | | |
|---|---|---|
| audio set | 음성 안내 세트 | ŭm·sŏng an·nae se·t'ŭ |
| catalogue | 안내 책자 | an·nae ch'aek·cha |
| guide (in English) | (영어로 된) 여행안내서 | (yŏng·ŏ·ro·doén) yŏ·haeng an·nae·sŏ |
| map | 지도 | chi·do |

I'd like to go somewhere off the beaten track.

흔하지 않은 새로운 곳에 가고 싶어요.
hŭn·ha·ji a·nŭn sae·ro·un·go·sé ka·go shi·p'ŏ·yo

| | | |
|---|---|---|
| **Do you have information on sights?** | | ... 관광지 정보 있나요?<br>... kwan·gwang·ji chŏng·bo<br>in·nâ·yo |
| **cultural** | 문화에<br>관련된 | mun·hwa·é<br>kwal·lyŏn·doén |
| **historical** | 역사에 관련된 | yŏk·sa·é kwal·lyŏn·doén |
| **natural** | 자연이 있는 | cha·yŏ·ni in·nŭn |
| **religious** | 종교에<br>관련된 | chong·gyo·é<br>kwal·lyŏn·doén |

| | |
|---|---|
| **I'd like to see ...** | ... 보고 싶어요.<br>... po·go shi·p'ŏ·yo |
| **What's that?** | 저게 뭐예요?<br>chŏ·gé mŏ·ye·yo |
| **How old is it?** | 얼마나 오래 되었나요?<br>ŏl·ma·na o·rae doé·ŏn·na·yo |
| **Who built/made it?** | 누가<br>지었나요/만들었나요?<br>nu·ga<br>chi·ŏn·na·yo/man·dŭ·rŏn·na·yo |
| **Could you take a photo of me/us?** | 제/우리 사진 좀 찍어<br>주시겠어요?<br>ché/u·ri sa·jin chom tchi·gŏ<br>ju·shi·gess·ŏ·yo |
| **Can I take a photo (of you)?** | (당신) 사진 찍어도 될까요?<br>(tang·shin) sa·jin tchi·gŏ·do<br>doélk·ka·yo |

## Getting In

| | |
|---|---|
| **What time does it open/close?** | 언제 여나요/닫나요?<br>ŏn·jé yŏn·na·yo/tan·na·yo |
| **What's the admission charge?** | 입장료 얼마예요?<br>ip·chang·nyo ŏl·ma·ye·yo |

| Is there a discount for ...? | ... 할인 있나요? |
|---|---|
| | ... ha·rin in·na·yo |

| children | 어린이 | ŏ·ri·ni |
| families | 가족 | ka·jok |
| groups | 단체 | tan·ch'é |
| senior citizens | 경로 | kyŏng·no |
| students | 학생 | hak·saeng |

## Galleries & Museums

| When's the gallery/ museum open? | 미술관/박물관 문 언제 여나요? mi·sul·gwan/pang·mul·gwan mun ŏn·jé yŏ·na·yo |
|---|---|
| 🇶 What kind of art are you interested in? | 어떤 종류의 미술을 좋아하세요? ŏt·tŏn chong·nyu·é mi·su·rŭl cho·a·ha·se·yo |
| 🇦 I'm interested in ... | ...을/를 좋아해요 ...·ŭl/·rŭl cho·a·hae·yo |
| 🇶 What's in the collection? | 어떤 전시회예요? ŏt·tŏn chŏn·shi·hoé·ye·yo |
| 🇦 It's an exhibition of ... | ... 전시회예요. ... chŏn·shi·hoé·ye·yo |
| 🇶 What do you think of ...? | ...에 대해 어떻게 생각하세요? ...·é dae·hae ŏt·tŏ·k'é saeng·ga·k'a·se·yo |
| 🇦 It reminds me of ... | ... 생각이 나게 하네요. ... saeng·ga·gi na·gé ha·ne·yo |

## Tours

| Can you recommend a ...? | ... 추천해 주시겠어요? ... ch'u·ch'ŏn·hae ju·shi·gess·ŏ·yo |
|---|---|

| | |
|---|---|
| **When's the next boat trip?** | 다음 선박 여행 언제예요?<br>ta·ŭm sŏn·bak yŏ·haeng<br>ŏn·je·ye·yo |
| **When's the next day trip?** | 다음 일일 여행 언제예요?<br>ta·ŭm i·ril yŏ·haeng ŏn·je·ye·yo |
| **When's the next (sightseeing) tour?** | 다음 (관광) 투어<br>언제예요?<br>ta·ŭm (kwan·gwang) t'u·ŏ<br>ŏn·je·ye·yo |
| **Is accommodation included?** | 숙박 포함인가요?<br>suk·pak p'o·ha·min·ga·yo |
| **Is food included?** | 음식 포함인가요?<br>ŭm·shik p'o·ha·min·ga·yo |
| **Is transport included?** | 교통비 포함인가요?<br>kyo·t'ong·bi p'o·ha·min·ga·yo |

사진 찍어도 될까요?
sa·jin tchi·gŏ·do doélk·ka·yo
*Can I take a photo?*

**LOOK FOR**

| 휴무 | hyu·mu | Closed |
|------|--------|--------|
| 비상구 | pi·sang·gu | Emergency Exit |
| 무료 입장 | mu·ryo ip·chang | Free Admission |
| 안내 | an·nae | Information |
| 신사용 | shin·sa·yong | Men |
| 출입 금지 | ch'u·rip kŭm·ji | No Entry |
| 금연 구역 | kŭ·myŏn gu·yŏk | No Smoking Area |
| 영업 중 | yŏng·ŏp·jung | Open |
| 사진 촬영 | sa·jin ch'wa·ryŏng | Photography |
| 금지 | gŭm·ji | Prohibited |
| ... 금지 | ... kŭm·ji | ... Prohibited |
| 예약 | ye·yak | Reserved |
| 흡연 구역 | hŭ·byŏn gu·yŏk | Smoking Area |
| 화장실 | hwa·jang·shil | Toilets |
| 숙녀용 | sung·nyŏ·yong | Women |

| **I'd like to hire a local guide.** | 현지 가이드가 있었으면 해요. hyŏn·ji ga·i·dŭ·ga iss·ŏss·ŭ·myŏn hae·yo |
|---|---|
| **How long is the tour?** | 투어가 얼마나 걸리나요? t'u·ŏ·ga ŏl·ma·na kŏl·li·na·yo |
| **What time should we be back?** | 언제까지 돌아와야 되나요? ŏn·jek·ka·ji to·ra·wa·ya doé·na·yo |
| **I've lost my group.** | 우리 그룹을 놓쳐 버렸어요. u·ri gŭ·ru·bŭl no·ch'ŏ·bŏ·ryŏss·ŏ·yo |
| **I'm with them.** | 저 팀이랑 같이 왔어요. chŏ t'i·mi·rang ka·ch'i wass·ŏ·yo |

# Senior & Disabled Travellers

## KEY PHRASES

| | | |
|---|---|---|
| I need assistance. | 도움이 필요해요. | to·u·mi p'i·ryo·hae·yo |
| Is there wheelchair access? | 휠체어 출입구가 있나요? | hwil·ch'e·ŏ ch'u·rip·ku·ga in·na·yo |
| Are there toilets for people with a disability? | 장애인 전용 화장실 있나요? | chang·ae·in chŏ·nyong hwa·jang·shil in·na·yo |

| | |
|---|---|
| I have a disability. | 전 장애인인데요. chŏn chang·ae·in in·de·yo |
| I need assistance. | 도움이 필요해요. to·u·mi p'i·ryo·hae·yo |
| What facilities do you have for people with a disability? | 장애인 시설이 뭐가 있나요? chang·ae·in shi·sŏ·ri mwŏ·ga in·na·yo |
| Are guide dogs permitted? | 맹인 안내견 출입 가능한가요? maeng·in an·nae·gyŏn ch'u·rip ka·nŭng·han·ga·yo |
| Are there parking spaces for people with a disability? | 장애인 전용 주차 공간이 있나요? chang·ae·in chŏ·nyong chu·ch'a·gong·ga·ni in·na·yo |
| Is there wheelchair access? | 휠체어 출입구가 있나요? hwil·ch'e·ŏ ch'u·rip·ku·ga in·na·yo |

| | |
|---|---|
| How wide is the entrance? | 입구가 얼마나 넓은가요?<br>ip·ku·ga ŏl·ma·na nŏl·bŭn·ga·yo |
| How many steps are there? | 계단이 몇 개인가요?<br>kye·da·ni myŏk·kae in·ga·yo |
| Is there an elevator/ lift? | 엘리베이터 있나요?<br>el·li·be·i·t'ŏ in·na·yo |
| Are there toilets for people with a disability? | 장애인 전용<br>화장실 있나요?<br>chang·ae·in chŏ·nyong hwa·jang·shil in·na·yo |
| Are there rails in the bathroom? | 욕실에 핸드레일 있나요?<br>yok·shi·ré haen·dŭ·re·il in·na·yo |
| Please call me a taxi for people with a disability. | 장애인용 택시 불러<br>주세요.<br>chang·ae·in·nyong t'aek·shi pul·lŏ ju·se·yo |
| Could you help me cross the street safely? | 길 건너는 데 좀<br>도와 주시겠어요?<br>kil kŏn·nŏ·nŭn·dé chom to·wa·ju·shi·gess·ŏ·yo |
| Is there somewhere I can sit down? | 앉을 수 있는 곳 있나요?<br>an·jŭl·su in·nŭn·got in·na·yo |
| guide dog | 맹인 안내견<br>maeng·in an·nae·gyŏn |
| person with a disability | 장애인<br>chang·ae·in |
| ramp | 램프<br>raem·p'ŭ |
| walking frame | 보행기/워커<br>po·haeng·gi/wŏ·k'ŏ |
| walking stick | 지팡이<br>chi·p'ang·i |
| wheelchair | 휠체어<br>hwil·ch'é·ŏ |

# Travel with Children

**KEY PHRASES**

| | | |
|---|---|---|
| **Are children allowed?** | 어린이 입장 할 수 있나요? | ŏ·ri·ni ip·chang hal·su in·na·yo |
| **Is there a discount for children?** | 어린이 할인 있나요? | ŏ·ri·ni ha·rin in·na·yo |
| **Is there a baby change room?** | 기저귀 가는 곳 있나요? | ki·jŏ·gwi ka·nŭn·got in·na·yo |

**Is there a ...?**
... 있나요?
... in·na·yo

| | | |
|---|---|---|
| **baby change room** | 기저귀 가는 곳 | ki·jŏ·gwi ka·nŭn·got |
| **child-minding service** | 아기 맡기는 곳 | a·gi mak·ki·nŭn·got |
| **children's menu** | 어린이 메뉴 | ŏ·ri·ni me·nyu |
| **discount for children** | 어린이 할인 | ŏ·ri·ni ha·rin |

**I need a/an ...**
...이/가 필요해요.
...i/·ga p'i·ryo·hae·yo

| | | |
|---|---|---|
| **baby seat** | 어린이 좌석 | ŏ·ri·ni jwa·sŏk |
| **cot** | 아기 침대 | a·gi ch'im·dae |
| **highchair** | 유아용 높은 의자 | yu·a·yong no·p'ŭn ŭi·ja |
| **pram/stroller** | 유모차 | yu·mo·ch'a |

| Do you sell ...? | | ... 있나요? |
|---|---|---|
| | | ... in·na·yo |
| baby wipes | 아기용 | a·gi·yong |
| | 물티슈 | mul·t'i·shyu |
| disposable nappies/diapers | 일회용 기저귀 | il·hoé·yong ki·jŏ·gwi |
| painkillers for infants | 어린이용 진통제 | ŏ·ri·ni·yong jin·t'ong·jé |
| tissues | 티슈 | t'i·shyu |

| | |
|---|---|
| **Are there any good places to take children around here?** | 주위에 아이들 데려 가기 좋은 곳 있나요? chu·wi·é a·i·dŭl te·ryŏ·ga·gi cho·ŭn·got in·na·yo |
| **Are children allowed?** | 어린이 입장 할 수 있나요? ŏ·ri·ni ip·chang hal·su in·na·yo |
| **Do you mind if I breastfeed here?** | 여기서 모유 줘도 될까요? yŏ·gi·sŏ mo·yu·jwŏ·do doél·ka·yo |
| **Is this suitable for (six)-year-old children?** | (여섯) 살에게 적당한가요? (yŏ·sŏs)·sa·re·gé chŏk·tang·han·ga·yo |
| **Is there a doctor who is good with children?** | 아이들 잘 다루는 의사 있나요? a·i·dŭl chal ta·ru·nŭn ŭi·sa in·na·yo |
| **Is there a dentist who is good with children?** | 아이들 잘 다루는 치과의사 있나요? a·i·dŭl chal ta·ru·nŭn ch'ik·kwa·ŭi·sa in·na·yo |

If your child is sick, see **health** (p178).

# Social

# Meeting People

## KEY PHRASES

| My name is... | 제 이름은<br>...입니다. | che i·rŭ·mŭn<br>...im·ni·da |
| I'm from ... | ...에서 왔어요. | ...e·sŏ wass·ŏ·yo |
| I work in ... | ... 에서 일을 해요. | ... e·sŏ i·rŭl hae·yo |
| I'm ... years old. | 저는 ...<br>살이에요. | chŏ·nŭn ...<br>sa·ri·e·yo |
| And you? | 당신은요? | tang·shi·nŭ·nyo |

## Basics

In Korean society a person with seniority or of higher age is accorded greater respect, which is demonstrated through language. A simple way to avoid offence, especially when speaking to older Koreans, is to add the polite ending ~yo ~요 to the end of your sentences, even if it's a one-word sentence!

Even when speaking to someone younger or with less seniority than yourself, it's considered good manners to use the polite forms. With the less formal younger generation, though, informal expressions are perfectly acceptable.

| Yes./No. | 네./아니요.<br>né/a·ni·yo |
| Thank you. pol | 고맙습니다.<br>ko·map·sŭm·ni·da<br>감사합니다.<br>kam·sa·ham·ni·da |
| Many thanks. pol | 정말 고맙습니다.<br>chŏng·mal ko·map·sŭm·ni·da |
| You're welcome. pol | 천만에요.<br>ch'ŏn·ma·ne·yo |

| | |
|---|---|
| **You're welcome.** inf | 아니에요./뭘요. <br> a·ni·e·yo/mwŏl·yo |
| **Excuse me.** pol <br> **(to get attention)** | 실례합니다. <br> shil·lé ham·ni·da |
| **Excuse me.** pol <br> **(to get past)** | 잠시만요. <br> cham·shi·man·nyo |
| **Sorry.** pol | 죄송합니다. <br> choé·song ham·ni·da |
| **May I?** | 해도 되나요? <br> hae·do toé·na·yo |

## Greetings & Goodbyes

At all times of the day, the greeting an·nyŏng ha·se·yo 안녕하세요 (hello) is appropriate. However, at lunchtime, dinnertime or immediately afterward, Koreans often greet someone they know by asking shik·sa ha·shŏss·ŏ·yo 식사 하셨어요? (Did you have a meal?). So ingrained is this habit that many Koreans will ask non-Koreans the same question in English. A simple né 네 (yes) is all that's expected in reply.

| | |
|---|---|
| **Hello.** pol | 안녕하세요. <br> an·nyŏng ha·se·yo |
| **Hi.** inf | 안녕. <br> an·nyŏng |
| **How are you?** | 안녕하세요? <br> (lit: Are you well?) <br> an·nyŏng ha·se·yo |
| **Fine, thanks. And you?** | 네. 안녕하세요? <br> (lit: Yes. Are you well?) <br> ne an·nyŏng ha·se·yo |
| **May I ask what your name is?** | 성함을 여쭤봐도 <br> 될까요? <br> sŏng·ha·mŭl yŏ·tchŏ·bwa·do <br> doélk·ka·yo |
| **My name is ...** | 제 이름은 ...입니다. <br> che i·rŭ·mŭn ...·im·ni·da |

When introducing people, the phrase i·bu·nŭn 이 분은 (lit: this person) may be omitted, but the introduction should be accompanied with an open palm gesturing toward the person being introduced.

| | | |
|---|---|---|
| **I'd like to introduce you to (Park Sujin).** | 이 분은 (박수진) 씨예요. | i·bu·nŭn (pak·su·jin)·shi·ye·yo |
| ✂ **This is ...** | …이에요/예요. | ....i·e·yo/·ye·yo |
| **This is my ...** | (이 분은) 제 … 이에요/예요. | (i·bu·nŭn) ché … ·i·e·yo/·ye·yo |
| child | 아이 | a·i |
| colleague | 동료 | tong·nyo |
| friend | 친구 | ch'in·gu |
| partner | 파트너 | p'a·tŭ·nŏ |
| **I'm pleased to meet you.** pol | 만나서 반갑습니다. | man·na·sŏ pan·gap·sŭm·ni·da |
| **See you later.** | 다음에 봬요. | ta·ŭ·mé pwae·yo |
| **Goodbye. (when leaving)** pol | 안녕히 계세요. | an·nyŏng·hi kye·se·yo |
| **Goodbye. (when staying)** pol | 안녕히 가세요. | an·nyŏng·hi ka·se·yo |
| **Bye.** inf | 안녕. | an·nyŏng |
| **Have a nice day!** | 좋은 하루 보내세요! | cho·ŭn ha·ru po·nae·se·yo |
| **Bon voyage!** | 즐거운 여행 하세요! | chŭl·gŏ·un yŏ·haeng ha·se·yo |

**Saying 'Please' & 'Sorry'**
To ask someone to do something, combine the main verb with ju·se·yo 수세요 (give). To offer something to someone, use the 'high form' of the verb 'receive' – pa·dŭ·se·yo 받으세요. When offering food or drink, though, tŭ·se·yo 드세요 (lit: eat this) or ma·ni dŭ·se·yo 많이 드세요 (lit: eat a lot) are more appropriate expressions. The word 'please' is rarely used on its own to reinforce a request. Actually, che·bal 제발 (lit: please) sounds like desperate pleading in Korean. Avoid using it, unless you desperately require someone's assistance.

In Korea people will rarely say anything when they bump into someone on the street. The expression choé·song ham·ni·da 죄송합니다 (sorry) is generally reserved for apologising for a more serious issue.

## Titles & Addressing People

Traditional forms of address are still the norm in Korea. They almost always follow the person's name. The less familiar you are with the speaker, the more likely it is you'll address that person by his or her surname. You'd never refer to a much older person by his or her given name.

| | |
|---|---|
| **Mr/Mrs/Miss** | … 씨<br>…·shi/·ssi |
| **Mr Donghun**<br>**(first name)** | 동헌 씨<br>tong·hŏn·shi |
| **Ms Taegyong**<br>**(first name)** | 태경 씨<br>t'ae·gyŏng·shi |
| **Mr Yang Donghun** | 양동헌 씨<br>yang·dong·hŏn·shi |
| **Ms Kim Taegyong** | 김태경 씨<br>kim·t'ae·gyŏng·shi |

When addressing or calling a child or a close friend (someone with similar social status), you can simply add a 아 (if the name ends in a consonant) or ya 야 (if the name ends in a vowel).

| Chong-un! | 정은아! |
| | chŏng·ŭ·na |
| Sangmi! | 상미야! |
| | sang·mi·ya |

There are also special forms of addressing people, such as sŏn·bae·nim 선배님 (a person in your group older than you, or at a higher social level), hu·bae 후배 (a person in your group younger than you, or at a lower social level). You can also use the following:

| Chairman (Kang) | (강) 사장님 |
| | (kang)·sa·jang·nim |
| Dr (Cho) | (조) 박사님 |
| | (cho)·pak·sa·nim |
| Professor (Lee) | (이) 교수님 |
| | (i)·kyo·su·nim |
| Teacher (Jonathan) | (조나단) 선생님 |
| | (cho·na·dan)·sŏn·saeng·nim |

---

**LANGUAGE TIP**

**'That' Person**

The titles sŏn·bae·nim 선배님 and sŏn·saeng·nim 선생님 (meaning 'higher person') are very useful if you're not sure how to address someone. Not knowing the relative position of an overseas 'guest', many Koreans will refer to him or her simply as sŏn·saeng·nim. If a traveller looks sufficiently young or not businesslike, they may be referred to simply as hak·saeng 학생 (lit: student).

Koreans frequently refer to each other in the third person. Rather than using nŏ 너 or tan·gshin 당신 (the informal and polite forms of 'you'), it's considered more polite to refer to a person's position or to use their name. See also **grammar** (p27).

**LANGUAGE TIP**

**Western Titles**

Koreans have adopted the Western titles Mr and Miss, adapting them into mi·su·t'ŏ 미스터 and mi·sŭ 미스. The latter is used even for married women, although mi·shi·jŭ 미시즈 is also becoming common. These titles precede the surname of the addressee (note that Korean women don't take their husband's surname). When addressing Westerners, though, many Koreans will use mi·sŭ·t'ŏ or mi·sŭ before the person's given name (eg 'Mr David' or 'Miss Amanda').

## Making Conversation

| | |
|---|---|
| **Nice weather, isn't it?** | 날씨가 좋지요?<br>nal·shi·ga cho·chi·yo |
| **Awful weather, isn't it?** | 날씨가 안 좋지요?<br>nal·shi·ga an·jo·chi·yo |
| **Do you live here?** | 여기서 사시나요?<br>yŏ·gi·sŏ sa·shi·na·yo |
| **Where are you going?** | 어디 가세요?<br>ŏ·di ka·se·yo |
| **What are you doing?** | 뭐 하세요?<br>mwŏ ha·se·yo |
| **Q Do you like it here?** | 여기 마음에 드시나요?<br>yŏ·gi ma·ŭ·mé dŭ·shi·na·yo |
| **A I love it here.** | 여기 정말 좋아요.<br>yŏ·gi chŏng·mal cho·a·yo |
| **What's this called?** | 이걸 뭐라고 하나요?<br>i·gŏl mwŏ·ra·go ha·na·yo |
| **That's beautiful, isn't it?** | 아름답지요?<br>a·rŭm·dap·chi·yo |
| **Can I take a photo (of you)?** | (당신) 사진 찍어도 될까요?<br>(tang·shin) sa·jin tchi·gŏ·do doélk·ka·yo |

**CULTURE TIP**  **Addressing Service Personnel**
In modern Korean culture, there's some uncertainty as to how to refer to a young person (eg a waiter or a shop assistant) unknown to the speaker. Calling a young man a·jŏ·shi 아저씨 (lit: uncle) seems odd, but there's no other appropriate 'relative' expression. On the other hand, calling a young woman a·ga·shi 아가씨 (lit: sister-in-law) is now out of favour. In restaurants, young people tend to call someone over by simply saying yŏ·gi·yo 여기요 ('over here' with a polite ending).

| | |
|---|---|
| I'll send you the photo. | 사진 보내 드릴게요.<br>sa·jin po·nae dŭ·rilk·ke·yo |
| **Q** How long are you here for? | 여기에 얼마 동안<br>계시나요?<br>yŏ·gi·é ŏl·ma·dong·an<br>kye·shi·na·yo |
| **A** I'm here for (10) days. | (십) 일 동안 있을 거예요.<br>(shib)·il dong·an iss·ŭl·kŏ·ye·yo |
| **A** I'm here for (three) weeks. | (삼) 주 동안<br>있을 거예요.<br>(sam)·ju dong·an<br>iss·ŭl·kŏ·ye·yo |
| **A** I'm here for (two) months. | (두) 달 동안 있을 거예요.<br>(tu)·dal dong·an iss·ŭl·kŏ·ye·yo |
| **Q** Are you here on holiday? | 여행하러 오셨나요?<br>yŏ·haeng·ha·rŏ o·shŏn·na·yo |
| **A** I'm here for a holiday. | 여행하러 왔어요.<br>yŏ·haeng ha·rŏ wass·ŏ·yo |
| **A** I'm here on business. | 사업 때문에 왔어요.<br>sa·ŏp·ttae·mu·né wass·ŏ·yo |
| **A** I'm here to study. | 공부하러 왔어요.<br>kong·bu ha·rŏ wass·ŏ·yo |

| We're here with our family. | 저희는 가족들과<br>왔어요.<br>çhŏ·hi·nŭn ka·jok·dŭl·gwa<br>wass·ŏ·yo |
| I'm here with my friend. | 저는 친구랑<br>왔어요.<br>chŏ·nŭn ch'in·gu·rang<br>wass·ŏ·yo |

## Nationalities

Koreans have two different ways of naming countries: a Hangulisation of the original name (for example sing·ga·p'o·rŭ 싱가포르 for Singapore), and the Korean pronunciation of the Chinese version of that country – eg il·bon 일본 (lit: sun's origin) for Japan.

Making words for nationalities out of country names is easy – simply add sa·ram 사람 or in 인 (the pure Korean and Sino-Korean words for 'person'). Keep in mind, though, that the pronunciation may change. Thus, a person from mi·guk 미국 (America, lit: beautiful country) becomes a mi·gu·gin 미국인 (lit: America-person).

| 🔲 Where are you from? | 어디서 오셨어요?<br>ŏdi·sŏ o·shŏn·na·yo |
| 🔺 I'm from ... | ...에서 왔어요.<br>...e·sŏ wass·ŏ·yo |

| Australia | 호주 | ho·ju |
| Britain | 영국 | yŏng·guk |
| Canada | 캐나다 | k'ae·na·da |
| New Zealand | 뉴질랜드 | nyu·jil·laen·dŭ |
| the USA | 미국 | mi·guk |

## Age

| 🔲 How old are you?<br>(to a child) | 몇 살이니?<br>myŏs·sa·ri·ni |

| | |
|---|---|
| How old are you? (to an adult around your age or younger) | 나이가 어떻게 되세요?<br>na·i·ga ŏt·tŏ·k'é toé·se·yo |
| How old are you? (to an adult older than you) | 연세가 어떻게 되세요?<br>yŏn·se·ga ŏt·tŏ·k'é toé·se·yo |
| I'm ... years old. | 저는 ... 살이에요.<br>chŏ·nŭn ... sa·ri·e·yo |
| How old is your daughter/son? | 딸/아들 나이가 어떻게 되나요?<br>ddal/a·dŭl na·i·ga ŏt·tŏ·k'é toé·na·yo |
| He/She is ... years old. (while pointing to them) | ... 살이에요.<br>... sa·ri·e·yo |
| Too old! | 너무 늙었어요!<br>nŏ·mu nŭl·gŏss·ŏ·yo |
| I'm younger than I look. | 전 보기보다 젊어요.<br>chŏn po·gi·bo·da chŏl·mŏ·yo |

For your age, see **numbers & amounts** (p38).

## Occupations & Studies

| | |
|---|---|
| What's your occupation? | 무슨 일 하세요?<br>mu·sŭn nil ha·se·yo |
| I work in administration. | 행정 일을 해요.<br>haeng·jŏng i·rŭl hae·yo |
| I'm retired. | 퇴직 했어요.<br>t'oé·jik haess·ŏ·yo |
| I'm self-employed. | 자영업을 해요.<br>cha·yŏng·ŏ·bŭl hae·yo |
| I'm unemployed. | 현재 직업이 없어요.<br>hyŏn·jae chi·gŏ·bi ŏp·sŏ·yo |
| What are you studying? | 뭘 공부하시나요?<br>mwŏl kong·bu·ha·shi·na·yo |

| **A** I'm studying ... | 저는 ...을/를 공부해요.<br>chŏ·nŭn ...·ŭl/·rŭl kong·bu<br>hae·yo |
|---|---|

| **English** | 영어 | yŏng·ŏ |
| **humanities** | 인문학 | in·mun·hak |
| **Korean** | 한국어 | han·gu·gŏ |
| **science** | 과학 | kwa·hak |

## Family

| **Q** Do you have a ...? | ... 있으세요?<br>... iss·ŭ·se·yo |
|---|---|
| **A** I have a ... | ...이/가 있어요.<br>...·i/·ga iss·ŏ·yo |
| **A** I don't have a ... | ...이/가 없어요.<br>...·i/·ga ŏp·sŏ·yo |

| **brother** | 형제 | hyŏng·je |
| **daughter** | 딸 | ddal |
| **granddaughter** | 손녀 | son·nyŏ |
| **grandson** | 손자 | son·ja |
| **husband** | 남편 | nam·p'yŏn |
| **sister** | 자매 | cha·mae |
| **son** | 아들 | a·dŭl |
| **wife** | 아내 | a·nae |

| **Q** Are you married? | 결혼 하셨나요?<br>kyŏl·hon ha·shŏn·na·yo |
|---|---|
| **A** I'm married. | 전 결혼했어요.<br>chŏn kyol·hon haess·ŏ·yo |
| **A** I'm single. | 전 미혼이에요.<br>chŏn mi·hon·i·e·yo |

SOCIAL

MEETING PEOPLE

| I live with someone. | 어떤 사람과 같이 살아요. |
| | ŏt·ton sa·ram·gwa ka·ch'i sa·ra·yo |
| We don't have any children. | 아이가 없어요. |
| | a·i·ga ŏp·sŏ·yo |

## Talking with Children

The phrases used in this section are only appropriate for talking to children – using them with adults may cause offense. For more information, see **personal pronouns** in the **grammar** chapter (p27).

| What's your name? | 이름이 뭐야? |
| | i·rŭ·mi mwŏ·ya |
| When's your birthday? | 생일이 언제야? |
| | saeng·ir·i ŏn·je·ya |
| What grade are you in? | 몇 학년이야? |
| | myŏt'·ang·nyŏ·ni·ya |
| Do you learn (English)? | (영어) 배우니? |
| | (yŏng·ŏ) pae·u·ni |
| What do you do after school? | 학교 끝나고 뭐 해? |
| | hak·kyo kkŭn·na·go mwŏ·hae |
| Do you like school? | 학교 좋아하니? |
| | hak·kyo cho·a·ha·ni |
| Do you like sport? | 운동 좋아하니? |
| | un·dong cho·a·ha·ni |
| Do you like your teacher? | 선생님 좋아하니? |
| | sŏn·saeng·nim cho·a·ha·ni |
| I come from very far away. | 난 먼 나라에서 왔어. |
| | nan mŏn na·ra·e·sŏ wass·ŏ |
| Do you go to school or kindergarten? | 학교 다녀, 유치원 다녀? |
| | hak·kyo ta·nyŏ yu·ch'i·wŏn ta·nyŏ |

## LISTEN FOR

Koreans consider themselves one big family, and there are several ways of referring to a person that reflect this:

| | | |
|---|---|---|
| 할아버지 | ha·ra·bŏ·ji | elderly man (lit: grandfather) |
| 할머니 | hal·mŏ·ni | elderly woman (lit: grandmother) |
| 아저씨 | a·jŏ·shi | older man (lit: uncle) |
| 아주머니/ 아줌마 | a·ju·mŏ·ni/ a·jum·ma | older woman (lit: aunt) |

Younger and middle-aged Koreans refer to 'close' people of similar age as 'older brother', 'older sister' or 'younger sibling'. Which word to use depends on the gender of the speaker. These words are sometimes attached to the person's name.

| | | |
|---|---|---|
| 오빠 | op·pa | older brother (if speaker is female) |
| 형 | hyŏng | older brother (if speaker is male) |
| 언니 | ŏn·ni | older sister (if speaker is female) |
| 누나 | nu·na | older sister (if speaker is male) |
| 남동생 | nam·dong·saeng | younger brother (regardless of speaker's gender) |
| 여동생 | yŏ·dong·saeng | younger sister (regardless of speaker's gender) |

## Talking about Children

| | |
|---|---|
| When's the baby due? | 출산 예정일이<br>언제예요?<br>ch'ul·san ye·jŏng·i·ri<br>ŏn·je·ye·yo |
| What are you going to call the baby? | 아기 이름은 뭘로<br>하실 거예요?<br>a·gi i·rŭ·mŭn mwŏl·lo<br>ha·shilk·kŏ·ye·yo |
| Is this your first child? | 첫째인가요?<br>chŏt·tchae·in·ga·yo |
| How many children do you have? | 자녀가 몇 명이에요?<br>cha·nyŏ·ga myŏn·myŏng·i·e·yo |
| What's his/her name? | 이름이 뭐예요?<br>i·rŭ·mi mwŏ·ye·yo |
| Does he/she go to school? | 학교 다니나요?<br>hak·kyo ta·ni·na·yo |
| He/She looks like you. | 닮았어요.<br>tal·mass·ŏ·yo |

## Farewells

Koreans greet each other with a bow, or a bow and a simultaneous handshake. The same is done when saying goodbye. They rarely hug in public, except for emotional goodbyes.

| | |
|---|---|
| Tomorrow is my last day here. | 내일이 마지막 날이에요.<br>nae·i·ri ma·ji·mang·na·ri·e·yo |
| It's been great meeting you. | 만나서 반가웠어요.<br>man·na·sŏ pan·ga·wŏss·ŏ·yo |
| Keep in touch! | 우리 서로 연락해요!<br>u·ri sŏ·ro yŏl·la·k'ae·yo |
| If you come to (Scotland), you can visit my place. | (스코틀랜드)에<br>오시면, 저희 집에 오세요.<br>(sŭ·k'o·t'ŭl·laen·dŭ)·e<br>o·shi·myŏn chŏ·hi ji·bé o·se·yo |

| | |
|---|---|
| **I plan to come back to Korea (next year).** | (내년에) 한국에 돌아 올 거예요. <br> (nae·nyŏ·né) han·gu·gé to·rá·ôlk·kŏ·ye·yo |
| **What's your (email) address?** | (이메일) 주소가 뭐예요? <br> (i·me·il) chu·so·ga mwŏ·ye·yo |
| **Here's my (email) address.** | 제 (이메일) 주소예요. <br> ché (i·me·il) chu·so·ye·yo |
| **What's your phone number?** | 전화번호가 뭐예요? <br> chŏn·hwa bŏn·ho·ga mwŏ·ye·yo |
| **Here's my phone number.** | 제 전화번호예요. <br> ché chŏn·hwa bŏn·ho·ye·yo |

## Well-Wishing

A distinctively Korean phrase is the call of encouragement p'a·i·t'ing 파이팅 (from the English word 'fighting'), used especially when the listener is feeling down or has just suffered a setback, as if saying 'Cheer up, things will get better'. Here are some other well-wishing phrases:

| | |
|---|---|
| **Congratulations!** | 축하해요! <br> ch'u·k'a hae·yo |
| **Good luck!** | 행운을 빌어요! <br> haeng·u·nŭl pi·rŏ·yo |
| **Happy birthday!** | 생일 축하해요! <br> saeng·il ch'u·k'a hae·yo |
| **Happy New Year!** | 새해 복 많이 받으세요! <br> sae·hae·bok ma·ni pa·dŭ·se·yo |
| **Merry Christmas!** | 즐거운 성탄절 보내세요! <br> chŭl·gŏ·un sŏng·t'an·jŏl po·nae·se·yo |

# Interests

### KEY PHRASES

| | | |
|---|---|---|
| What do you do in your spare time? | 시간 있을 때 뭐 하세요? | shi·gan iss·ŭlt·tae mwŏ ha·se·yo |
| Do you like ...? | ... 좋아하세요? | ... cho·a·ha·se·yo |
| I like/ don't like ... | ... 좋아해요/ 싫어해요. | ... cho·a·hae·yo/ shi·rŏ·hae·yo |

## Common Interests

| | |
|---|---|
| What do you do in your spare time? | 시간 있늘 때 뭐 하세요? shi·gan iss·ŭlt·tae mwŏ ha·se·yo |
| Q Do you like ...? | ... 좋아하세요? ... cho·a·ha·se·yo |
| A I like ... | ... 좋아해요. ... cho·a·hae·yo |
| A I don't like ... | ... 싫어해요. ... shi·rŏ·hae·yo |

| | | |
|---|---|---|
| cooking | 요리 | yo·ri |
| gardening | 정원 가꾸기 | chŏng·won kak·ku·gi |
| hiking | 등산 | tŭng·san |
| reading | 독서 | tok·sŏ |
| sport | 운동 | un·dong |
| travelling | 여행 | yŏ·haeng |

For types of sports, see **sports** (p158), and the **dictionary** (p221).

## Music

| Do you dance? | 춤 추시나요?<br>ch'um ch'u·shi·na·yo |
| Do you go to concerts? | 공연 가시나요?<br>kong·yŏn ka·shi·na·yo |
| Do you listen to music? | 음악 들으시나요?<br>ŭ·mak tŭ·rŭ·shi·na·yo |
| Do you play an instrument? | 악기 다루시나요?<br>ak·ki ta·ru·shi·na·yo |
| Do you sing? | 노래 부르시나요?<br>no·rae pu·rŭ·shi·na·yo |
| What ... do you like? | 어떤 ...을/를<br>좋아하시나요?<br>ŏt·tŏn ...·ŭl/·rŭl<br>cho·a·ha·shi·na·yo |

| bands | 밴드 | paen·dŭ |
| music | 음악 | ŭ·mak |
| performers | 공연가 | kong·yŏn·ga |
| singers | 가수 | ka·su |

| contemporary music | 현대 음악<br>hyŏn·dae ŭ·mak |
| electronic music | 전자 음악<br>chŏn·ja ŭ·mak |
| Korean traditional music | 국악<br>ku·gak |
| traditional opera | 판소리<br>p'an·so·ri |

Planning to go to a concert? See **buying tickets** (p54), and **going out** (p144).

**CULTURE TIP**

**Korean Names**

In Korea, a person may have a Korean given name and also a se·rye·myŏng 세례명 (Christian name) if they're Catholic or belong to some Protestant churches. This name usually isn't used in Korea (though it's often adopted as one's English name) and it isn't an i·rŭm 이름 (a given name) in the Western sense.

Nevertheless, many Koreans try to make their Korean names easier for foreigners to read or pronounce. When a syllable in someone's name sounds like a word in English, they may use that word's spelling in their name. So a person named sŏng·dŏk 성덕 might spell his name Sung-Duck, and yŏng·ju 영주 might write her name as Young-Jew. Members of the won 원, yu 유 and pak or park (both written 박) clans sometimes write their surnames as One, You and Bach.

## Cinema & Theatre

| I feel like going to a/an ... | ... 보러 가고 싶어요.<br>... po·rŏ ka·go shi·p'ŏ·yo |
| --- | --- |
| **Q** How was the ...? | ... 어땠나요?<br>... ŏt·taen·na·yo |

| | | |
| --- | --- | --- |
| **ballet** | 발레 | pal·lé |
| **film** | 영화 | yŏng·hwa |
| **musical** | 뮤지컬 | myu·ji·k'ŏl |
| **opera** | 오페라 | o·p'e·ra |
| **performance** | 공연 | kong·yŏn |
| **play** | 연극 | yŏn·gŭk |

**A** I thought it was ...   ... 같아요.
... ka·t'a·yo

| boring | 지루했던 것 | chi·ru·haet·tŏn·gŏt |
| entertaining | 재미있었던 것 | chae·mi iss·ŏt·tŏn·gŏt |
| excellent | 좋았던 것 | cho·at·tŏn·gŏt |
| long | 길었던 것 | ki·rŏt·tŏn·gŏt |
| OK | 괜찮았던 것 | kwaen·cha·nat·tŏn·gŏt |

| What's showing at the cinema/theatre tonight? | 오늘 밤 영화관에서/ 극장에서 뭐 하나요? o·nŭl·bam yŏng·hwa·gwa·ne·sŏ/ kŭk·chang·e·sŏ mwŏ ha·na·yo |
| Is it in (English)? | (영어)로 나오나요? (yŏng·ŏ)·ro na·o·na·yo |
| Does it have (English) subtitles? | (영어) 자막 나오나요? (yŏng·ŏ) cha·mang·na·o·na·yo |
| Is it dubbed? | 더빙 되었나요? tŏ·bing doé·ŏn·na·yo |
| Is this seat available? | 여기 자리 있나요? yŏ·gi cha·ri in·na·yo |
| Do you have tickets for ...? | ... 표 있나요? ... p'yo in·na·yo |
| Are there any extra tickets? | 남는 표 있나요? nam·nŭn p'yo in·na·yo |
| I'd like cheap tickets. | 싼 표 주세요. ssan p'yo ju·se·yo |

## ◀)) LISTEN FOR

죄송합니다,
매진입니다.

choé·song ham·ni·da
mae·jin im·ni·da
I'm sorry, it's sold out.

SOCIAL INTERESTS

| I'd like the best tickets. | 제일 좋은 표 주세요.<br>che·il cho·ŭn p'yo ju·se·yo |
|---|---|
| Is there a matinée show? | 낮 공연 있나요?<br>nat kong·yŏn in·na·yo |
| Is there a late-night showing for this film? | 이 영화 심야 상영 있나요?<br>i·yŏng·hwa shi·mya sang·yŏng in·na·yo |
| Have you seen ...? | ... 보셨나요?<br>... po·shŏn·na·yo |
| 🇶 Who's in it? | 누가 나오나요?<br>nu·ga na·o·na·yo |
| 🇦 It stars ... | ...이/가 나와요.<br>...·i/·ga na·wa·yo |
| I like ... | ... 좋아해요.<br>... cho·a·hae·yo |
| I don't like ... | ... 싫어해요.<br>... shi·rŏ·hae·yo |

| action movies | 액션 영화 | aek·shŏn yŏng·hwa |
|---|---|---|
| comedies | 코메디 | k'o·me·di |
| documentaries | 다큐멘터리 | da·k'yu·men·t'ŏ·ri |
| drama | 드라마 | tŭ·ra·ma |
| horror movies | 공포 영화 | kong·p'o yŏng·hwa |
| Korean cinema | 한국 영화 | han·guk yŏng·hwa |
| martial arts films | 무술 영화 | mu·sul yŏng·hwa |
| period dramas | 사극 | sa·gŭk |
| sci-fi films | 공상 과학 영화 | kong·sang kwa·hak yŏng·hwa |
| thrillers | 스릴러 영화 | sŭ·ril·lŏ yŏng·hwa |
| war movies | 전쟁 영화 | chŏn·jaeng yŏng·hwa |

# Feelings & Opinions

**KEY PHRASES**

| | | |
|---|---|---|
| **How do you feel today?** | 오늘 기분이 어떠세요? | o·nŭl ki·bu·ni ŏt·tŏ·se·yo |
| **I'm ...** | 저는 ... | chŏ·nŭn ... |
| **What do you think of ...?** | ...에 대해 어떻게 생각하시나요? | ...é dae·hae ŏt·tŏ·k'é saeng·gak ha·shi·na·yo |
| **I think it's interesting.** | 재미있는 것 같아요. | chae·mi·in·nŭn·gŏt ka·t'a·yo |
| **Did you hear about ...?** | ... 이야기 들으셨나요? | ... i·ya·gi dŭ·rŭ·shŏn·na·yo |

## Feelings

When describing oneself or another person, the subject – eg chŏ·nŭn 저는 ('I') – is omitted if it's clear from the context who is meant.

**How do you feel today?**    오늘 기분이 어떠세요?
o·nŭl ki·bu·ni ŏt·tŏ·se·yo

**Are you ...?**

| | | |
|---|---|---|
| **cold** | 추우세요? | ch'u·u·se·yo |
| **happy** | 행복하세요? | haeng·bo·k'a·se·yo |
| **hot** | 더우세요? | tŏ·u·se·yo |
| **hungry** | 시장하세요? | shi·jang·ha·se·yo |
| **sad** | 슬프세요? | sŭl·p'ŭ·se·yo |
| **thirsty** | 목 마르세요? | mong·ma·rŭ·se·yo |
| **tired** | 피곤하세요? | p'i·gon·ha·se·yo |
| **well** | 건강하세요? | kŏn·gang·ha·se·yo |

| 🅰 I'm ... | | 저는 ...<br>chŏ·nŭn ... |
|---|---|---|
| **cold** | 추워요 | ch'u·wŏ·yo |
| **happy** | 행복해요 | haeng·bo·k'ae·yo |
| **hot** | 더워요 | tŏ·wŏ·yo |
| **hungry** | 배고파요 | pae·go·p'a·yo |
| **sad** | 슬퍼요 | sŭl·p'ŏ·yo |
| **thirsty** | 목 말라요 | mong·mal·la·yo |
| **tired** | 피곤해요 | p'i·gon·hae·yo |
| **well** | 건강해요 | kŏn·gang·hae·yo |

If you're not feeling well, see **health** (p178).

## Opinions

| ❓ **Did you like it?** | 좋았나요?<br>cho·an·na·yo |
|---|---|
| ❓ **What do you think of ...?** | ...에 대해 어떻게 생각하시나요?<br>...é dae·hae ŏt·tŏ·k'é saeng·gak ha·shi·na·yo |
| 🅰 **I think it's ...** | 제 생각에는 ... 같아요.<br>ché saeng·ga·ge·nŭn ... ka·t'a·yo |

| **awful** | 형편 없는 것 | hyŏng·p'yŏn ŏm·nŭn·gŏt |
|---|---|---|
| **beautiful** | 아름다운 것 | a·rŭm·da·un·gŏt |
| **boring** | 지루한 것 | chi·ru·han·gŏt |
| **great** | 좋은 것 | cho·ŭn·gŏt |
| **interesting** | 재미있는 것 | chae·mi·in·nŭn·gŏt |
| **strange** | 이상한 것 | i·sang·han·gŏt |

아름다워요.
a·rŭm·da·wŏ·yo

*I think it's beautiful.*

## Politics & Social Issues

**Who will you vote for?**
누구 찍으실 거예요?
nu·gu tchi·gŭ·shilk·kŏ·ye·yo

**I support the ... party.**
전 ...을/를 지지해요.
chŏn ...·ŭl/·rŭl chi·ji·hae·yo

| | | |
|---|---|---|
| **conservative** | 보수당 | po·su·dang |
| **democratic** | 민주당 | min·ju·dang |
| **green** | 녹색당 | nok·saek·tang |
| **liberal** | 자유당 | cha·yu·dang |
| **social-democratic** | 사회 민주당 | sa·hoé min·ju·dang |
| **socialist** | 사회당 | sa·hoé·dang |

| | |
|---|---|
| I'm (American), but I didn't vote for ... | 전 (미국인)인데, ... 찍지 않았어요. |
| | chŏn (mi·gu·gin) in·dé ... tchik·chi a·nass·ŏ·yo |
| **Q** How do people feel about ...? | ...에 대해 사람들이 어떻게 생각하나요? |
| | ...é dae·hae sa·ram·dŭ·ri ŏt·tŏ·k'é saeng·ga·k'a·na·yo |
| **A** I agree/disagree with the policy on ... | ...에 대한 정책에 찬성해요/반대해요. |
| | ...é dae·han chŏng·ch'ae·gé ch'an·sŏng·hae·yo/pan·dae·hae·yo |
| Did you hear about ...? | ... 이야기 들으셨나요? |
| | ... i·ya·gi dŭ·rŭ·shŏn·na·yo |
| the economy | 경제 |
| | kyŏng·jé |
| immigration | 이민 |
| | i·min |
| the war (in ...) | (...의) 전쟁 |
| | (...é) jŏn·jaeng |
| Is there help for (the) ...? | ...에게 도움을 주나요? |
| | ...é·gé to·u·mŭl ju·na·yo |
| aged | 노인 | no·in |
| disabled | 장애인 | chang·ae·in |
| homeless | 노숙자 | no·suk·cha |
| unemployed | 실업자 | shi·rŏp·cha |

## The Environment

| | |
|---|---|
| Is there a ... problem here? | 여기 ... 문제 있나요? |
| | yŏ·gi ... mun·jé in·na·yo |

##  LOOK FOR

In Korea, recycling (chae·hwa·ryong 새활룡) is the law in many places. In public, separate bins are marked 'for plastic only', 'for cans only' etc. At home, nonrecyclables can only be disposed of using special garbage bags (ssǔ·re·gi chong·nyang·jé bong·t'u 쓰레기 종량제 봉투). Food waste is also disposed of separately.

| | | |
|---|---|---|
| 병/유리 | pyŏng/yu·ri | bottles only |
| 알루미늄/캔 | al·lu·mi·nyum/k'aen | cans only |
| 종이 | chong·i | paper products only |
| 플라스틱 | p'ǔl·la·sǔ·t'ik | plastic only |
| 일반 쓰레기 | il·ban ssǔ·re·gi | regular garbage |
| 음식물<br>쓰레기 | ǔm·shing·mul<br>ssǔ·re·gi | food waste |

SOCIAL FEELINGS & OPINIONS

| | |
|---|---|
| **What should be done about ...?** | ...을/를 어떻게 해야 할까요?<br>...·ǔl/·rǔl ŏt·tŏ·k'é hae·ya halk·ka·yo |
| **Is this a protected area?** | 여기 자연 보호 구역인가요?<br>yŏ·gi cha·yŏn·bo·ho ku·yŏ·gin·ga·yo |
| **Is this a protected species?** | 천연기념물인가요?<br>ch'ŏ·nyŏn·gi·nyŏm·mu·rin·ga·yo |
| **Does (Kwangju) have a recycling program?** | (광주)에서는<br>재활용을 하나요?<br>(kwang·ju)·e·sŏ·nǔn<br>chae·hwa·ryong·ǔl ha·na·yo |
| **Is this recyclable?** | 이것 재활용 되나요?<br>i·gŏt chae·hwa·ryong doé·na·yo |
| **Do we separate our garbage?** | 분리수거 해야 되나요?<br>pul·li·su·gŏ hae·ya doé·na·yo |
| **climate change** | 기후 변화<br>ki·hu·byŏn·hwa |
| **pollution** | 오염<br>o·yŏm |

SOCIAL GOING OUT

# Going Out

## KEY PHRASES

| | | |
|---|---|---|
| **Is there anything interesting on tonight?** | 오늘 밤에 뭐 재미있는 것 없나요? | o·nŭl ba·mé mwŏ chae·mi in·nŭn·gŏt ŏm·na·yo |
| **Where can I find clubs?** | 클럽 어디에 있나요? | k'ŭl·lŏp ŏ·di·é in·na·yo |
| **Would you like to go for a coffee?** | 커피 마시러 가시겠어요? | k'ŏ·p'i ma·shi·rŏ ka·shi·gess·ŏ·yo |
| **What time will we meet?** | 몇 시에 만날까요? | myŏs·shi·é man·nalk·ka·yo |
| **Where shall we meet?** | 어디서 만날까요? | ŏ·di·sŏ man·nalk·ka·yo |

## Where to Go

| | |
|---|---|
| **What's there to do in the evenings?** | 저녁에 뭐 재미있게 할 것 없나요? <br> chŏ·nyŏ·gé mwŏ chae·mi ik·ké hal·gŏt ŏm·na·yo |
| **Where can I find out what's on?** | 재미있는 할 거리 있는지 어디서 알아보나요? <br> chae·mi in·nŭn hal·gŏ·ri in·nŭn·ji ŏ·di·sŏ a·ra·bo·na·yo |
| **Which paper are the (concerts) listed in?** | (공연) 목록이 있는 신문이 뭔가요? <br> (kong·yŏn) mong·no·gi in·nŭn shin·mu·ni mwŏn·ga·yo |

| Is there anything interesting on tonight? | 오늘 밤에 뭐 재미있는 것 없나요? | o·nŭl ba·me mwŏ chae·mi in·nŭn·gŏt ŏm·na·yo |
|---|---|---|
| Is there anything interesting on this weekend? | 이번 주말에 뭐 재미있는 것 없나요? | i·bŏn ju·ma·ré mwŏ chae·mi in·nŭn·gŏt ŏm·na·yo |
| Where can I find ...? | ... 어디에 있나요? | ... ŏ·di·é in·na·yo |

| bars | 술집 | sul·chip |
|---|---|---|
| clubs | 클럽 | k'ŭl·lŏp |
| gay/lesbian bars | 게이바 | ke·i·ba |
| music venues | 음악 공연장 | ŭ·mak kong·yŏn·jang |
| restaurants | 음식점 | ŭm·shik·chŏm |

| I feel like going to a ... | ...에 가고 싶어요. | ...·é ka·go shi·p'ŏ·yo |
|---|---|---|

| bar | 술집 | sul·chip |
|---|---|---|
| cafe | 카페 | k'a·p'é |
| concert | 콘서트 | k'on·sŏ·t'ŭ |
| film | 영화관 | yŏng·hwa·gwan |
| karaoke bar | 가라오케 | ka·ra·o·k'é |
| nightclub | 나이트 클럽 | na·i·t'ŭ k'ŭl·lŏp |
| play | 연극 공연 | yŏn·gŭk kong·yŏn |
| restaurant | 식당 | shik·tang |
| teashop | 찻집 | ch'at·chip |
| traditional music performance | 국악 공연 | ku·gak kong·yŏn |

For more on bars, drinks and partying, see **romance** (p150), and **eating out** (p201 and p202).

## Invitations

| | |
|---|---|
| **What are you doing tonight?** | 오늘 밤에 뭐 하세요? <br> o·nŭl ba·mé mwŏ ha·se·yo |
| **What are you doing this weekend?** | 이번 주말에 뭐 하세요? <br> i·bŏn ju·ma·ré mwŏ ha·se·yo |
| **Would you like to go (for a) ...?** | … 가시겠어요? <br> … ka·shi·gess·ŏ·yo |
| **I feel like going (for a) ...** | … 가고 싶어요. <br> … ka·go shi·p'ŏ·yo |

| | | |
|---|---|---|
| **coffee** | 커피 마시러 | k'ŏ·p'i ma·shi·rŏ |
| **dancing** | 춤추러 | ch'um·ch'u·rŏ |
| **drink** | 술 마시러 | sul ma·shi·rŏ |
| **meal** | 밥 먹으러 | pam·mŏg·ŭ·rŏ |
| **walk** | 산책하러 | san·ch'ae·k'a·rŏ |

| | |
|---|---|
| **Do you want to come to the (BoA) concert with me?** | (보아) 공연에 같이 가시겠어요? <br> (po·a) kong·yŏ·né ka·ch'i ka·shi·gess·ŏ·yo |
| **We're having a party.** | 우리 파티 할 거예요. <br> u·ri p'a·t'i halk·kŏ·ye·yo |
| **You should come along.** | 같이 가요. <br> ka·ch'i ka·yo |

## Responding to Invitations

| | |
|---|---|
| **Sure!** | 물론이죠! <br> mul·lo·ni·jo |
| **Yes, I'd love to.** | 네, 가고 싶어요. <br> né ka·go shi·p'ŏ·yo |
| **Where shall we go?** | 어디 갈까요? <br> ŏ·di kalk·ka·yo |

**CULTURE TIP**

### Entertainment Venues

In Korea, going out often means visiting various pang/bang 방 (lit: room), venues which offer affordable entertainment options. Here are some of them:

노래방     no·rae·bang     song-room

small rooms with karaoke machines, perfect for up to a dozen people to sing along to their favourite songs

디브이디 방     di·bǔ·i·di·bang     DVD-room

a place where you can watch movies on DVD in a small room with a sofa – popular with groups of friends and couples, especially when the weather's bad

찜질방     jjim·jil·bang     steam-room

special facilities in a public bath, with a room for men and women to watch TV, read or relax and do nothing – often open 24 hours, allowing guests to sleep overnight

피시방     p'i·shi·bang     PC-room

the Korean equivalent of an internet cafe – a big room, often dark and crowded, which attracts more computer-game addicts than internet users

| | |
|---|---|
| **I'm afraid I can't.** | 죄송하지만<br>못 갈 것 같아요.<br>choé·song·ha·ji·man<br>mok·kal·gǒt ka·t'a·yo |
| **What about tomorrow?** | 내일은 어떠세요?<br>nae·i·rǔn ǒt·tǒ·se·yo |

## Arranging to Meet

Most Koreans don't meet up at a friend's home when they go out. Instead, they'll suggest meeting near a subway station, in front of a department store, or at the restaurant where they plan to go.

| | |
|---|---|
| **Q** What time will we meet? | 몇 시에 만날까요?<br>myŏs·shi·é man·nalk·ka·yo |
| **A** Let's meet at (eight) o'clock. | (여덟) 시에 만나요.<br>(yŏ·dŏl)·shi·é man·na·yo |
| **Q** Where shall we meet? | 어디서 만날까요?<br>ŏ·di·sŏ man·nalk·ka·yo |
| **A** Let's meet at the entrance. | 입구에서 만나요.<br>ip·ku·é·sŏ man·na·yo |
| **A** I'll pick you up at (six). | (여섯) 시에 태워 드리러<br>올게요.<br>(yŏ·sŏs) shi·é t'ae·wŏ dŭ·ri·rŏ<br>olk·ke·yo |
| **Q** Are you ready? | 준비 되셨나요?<br>chun·bi doé·shŏn·na·yo |
| **A** I'm ready. | 전 준비 됐어요.<br>chŏn jun·bi dwaess·ŏ·yo |
| **A** I'll be (15 minutes) late. | (십오 분) 늦을 것<br>같아요.<br>(shi·bo·bun) nŭ·jŭl·gŏt<br>ka·t'a·yo |
| I'll try to make it. | 노력해 볼게요.<br>no·ryŏ·k'ae bol·ke·yo |
| If I'm not there by (nine), don't wait for me. | 제가 (아홉) 시까지<br>안 오면, 기다리지 마세요.<br>che·ga (a·hop) shik·ka·ji<br>a·no·myŏn ki·da·ri·ji ma·se·yo |
| OK, I'll see you then. | 네, 그때 뵐게요.<br>né kŭt·tae boélk·ke·yo |
| I'm looking forward to it. | 기대 돼요.<br>ki·dae dwae·yo |
| Sorry, I'm late. | 늦어서 죄송합니다.<br>nŭ·jŏ·sŏ choé·song·ham·ni·da |
| Never mind. | 괜찮아요.<br>kwaen·ch'a·na·yo |

어디 갈까요?
ŏ·di kalk·ka·yo

***Where shall we go?***

## Drugs

| | |
|---|---|
| **I don't take drugs.** | 전 마약 안 해요.<br>chŏn ma·yak an·hae·yo |
| **I'm addicted to (coffee).** | 전 (커피) 중독이에요.<br>chŏn (k'ŏ·p'i) chung·do·gi·e·yo |
| **I'm trying to quit.** | 끊으려고 노력 중이에요.<br>ggŭ·nŭ·ryŏ·go no·ryŏk·chung<br>i·e·yo |
| **Do you want to have a smoke?** | 담배 피우시겠어요?<br>tam·bae p'i·u·shi·gess·ŏ·yo |
| **Do you have a light?** | 불 있으세요?<br>pu·riss·ŭ·se·yo |

If the police are talking to you about drugs, see **police** (p177), for useful phrases.

# Romance

## KEY PHRASES

| | | |
|---|---|---|
| Would you like to do something with me? | 같이 뭐 할까요? | ka·ch'i mwŏ halk·ka·yo |
| I love you. | 사랑해요. | sa·rang·hae·yo |
| Excuse me, I have to go now. | 죄송하지만 지금 어디 가야 돼요. | choé·song·ha·ji·man chi·gŭm ŏ·di ka·ya dwae·yo |

## Asking Someone Out

| | |
|---|---|
| Where would you like to go (tonight)? | (오늘 밤) 어디 가고 싶으신가요? (o·nŭl·bam) ŏ·di ka·go shi·p'ŭ·shin·ga·yo |
| **Q** Would you like to do something with me (tomorrow)? | (내일) 같이 뭐 할까요? (nae·il) ka·ch'i mwŏ halk·ka·yo |
| **A** Yes, I'd love to. | 네, 좋아요. né cho·a·yo |
| **A** Sorry, I can't. | 죄송하지만 안 돼요. choé·song·ha·ji·man an·dwae·yo |

## Pick-up Lines

| | |
|---|---|
| Would you like a drink? | 뭐 같이 마실까요? mwŏ ka·ch'i ma·shilk·ka·yo |
| Do you have a light? | 라이터 있으신가요? ra·i·t'ŏ iss·ŭ·shin·ga·yo |

| | |
|---|---|
| **Shall we get some fresh air?** | 산책 할까요?<br>san·ch'aek halk·ka·yo |
| **Can I dance with you?** | 같이 춤춰도<br>될까요?<br>ka·ch'i ch'um·ch'wŏ·do<br>doélk·ka·yo |
| **Can I take you home?** | 집에 데려다 드려도<br>될까요?<br>chi·bé te·ryŏ·da dŭ·ryŏ·do<br>doélk·ka·yo |

## Rejections

| | |
|---|---|
| **I'm here with my girlfriend/boyfriend.** | 여자친구랑/<br>남자친구랑 같이<br>왔어요.<br>yŏ·ja·ch'in·gu·rang/<br>nam·ja·ch'in·gu·rang ka·ch'i<br>wass·ŏ·yo |
| **I'm sorry, but I'd rather not.** | 죄송하지만 안 돼요.<br>choé·song·ha·ji·man<br>an·dwae·yo |
| **Excuse me, I have to go now.** | 죄송하지만 지금<br>어디 가야 돼요.<br>choé·song·ha·ji·man chi·gŭm<br>ŏ·di ka·ya dwae·yo |

## Getting Closer

| | |
|---|---|
| **I really like you.** | 당신이 정말 좋아요.<br>tang·shi·ni chŏng·mal cho·a·yo |
| **Can I kiss you?** | 키스해도 돼요?<br>k'i·sŭ·hae·do dwae·yo |
| **Do you want to come inside for a while?** | 안에 잠시<br>들어오시겠어요?<br>a·né cham·shi dŭ·rŏ<br>o·shi·gess·ŏ·yo |

| | |
|---|---|
| **Would you like to stay over?** | 자고 가시겠어요?<br>cha·go ka·shi·gess·ŏ·yo |

## Sex

| | |
|---|---|
| **Kiss me.** | 키스해 주세요.<br>k'i·sŭ·hae·ju·se·yo |
| **I want you.** | 당신을 원해요.<br>tang·shi·nŭl wŏn·hae·yo |
| **Let's go to bed.** | 잠자리에 들어요.<br>cham·ja·ri·é dŭ·rŏ·yo |
| **Do you like this?** | 좋아요?<br>cho·a·yo |
| **I like that.** | 좋아요.<br>cho·a·yo |
| **I don't like that.** | 싫어요.<br>shi·rŏ·yo |
| **That's great.** | 좋아요.<br>cho·a·yo |
| **I think we should stop now.** | 그만해야 될 것 같아요.<br>kŭ·man·hae·ya doél·gŏt ka·t'a·yo |
| **Do you have a (condom)?** | (콘돔) 있나요?<br>(k'on·dom) in·na·yo |
| **We need to use a (condom).** | (콘돔) 써야 해요.<br>(k'on·dom) ssŏ·ya hae·yo |
| **I won't do it without protection.** | 피임 없이 안 할 거예요.<br>p'i·im ŏp·shi an·halk·kŏ·ye·yo |

## Love

| | |
|---|---|
| **I think we're good together.** | 우리 잘 어울리는 것 같아요.<br>u·ri chal ŏ·ul·li·nŭn·gŏt ka·t'a·yo |

| I'm really happy with you. | 당신과 있으면 행복해요.<br>tang·shin·gwa iss·ŭ·myŏn<br>haeng·bo·k'ae·yo |
| I love you. | 사랑해요.<br>sa·rang·hae·yo |
| Will you marry me? | 결혼해 주시겠어요?<br>kyŏl·hon hae·ju·shi·gess·ŏ·yo |
| I'd like you to meet my parents. | 부모님께 인사드리러 가요.<br>pu·mo·nimk·ké in·sa·dŭ·ri·rŏ<br>ka·yo |

## Problems

| I don't think it's working out. | 안 될 것 같네요.<br>an·doél·gŏt ka·t'a·yo |
| Q Are you seeing someone else? | 다른 사람 만나나요?<br>ta·rŭn sa·ram man·na·na·yo |
| A He/She is just a friend. | 그냥 친구예요.<br>kŭ·nyang ch'in·gu·ye·yo |
| We'll work it out. | 잘 해결할 수<br>있을 거예요.<br>chal hae·gyŏl hal·su<br>iss·ŭlk·kŏ·ye·yo |
| I want to stay friends. | 친구로 남았으면 좋겠어요.<br>ch'in·gu·ro na·mass·ŭ·myŏn<br>cho·k'ess·ŏ·yo |

## Leaving

| I have to leave (tomorrow). | 저 (내일) 떠나야 돼요.<br>chŏ (nae·il) ddŏ·na·ya dwae·yo |
| I'll keep in touch. | 연락할게요.<br>yŏl·la·k'alk·ke·yo |
| I'll miss you. | 보고 싶을 거예요.<br>po·go shi·p'ŭlk·kŏ·ye·yo |

# Beliefs & Culture

## KEY PHRASES

| What's your religion? | 종교가 뭐예요? | chong·gyo·ga mwǒ·ye·yo |
| I'm ... | 전 ... | chǒn ... |
| I'm sorry, it's against my beliefs. | 죄송하지만, 그것은 저의 믿음에 위배돼요. | choé·song·ha·ji·man kǔ·gǒ·sǔn chǒ·é mi·dǔm·é wi·bae dwae·yo |

## Religion

**Q** What's your religion?
종교가 뭐예요?
chong·gyo·ga mwǒ·ye·yo

**A** I'm agnostic.
전 불가지론자예요.
chǒn pul·ga·ji·ron·ja·ye·yo

**A** I'm an atheist.
전 무신론자예요.
chǒn mu·shin·non·ja·ye·yo

**A** I'm (a/an) ...
전 ...
chǒn ...

| Buddhist | 불교예요 | pul·gyo·ye·yo |
| Catholic | 천주교예요 | ch'ǒn·ju·gyo·ye·yo |
| Christian | 기독교예요 | ki·dok·kyo·ye·yo |
| Confucianist | 유교예요 | yu·gyo·ye·yo |
| Hindu | 힌두교예요 | hin·du·gyo·ye·yo |
| Jewish | 유태교예요 | yu·t'ae·gyo·ye·yo |
| Muslim | 이슬람교예요 | i·sǔl·lam·gyo·ye·yo |

| | |
|---|---|
| **A** I believe in religious freedom. | 전 종교의 자유를 믿어요. <br> chŏn jong·gyo·é ja·yu·rŭl mi dŏ·yo |
| **A** I don't have any religion. | 전 종교가 없어요. <br> chŏn jong·gyo·ga ŏp·sŏ·yo |
| I (don't) believe in ... | 전 ...을/를 (안) 믿어요. <br> chŏn ...ŭl/·rŭl (an) mi·dŏ·yo |

| | | |
|---|---|---|
| a god | 신 | shin |
| astrology | 점성학 | chŏm·sŏng·hak |
| fate | 운명 | un·myŏng |
| God (Judeo-Christian) | 하나님 | ha·na·nim |

| | |
|---|---|
| Can I attend a service/mass here? | 여기서 예배/미사 드려도 되나요? <br> yŏ·gi·sŏ ye·bae/mi·sa dŭ·ryŏ·do doé·na·yo |
| Can I pray here? | 여기서 기도해도 되나요? <br> yŏ·gi·sŏ ki·do·hae·do doé·na·yo |
| Can I worship here? | 여기서 찬양 예배 드려도 되나요? <br> ch'a·nyang ye·bae dŭ·ryŏ·do |
| Where can I attend a service/mass? | 어디서예배/미사 드릴 수 있나요? <br> ŏ·di·sŏ ye·bae/mi·sa dŭ·ril·su in·na·yo |
| Where can I pray? | 어디서 기도할 수 있나요? <br> ŏ·di·sŏ ki·do·hal·su in·na·yo |
| Where can I worship? | 어디서 찬양 예배 드릴 수 있나요? <br> ŏ·di·sŏ ch'a·nyang ye·bae dŭ·ril·su in·na·yo |

## Cultural Differences

| | |
|---|---|
| **How do you do this in (Korea)?** | (한국)에서는 이걸 어떻게 하나요?<br>(han·gug)·e·sŏ·nŭn i·gŏl ŏt·to·k'é ha·na·yo |
| **I didn't mean to do/say anything wrong.** | 일부러 그런 게 아니예요.<br>il·bu·rŏ kŭ·rŏn·gé a·ni·ye·yo |
| **Is this a local or national custom?** | 이 지방의 관습인가요, 한국 전체의 관습인가요?<br>i·ji·bang·é kwan·sŭ·bin·ga·yo han·guk chŏn·ch'e·é kwan·sŭ·bin·ga·yo |
| **I don't want to offend you.** | 기분 나쁘게 하려던 게 아니예요.<br>ki·bun nap·pŭ·gé ha·ryŏ·dŏn·gé a·ni·ye·yo |
| **I respect your beliefs.** | 당신의 믿음을 존중해요.<br>tang·shi·né mi·dŭm·ŭl jon·jung·hae·yo |
| **I'm not used to this.** | 이것에 익숙하지 않아요.<br>i·gŏ·sé ik·su·k'a·ji a·na·yo |

**CULTURE TIP**

**Shamanism**

An important part of Korean spirituality is mu·sok·shi·nang 무속신앙 (shamanism). It's not a religion, but it does involve communication with spirits through intermediaries known as mu·dang 무당 (female shamans). Shamanist ceremonies are held for a variety of reasons: to cure illness, to ward off financial problems or to guide a deceased family member safely into the spirit world. A kut 굿 (exorcism ceremony) might be held by a village on a regular basis to ensure the safety of its citizens and a good harvest of rice or fish.

**CULTURE TIP**

## Superstitions

In Korean the number four, sa 사, sounds like one of the Chinese characters for 'death' – the Korean word for 'death', sa·mang 사망, is based on this. The resulting superstition is the reason the 4th floor in elevators and office listings is often named with the letter 'F' instead of the number four.

When writing a person's name, it's preferable to use any colour except bbal·gang 빨강 (red). Though the source of this superstition is uncertain, many older people associate writing someone's name in red ink with death.

Finally, a twae·ji 돼지 (pig) appearing in a dream is considered a sign of good luck – if it happens to you, Korean friends might advise you to buy a lottery ticket!

| | |
|---|---|
| **I'd rather not join in.** | 하지 않는 게 낫겠어요. <br> ha·ji an·nŭn·gé nak·kess·ŏ·yo |
| **I'll try it.** | 한번 해 볼게요. <br> han·bŏn hae·bolk·ke·yo |
| **I'm sorry, it's against my beliefs.** | 죄송하지만, 그것은 <br> 저의 믿음에 위배돼요. <br> choé·song·ha·ji·man kŭ·gŏ·sŭn <br> chŏ·é mi·dŭm·é wi·bae dwae·yo |
| **I'm sorry, it's against my culture.** | 죄송하지만, 그것은 <br> 저의 문화에 위배돼요. <br> choé·song·ha·ji·man kŭ·gŏ·sŭn <br> chŏ·é mun·hwa·é wi·bae dwae·yo |
| **I'm sorry, it's against my religion.** | 죄송하지만, 그것은 <br> 저의 종교에 위배돼요. <br> choé·song·ha·ji·man kŭ·gŏ·sŭn <br> chŏ·é chong·gyo·é wi·bae dwae·yo |
| **This is different.** | 이건 색달라요. <br> i·gŏn saek·tal·la·yo |
| **This is interesting.** | 이건 흥미로워요. <br> i·gŏn hŭng·mi·ro·wŏ·yo |

# Sports

## KEY PHRASES

| | | |
|---|---|---|
| Which sport do you play? | 어떤 운동 하세요? | ŏt·tŏn un·dong ha·se·yo |
| What's your favourite team? | 제일 좋아하는 팀이 뭐예요? | che·il cho·a·ha·nŭn t'i·mi mwŏ·ye·yo |
| What's the score? | 점수가 어떻게 되나요? | chŏm·su·ga ŏt·tŏ·k'é doé·na·yo |

## Sporting Interests

| | |
|---|---|
| **Q** Which sport do you follow? | 어떤 운동 관심 있으세요? ŏt·tŏn un·dong kwan·shim iss·ŭ·se·yo |
| **Q** Which sport do you play? | 어떤 운동 하세요? ŏt·tŏn un·dong ha·se·yo |
| **A** I follow ... | ...에 관심 있어요. ...é kwan·shim iss·ŏ·yo |
| **A** I play/do ... | 저는 ...을/를 해요. chŏ·nŭn ...ŭl/·rŭl hae·yo |

| | | |
|---|---|---|
| **aerobics** | 에어로빅 | e·ŏ·ro·bik |
| **archery** | 양궁 | yang·gung |
| **football/soccer** | 축구 | ch'uk·ku |
| **karate** | 가라테 | ka·ra·t'e |
| **martial arts** | 무술 | mu·sul |
| **scuba diving** | 스쿠버 다이빙 | sŭ·k'u·bŏ da·i·bing |
| **tennis** | 테니스 | t'e·ni·sŭ |
| **weightlifting** | 역도 | yŏk·to |

| | | |
|---|---|---|
|  **I cycle.** | 전 자전거를 타요.<br>chŏn cha·jŏn·gŏ·rŭl t'a·yo | |
| **I run.** | 선 달리기를 해요.<br>chŏn tal·li·gi·rŭl hae·yo | |
| **I walk.** | 전 걷기를 해요.<br>chŏn kŏk·ki·rŭl hae·yo | |
| **I swim.** | 전 수영을 해요.<br>chŏn su·yŏng·ŭl hae·yo | |
| **Do you like (baseball)?** | (야구) 좋아하시나요?<br>(ya·gu) cho·a·ha·shi·na·yo | |
| **Yes, very much.** | 많이 좋아해요.<br>ma·ni cho·a·hae·yo | |
| **Not really.** | 별로요.<br>pyŏl·lo·yo | |

SOCIAL

SPORTS

어떤 운동 하세요?
ŏt·tŏn un·dong ha·se·yo
*Which sport do you play?*

| **A** I like watching it. | 보는 것은 좋아해요.<br>po·nŭn·gŏ·sŭn cho·a·hae·yo |
| **Who's your favourite sportsperson?** | 특히 좋아하는 운동<br>선수가 누구예요?<br>t'ŭ·k'i cho·a·ha·nŭn un·dong<br>sŏn·su·ga nu·gu·ye·yo |
| **What's your favourite team?** | 제일 좋아하는 팀이<br>뭐예요?<br>che·il cho·a·ha·nŭn t'i·mi<br>mwŏ·ye·yo |

For more sports, see the **dictionary**.

## Going to a Game

| **Would you like to go to a game?** | 경기 보러<br>가시겠어요?<br>kyŏng·gi bo·rŏ<br>ka·shi·gess·ŏ·yo |
| **Who are you supporting?** | 어느 팀을 응원하세요?<br>ŏ·nŭ t'i·mŭl ŭng·wŏn·ha·se·yo |
| **What's the score?** | 점수가 어떻게 되나요?<br>chŏm·su·ga ŏt·tŏ·k'é doé·na·yo |
| **Who's playing?** | 누가 경기해요?<br>nu·ga kyŏng·gi·hae·yo |
| **Who's winning?** | 누가 이기고 있나요?<br>nu·ga i·gi·go in·na·yo |

### 🔊 LISTEN FOR

| 무승부 | mu·sŭng·bu | draw/even |
| 무득점 | mu·dŭk·chŏm | love (zero) |
| 매치포인트 | mae·ch'i·p'o·in·t'ŭ | match point |
| 영점 | yŏng·jŏm | nil (zero) |

| | |
|---|---|
| That was a boring game! | 지루한 경기였어요!<br>chi·ru·han kyŏng·gi·yŏss·ŏ·yo |
| That was a great game! | 굉장한<br>경기였어요!<br>koéng·jang·han<br>kyŏng·gi·yŏss·ŏ·yo |

## Playing Sport

| | |
|---|---|
| Q Do you want to play a game? | 저랑 운동경기 하시겠어요?<br>chŏ·rang un·dong·gyŏng·gi<br>ha·shi·gess·ŏ·yo |
| A I'm sorry, I can't. | 죄송하지만, 안 돼요.<br>choé·song·ha·ji·man<br>an·dwae·yo |
| Can I join in? | 같이 해도 되나요?<br>ka·ch'i hae·do doé·na·yo |
| Your/My point. | 제/당신 점수예요.<br>ché/tang·shin chŏm·su·ye·yo |
| Kick/Pass it to me! | 저한데 치/패스해<br>주세요!<br>chŏ·han·t'e ch'a/p'ae·sŭ·hae<br>ju·se·yo |
| Where's a good place to ...? | ...하기 좋은 곳이<br>어디예요?<br>... ha·gi cho·ŭn go·shi<br>ŏ·di·ye·yo |

| | | |
|---|---|---|
| fish | 낚시 | nakk·shi |
| go hiking | 등산 | tŭng·san |
| go horse riding | 승마 | sŭng·ma |
| go scuba diving | 스쿠버 다이빙 | sŭ·k'u·bŏ da·i·bing |
| go windsurfing | 윈드서핑 | win·dŭ·sŏ·p'ing |
| run | 육상 | yuk·sang |
| ski | 스키 | sŭ·k'i |

| Where's the nearest ...? | | 제일 가까운 ...<br>어디예요?<br>che·il kak·ka·un ...<br>ŏ·di·ye·yo |
|---|---|---|
| basketball court | 야구장 | ya·gu·jang |
| golf course | 골프장 | kol·p'ŭ·jang |
| gym | 헬스장 | hel·sŭ·jang |
| ice rink | 빙상경기장 | ping·sang·gyŏng·gi·jang |
| swimming pool | 수영장 | su·yŏng·jang |
| tennis court | 테니스장 | t'e·ni·sŭ·jang |

| Can I hire a ...? | | ... 빌릴 수 있나요?<br>... pil·lil·su in·na·yo |
|---|---|---|
| ball | 공 | kong |
| bicycle | 자전거 | cha·jŏn·gŏ |
| court | 경기장 | kyŏng·gi·jang |
| racquet | 라켓 | ra·k'et |

| What's the charge per day? | 하루당 얼마예요?<br>ha·ru·dang ŏl·ma·ye·yo |
|---|---|
| What's the charge per game? | 게임당 얼마예요?<br>ke·im·dang ŏl·ma·ye·yo |
| What's the charge per hour? | 시간당 얼마예요?<br>shi·gan·dang ŏl·ma·ye·yo |
| Is there a women-only session/pool? | 여성 전용<br>강습/수영장<br>있나요?<br>yŏ·sŏng·jŏ·nyong<br>kang·sŭp/su·yŏng·jang<br>in·na·yo |
| Where are the changing rooms? | 탈의실이 어디예요?<br>t'a·ri·shi·ri ŏ·di·ye·yo |

## Soccer/Football

| | |
|---|---|
| **Who plays for (the Korean National Soccer Team)?** | (한국 국가대표팀)에 이떤 선수가 뛰나요? (han·guk kuk·ka·dae·p'yo·t'im)·é ŏt·tŏn sŏn·su·ga ttwi·na·yo |
| **He's a great player.** | 그는 실력있는 선수예요. kŭ·nŭn shil·lyŏ·gin·nŭn sŏn·su·ye·yo |
| **What a great/terrible team!** | 굉장한/ 형편없는 팀이네요! koéng·jang·han/ hyŏng·p'yŏn·ŏm·nŭn t'i·mi·ne·yo |
| **Down with ...!** | ... 져라! ... jŏ·ra |
| **What a goal!** | 골 멋져요! kol mŏt·chŏ·yo |
| **What a pass!** | 패스 멋져요! p'ae·sŭ mŏt·chŏ·yo |
| **What a kick!** | 킥 멋져요! k'ik mŏt·chŏ·yo |

Off to see a match? Check out **going to a game** (p160), and **buying tickets** (p54).

🔊 **LISTEN FOR**

| | | |
|---|---|---|
| 공 | kong | ball |
| 퇴장 | t'oé·jang | expulsion |
| 골대 | kol·dae | goal posts |
| 선수 | sŏn·su | player |
| 심판 | shim·p'an | referee |
| 공격수 | kong·gyŏk·su | striker |

SOCIAL

SPORTS

# Outdoors

**KEY PHRASES**

| | | |
|---|---|---|
| Where can we buy hiking supplies? | 등산 용품 어디서 살 수 있나요? | tŭng·san yong·p'um ŏ·di·sŏ sal·su in·na·yo |
| Are there guided treks? | 따라갈 수 있는 길이 있나요? | dda·ra·gal·su in·nŭn gi·ri in·na·yo |
| I'm lost. | 길을 잃었어요. | ki·rŭl i·rŏss·ŏ·yo |
| Is it safe to dive/swim here? | 여기서 다이빙해도/ 수영해도 안전한가요? | yŏ·gi·sŏ da·i·bing·hae·do/ su·yŏng·hae·do an·jŏn han·ga·yo |
| What's the weather like? | 날씨 어떤가요? | nal·shi ŏt·tŏn·ga·yo |

## Hiking

| Are there guided treks? | 따라갈 수 있는 길이 있나요? dda·ra·gal·su in·nŭn gi·ri in·na·yo |
|---|---|
| How long is the trail? | 등산로가 얼마나 긴가요? tŭng·san·no·ga ŏl·ma·na kin·ga·yo |
| Is it possible to go rock climbing here? | 여기서 암벽 등반해도 되나요? yŏ·gi·sŏ am·byŏk tŭng·ban hae·do doé·na·yo |
| Is it safe to climb this mountain? | 이 산 올라가기에 안전한가요? i·san ol·la·ga·gi·é an·jŏn·han·ga·yo |

| | |
|---|---|
| **How high is the climb?** | 얼마나 높나요?<br>ŏl·ma·na nom·na·yo |
| **Is it very scenic?** | 경치가 아주 좋은가요?<br>kyŏng·ch'i·ga a·ju cho·ŭn ga·yo |
| **When does it get dark?** | 언제 어두워 지나요?<br>ŏn·jé ŏ·du·wŏ ji·na·yo |
| **Where's the nearest village?** | 가장 가까운 마을이 어디<br>있나요?<br>ka·jang kak·ka·un ma·ŭ·ri ŏ·di<br>in·na·yo |
| **Where's the nearest temple?** | 가장 가까운 절이 어디<br>있나요?<br>ka·jang kak·ka·un chŏ·ri ŏ·di<br>in·na·yo |
| **Is there a mountain hut up there?** | 저 위에 산장이 있나요?<br>chŏ wi·é san·jang·i in·na·yo |
| **Where can we buy hiking supplies?** | 등산 용품 어디서<br>살 수 있나요?<br>tŭng·san yong·p'um ŏ·di·sŏ<br>sal·su in·na·yo |
| **Do you employ local guides?** | 현지 가이드가 있나요?<br>hyŏn·ji ga·i·dŭ·ga in·na·yo |
| **Where can we spend the night?** | 어디서 잘 수 있나요?<br>ŏ·di·sŏ chal·su in·na·yo |
| **Can I leave some things here for a while?** | 여기 잠깐 물건<br>놔둬도 되나요?<br>yŏ·gi chamk·kan mul·gŏn<br>nwa·dwŏ·do doé·na·yo |
| **Do we have to pay?** | 돈 내야 하나요?<br>ton nae·ya ha·na·yo |
| **Can I cook here?** | 여기서 취사해도<br>되나요?<br>yŏ·gi·sŏ ch'wi·sa·hae·do<br>doé·na·yo |

| | | |
|---|---|---|
| **Where can I ...?** | 어디서 … 있나요? | ŏ·di·sŏ … in·na·yo |
| buy things | 물건 살 수 | mul·gŏn sal·su |
| find someone who knows this area | 여기 잘 아는 사람을 찾을 수 | yŏ·gi chal a·nŭn sa·ra·mŭl ch'a·jŭl·su |
| get a map | 지도 구할 수 | chi·do ku·hal·su |
| hire hiking gear | 등산 장비 빌릴 수 | tŭng·san jang·bi pil·lil·su |

| | | |
|---|---|---|
| **Where can I find the ...?** | … 어디 있나요? | … ŏ·di in·na·yo |
| campsite | 야영 장소 | ya·yŏng jang·so |
| nearest village | 제일 가까운 마을 | che·il kak·ka·un ma·ŭl |
| showers | 샤워 시설 | sha·wŏ shi·sŏl |
| toilets | 화장실 | hwa·jang·shil |

| | | |
|---|---|---|
| **Do we need to take food?** | 음식 가져 가야 되나요? | ŭm·shik ka·jŏ·ga·ya doé·na·yo |
| **Do we need to take water?** | 물 가져 가야 되나요? | mul ka·jŏ·ga·ya doé·na·yo |
| **Which is the easiest route?** | 제일 쉬운 경로가 뭐예요? | che·il shi·un kyŏng·no·ga mwŏ·ye·yo |
| **Which is the most interesting route?** | 제일 재미있는 경로가 뭐예요? | che·il chae·mi·in·nŭn kyŏng·no·ga mwŏ·ye·yo |

| | |
|---|---|
| **Which is the shortest route?** | 제일 짧은 경로가 뭐예요?<br>che·il tchal·bŭn kyŏng·no·ga mwŏ·ye·yo |
| **Is the track open?** | 이 길 개방되어 있나요?<br>i·gil kae·bang·doé·ŏ in·na·yo |
| **Is the track scenic?** | 이 길 경치가 좋은가요?<br>i·gil kyŏng·ch'i·ga cho·ŭn·ga·yo |
| **Is the track well-marked?** | 이 길 보기 쉽게 표시되어 있나요?<br>i·gil po·gi ship·ké p'yo·shi·doé·ŏ in·na·yo |
| **Where have you come from?** | 어디서 오시는 길이에요?<br>ŏ·di·sŏ o·shi·nŭn gi·ri·e·yo |
| **How long did it take?** | 얼마나 걸리셨나요?<br>ŏl·ma·na kŏl·li·shŏn·na·yo |
| **Does this path go to (Dobongsan)?** | 이 길이 (도봉산) 가는 길인가요?<br>i·gi·ri (to·bong·san) ka·nŭn gi·rin·ga·yo |
| **Can I go through here?** | 여기 지나가도 되나요?<br>yŏ·gi ji·na·ga·do doé·na·yo |
| **I'm lost.** | 길을 잃었어요.<br>ki·rŭl i·rŏss·ŏ·yo |
| **Is the water OK to drink?** | 마셔도 괜찮은 물인가요?<br>ma·shŏ·do kwaen·ch'a·nŭn mu·rin·ga·yo |

SOCIAL  OUTDOORS

### 🔊 LISTEN FOR

| | | |
|---|---|---|
| 물살<br>조심하세요! | mul·sal<br>cho·shim ha·se·yo | Be careful of the undertow! |
| 위험해요! | wi·hŏm·hae·yo | It's dangerous! |

SOCIAL OUTDOORS

## At the Beach

| | |
|---|---|
| **Is there a beach near here?** | 주위에 해수욕장 있나요? chu·wi·é hae·su·yok·chang in·na·yo |
| **Is it safe to dive/swim here?** | 여기서 다이빙해도/ 수영해도 안전한가요? yŏ·gi·sŏ da·i·bing·hae·do/ su·yŏng·hae·do an·jŏn han·ga·yo |
| **What time is high/low tide?** | 밀물이/썰물이 언제예요? mil·mu·ri/ssŏl·mu·ri ŏn·je·ye·yo |
| **How much to rent a chair?** | 의자 빌리는 데 얼마예요? ŭi·ja pil·li·nŭn·dé ŏl·ma·ye·yo |
| **How much to rent a parasol?** | 파라솔 빌리는 데 얼마예요? p'a·ra·sol pil·li·nŭn·dé ŏl·ma·ye·yo |

## Weather

| | |
|---|---|
|  **What will the weather be like tomorrow?** | 내일 날씨가 어떨까요? nae·il nal·shi·ga ŏt·tŏlk·ka·yo |
| **What's the weather like?** | 날씨 어떤가요? nal·shi ŏt·tŏn·ga·yo |

### 🔍 LOOK FOR

| | | |
|---|---|---|
| 낚시 금지 | nak·shi kŭm·ji | No Fishing |
| 다이빙 금지 | ta·i·bing kŭm·ji | No Diving |
| 수영 금지 | su·yŏng kŭm·ji | No Swimming |

**It's ...**

| cloudy | 구름이 많아요. | ku·rŭ·mi ma·na·yo |
| cold | 추워요. | ch'u·wŏ·yo |
| fine | 맑아요. | mal·ga·yo |
| freezing | 정말 추워요. | chŏng·mal ch'u·wŏ·yo |
| hot | 더워요. | tŏ·wŏ·yo |
| humid | 습도가 높아요. | sŭp·to·ga no·p'a·yo |
| muggy | 푹푹 쩌요. | p'uk·p'uk tchŏ·yo |
| raining | 비가 와요. | pi·ga wa·yo |
| snowing | 눈이 와요. | nu·ni wa·yo |
| sunny | 햇빛이 밝아요. | haep·pi·ch'i bal·ga·yo |
| warm | 따뜻해요. | ddat·tŭ·t'ae·yo |
| windy | 바람이 많이 불어요. | pa·ra·mi ma·ni pu·rŏ·yo |

| Where can I buy a rain jacket? | 우비 어디서 사나요? u·bi ŏ·di·sŏ sa·na·yo |
| Where can I buy an umbrella? | 우신 어디서 살 수 있어요? u·san ŏ·di·sŏ sal·su iss·ŏ·yo |

## Flora & Fauna

| Which ... is that? | 이게 무슨 ...이에요/예요? i·gé mu·sŭn ...·i·e·yo/·ye·yo |

| animal | 동물 | tong·mul |
| flower | 꽃 | ggot |
| plant | 식물 | shing·mul |
| tree | 나무 | na·mu |

 **LISTEN FOR**

| 진달래 | chin·dal·lae | azalea |
| 벚꽃 | pŏk·kot | cherry blossom |
| 개나리 | kae·na·ri | forsythia |
| 은행나무 | ŭn·haeng na·mu | gingko tree |
| 고라니 | ko·ra·ni | Korean water deer |
| 단풍나무 | tan·p'ung na·mu | maple tree |
| 무궁화 | mu·gung·hwa | Rose of Sharon |

**Is it ...?**

| **common** | 흔한가요? | hŭn·han·ga·yo |
| **dangerous** | 위험한가요? | wi·hŏm·han·ga·yo |
| **endangered** | 멸종 위기에 있나요? | myŏl·chong wi·gi·é in·na·yo |
| **poisonous** | 독이 있나요? | to·gi in·na·yo |
| **protected** | 보호를 받고 있나요? | po·ho·rŭl pak·ko in·na·yo |

| **What's it used for?** | 뭐에 쓰나요? mwŏ·é ssŭ·na·yo |
| **Can you eat the fruit?** | 열매 먹을 수 있나요? yŏl·mae mŏ·gŭl·su in·na·yo |

For geographical and agricultural terms, and more names of animals and plants, see the **dictionary**.

# Safe Travel

# Emergencies

## KEY PHRASES

| | | |
|---|---|---|
| **Help!** | 도와주세요! | to·wa·ju·se·yo |
| **There's been an accident.** | 사고가 났어요. | sa·go·ga nass·ŏ·yo |
| **It's an emergency!** | 응급 상황이에요! | ŭng·gŭp sang·hwang·i·e·yo |

| | |
|---|---|
| **Help!** | 도와주세요!<br>to·wa·ju·se·yo |
| **Stop!** | 그만 하세요!<br>kŭ·man ha·se·yo |
| **Go away!** | 저리 가세요!<br>chŏ·ri ka·se·yo |
| **Thief!** | 도둑이야!<br>to·du·gi·ya |
| **Fire!** | 불이야!<br>pu·ri·ya |
| **Watch out!** | 조심하세요!<br>cho·shim·ha·se·yo |
| **Call an ambulance!** | 구급차 불러주세요!<br>ku·gŭp·ch'a pul·lŏ·ju·se·yo |
| **Call a doctor!** | 의사 불러주세요!<br>ŭi·sa pul·lŏ·ju·se·yo |
| **Call the police!** | 경찰 불러주세요!<br>kyŏng·ch'al pul·lŏ·ju·se·yo |
| **It's an emergency!** | 응급 상황이에요!<br>ŭng·gŭp sang·hwang·i·e·yo |

## 🔍 LOOK FOR

| | | |
|---|---|---|
| 경찰서 | kyŏng·ch'al·sŏ | Police Station |
| 병원 | pyŏng·won | Hospital |
| 응급실 | ŭng·gŭp·shil | Emergency Department |
| 파출소 | p'a·ch'ul·so | Police Substation |

**There's been an accident.**
사고가 났어요.
sa·go·ga nass·ŏ·yo

**Can I use your phone?**
전화 좀 써도 되나요?
chŏn·hwa chom ssŏ·do doé·na·yo

**Could you help me, please?**
좀 도와주시겠어요?
chom to·wa·ju·shi·gess·ŏ·yo

**Where are the toilets?**
화장실이 어디예요?
hwa·jang·shi·ri ŏ·di·ye·yo

**I'm lost.**
길을 잃었어요.
ki·rŭl i·rŏss·ŏ·yo

**She's having a baby.**
아기가 곧 나올 것 같아요.
a·gi·ga kot na·ol·gŏt ka·t'a·yo

**He/She is having a/an ...**

| | | |
|---|---|---|
| **allergic reaction** | 알레르기 반응을 보여요. | al·le·rŭ·gi ba·nŭng·ŭl po·yŏ·yo |
| **asthma attack** | 천식 발작 해요. | ch'ŏn·shik bal·cha·k'ae·yo |
| **epileptic fit** | 간질 발작 해요. | kan·jil bal·cha·k'ae·yo |
| **heart attack** | 심장 마비예요. | shim·jang ma·bi·ye·yo |

SAFE TRAVEL

EMERGENCIES

**LANGUAGE TIP**

**Tongue Twisters**

Try rolling these two beauties off your tongue:

경찰청 쇠창살 외철창살,
검찰청 쇠창살 쌍철창살.
kyŏng·ch'al·ch'ŏng soé·ch'ang·sal oé·ch'ŏl·ch'ang·sal
kŏm·ch'al·ch'ŏng soé·ch'ang·sal ssang·ch'ŏl·ch'ang·sal
An iron bar in the National Police Agency window is a
single iron bar, and an iron bar in the Public Prosecutor's
Office window is a double iron bar.

간장 공장 공장장은 강 공장장이고,
된장 공장 공장장은 공 공장장이다.
kan·jang kong·jang kong·jang·jang·ŭn kang
kong·jang·jang·i·go toén·jang kong·jang
kong·jang·jang·ŭn kong kong·jang·jang·i·da
The manager of the soy sauce factory is manager Kang, and
the manager of the soy bean paste factory is manager Kong.

| **Is it safe ...?** | ... 안전한가요? |
| | ... an·jŏn han·ga·yo |

| **at night** | 밤에 | pa·mé |
| **for gay people** | 동성 커플에게 | tong·sŏng k'ŏ·p'ŭ·re·gé |
| **for travellers** | 여행자에게 | yŏ·haeng·ja·e·gé |
| **for women** | 여자에게 | yŏ·ja·e·gé |
| **on your own** | 혼자서도 | hon·ja·sŏ·do |

# Police

## KEY PHRASES

| | | |
|---|---|---|
| **Where's the police station?** | 경찰서가 어디예요? | kyŏng·chal·sŏ·ga ŏ·di·ye·yo |
| **I want to contact my embassy/ consulate.** | 대사관에/ 영사관에 연락하고 싶습니다. | tae·sa·gwa·né/ yŏng·sa·gwa·né yŏl·la·k'a·go ship·sŭm·ni·da |
| **My bags were stolen.** | 가방 도둑 맞았어요. | ka·bang to·dung·ma·jass·ŏ·yo |

Korean police in general are willing to give extra leeway to foreigners, but not if they cop attitude. Apologising and/or admitting fault can be a quick way to end a sticky situation, as the disadvantaged party is often only looking for a face-saving admission that they were wronged. Most police speak only rudimentary English. In a bind, you can call the taxi interpreting service for help.

| | |
|---|---|
| **Where's the police station?** | 경찰서가 어디예요? kyŏng·chal·sŏ·ga ŏ·di·ye·yo |
| **I want to report an offence.** | 신고하려고 해요. shin·go ha·ryŏ·go hae·yo |
| **I've been assaulted.** | 저는 폭행 당했어요. chŏ·nŭn p'o·k'aeng·dang haess·ŏ·yo |
| **I've been raped.** | 저는 강간 당했어요. chŏ·nŭn kang·gan·dang haess·ŏ·yo |
| **I've been robbed.** | 저는 도둑 맞았어요. chŏ·nŭn to·dung ma·jass·ŏ·yo |
| **I have insurance.** | 전 보험에 들었어요. chŏn po·hŏ·mé dŭ·rŏss·ŏ·yo |

| I've lost my ... | | ... 잃어버렸어요.<br>... i·rŏ·bŏ·ryŏss·ŏ·yo |
|---|---|---|
| My ... was/were stolen. | | ... 도둑 맞았어요.<br>... to·dung·ma·jass·ŏ·yo |

| backpack | 배낭 | pae·nang |
|---|---|---|
| bags | 가방 | ka·bang |
| car keys | 차 열쇠 | ch'a yŏl·soé |
| credit card | 신용 카드 | shi·nyong k'a·dŭ |
| handbag | 핸드백 | haen·dŭ·baek |
| jewellery | 보석 | po·sŏk |
| money | 돈 | ton |
| papers | 서류 | sŏ·ryu |
| passport | 여권 | yŏk·kwŏn |
| travellers<br>cheques | 여행자<br>수표 | yŏ·haeng·ja<br>su·p'yo |
| wallet | 지갑 | chi·gap |

| I need an (English)<br>interpreter. | (영어) 통역사가<br>필요해요.<br>(yŏng·ŏ) t'ong·yŏk·sa·ga<br>p'i·ryo·hae·yo |
|---|---|
| What am I accused of? | 제가 무슨 혐의가<br>있나요?<br>che·ga mu·sŭn hyŏ·mi·ga<br>in·na·yo |
| I didn't do it. | 전 그런 적 없습니다.<br>chŏn kŭ·rŏn·jŏk ŏp·sŭm·ni·da |
| I'm sorry. | 죄송합니다.<br>choé·song·ham·ni·da |
| I apologise. | 사과드립니다.<br>sa·gwa dŭ·rim·ni·da |

## 🔊 LISTEN FOR

| | |
|---|---|
| 교통 위반 벌금입니다. | kyo·t'ong wi·ban pŏl·gŭm im·ni·da<br>It's a traffic violation fine. |
| 속도 위반 벌금입니다. | sok·to wi·ban pŏl·gŭm im·ni·da<br>It's a speeding fine. |
| 주차 위반 벌금입니다. | chu·ch'a wi·ban pŏl·gŭm im·ni·da<br>It's a parking fine. |

| | |
|---|---|
| **I didn't realise I was doing anything illegal.** | 전 그게 불법인지<br>몰랐습니다.<br>chŏn kŭ·gé pul·bŏ·bin·ji<br>mol·lass·sŭm·ni·da |
| **Is there a fine we can pay to clear this?** | 벌금을 내면<br>됩니까?<br>pŏl·gŭ·mŭl nae·myŏn<br>doém·nik·ka |
| **I want to contact my embassy/consulate.** | 대사관에/영사관에<br>연락하고 싶습니다.<br>tae·sa·gwa·né/yŏng·sa·gwa·né<br>yŏl·la·k'a·go ship·sŭm·ni·da |
| **Can I make a phone call?** | 전화 좀 써도<br>되겠습니까?<br>chŏn·hwa chom ssŏ·do<br>doé·gess·sŭm·nik·ka |
| **Can I have a lawyer (who speaks English)?** | (영어하는) 변호사<br>쓸 수 있습니까?<br>(yŏng·ŏ·ha·nŭn) pyŏn·ho·sa<br>ssŭl·su iss·sŭm·nik·ka |
| **This medicine is for personal use.** | 이 약은 제가 쓸 겁니다.<br>i·ya·gŭn che·ga ssŭl gŏm·ni·da |
| **I have a prescription for this drug.** | 이 약 처방전이<br>있습니다.<br>i·yak chŏ·bang·jŏ·ni<br>iss·sŭm·ni·da |

# Health

### KEY PHRASES

| | | |
|---|---|---|
| Where's the nearest hospital? | 제일 가까운 병원 어디 있나요? | che·il kak·ka·un pyŏng·wŏn ŏ·di in·na·yo |
| I'm sick. | 전 아파요. | chŏn a·p'a·yo |
| I need a doctor. | 의사가 필요해요. | ŭi·sa·ga p'i·ryo hae·yo |
| I'm on medication for ... | 전 ... 약을 먹어요. | chŏn ... ya·gŭl mŏ·gŏ·yo |
| I'm allergic to ... | 전 ...에 알레르기가 있어요. | chŏn ...·é al·le·rŭ·gi·ga iss·ŏ·yo |

## Doctor

| Where's the nearest ...? | 제일 가까운 ... 어디 있나요? che·il kak·ka·un ... ŏ·di in·na·yo | |
|---|---|---|
| dental clinic | 치과 | ch'i·kwa |
| emergency department | 응급실 | ŭng·gŭp·shil |
| hospital | 병원 | pyŏng·wŏn |
| optometrist | 안경점 | an·gyŏng·jŏm |
| pharmacy | 약국 | yak·kuk |

| I need a doctor (who speaks English). | (영어 하는) 의사가 필요해요. (yŏng·ŏ ha·nŭn) ŭi·sa·ga p'i·ryo hae·yo |
|---|---|

| | | |
|---|---|---|
| **Could I see a female doctor?** | 여자 의사 있나요? | |
| | yŏ·ja ŭi·sa in·na·yo | |
| **Could the doctor come here?** | 왕진 올 수 있나요? | |
| | wang·jin ol·su in·na·yo | |
| **I've run out of my medication.** | 약이 다 떨어졌어요. | |
| | ya·gi ta ddŏ·rŏ·jŏss·ŏ·yo | |
| **This is my usual medicine.** | 제가 늘 먹는 약이에요. | |
| | che·ga nŭl mŏng·nŭn ya·gi·e·yo | |
| **My child weighs (20) kilos.** | 제 아이는 (이십) 킬로그램이에요. | |
| | ché a·i·nŭn (i·ship) k'il·lo·gŭ·rae·mi·e·yo | |
| **What's the correct dosage?** | 정확한 복용량이 뭐예요? | |
| | chŏng·hwa·k'an po·gyong·nyang·i mwŏ·ye·yo | |
| **I don't want a blood transfusion.** | 수혈은 싫어요. | |
| | su·hyŏ·rŭn shi·rŏ·yo | |
| **I've been vaccinated against ...** | 전 ... 예방주사 맞았어요. | |
| | chŏn ... ye·bang·ju·sa ma·jass·ŏ·yo | |

| | | |
|---|---|---|
| **diptheria and tetanus** | 디프테리아, 파상풍 | ti·p'ŭ·t'e·ri·a p'a·sang·p'ung |
| **hepatitis A/B** | A형/B형 간염 | e·i·hyŏng/bi·hyŏng ga·nyŏm |
| **Japanese B encephalitis** | 일본 뇌염 | il·bon noé·yŏm |
| **measles, mumps and rubella** | MMR | e·me·mal |
| **rabies** | 광견병 | kwang·gyŏn·byŏng |
| **tuberculosis** | 결핵 | kyŏl·haek |
| **typhoid** | 장티푸스 | chang·t'i·p'u·sŭ |
| **varicella/ chickenpox** | 수두 | su·du |

> **LANGUAGE TIP**
>
> **Addressing Doctors**
> Doctors and other medical professionals can be referred to as sŏn·saeng·nim 선생님 (a term for someone to whom you wish to show respect). Using English and calling your doctor or dentist 'Dr Kim', for example, is also perfectly acceptable.

| | |
|---|---|
| **I need new contact lenses.** | 새 콘택트렌즈가 필요해요.<br>sae k'on·t'aek·t'ŭ·ren·jŭ ga p'i·ryo·hae·yo |
| **I need new glasses.** | 새 안경이 필요해요.<br>sae an·gyŏng·i p'i·ryo·hae·yo |
| **I have foreign medical insurance.** | 외국 의료보험이 있어요.<br>oé·guk ŭi·ryo·bo·hŏ·mi iss·ŏ·yo |
| **I have Korean national medical insurance.** | 한국 의료보험이 있어요.<br>han·guk ŭi·ryo·bo·hŏ·mi iss·ŏ·yo |
| **Can I have a receipt for my insurance?** | 보험용 영수증 좀 주시겠어요?<br>po·hŏm·nyong yŏng·su·jŭng chom ju·shi·gess·ŏ·yo |

## Symptoms & Conditions

| | |
|---|---|
| **I'm sick.** | 전 아파요.<br>chŏn a·p'a·yo |
| **My friend/child is (very) sick.** | 제 친구가/아이가 (많이) 아파요.<br>ché ch'in·gu·ga/a·i·ga (ma·ni) a·p'a·yo |

| It hurts here. | 으<br>yŏ |
| --- | --- |
| I'm dehydrated. | 전 탈<br>chŏn t |
| I can't sleep. | 잠이 안 오<br>cha·mi an· |
| I'm on medication for ... | 전 ... 약을 먹<br>chŏn ... ya·gŭl |
| I have (a/an) ... | 저는 ...에 걸렸어<br>chŏ·nŭn ...·é kŏl·lyŏss·ŏ·yo |
| I've recently had (a/an) ... | 저는 최근에 ...에<br>걸렸어요.<br>chŏ·nŭn ch'oé·gŭ·né ...·é<br>kŏl·lyŏss·ŏss·ŏ·yo |

## 🔊 LISTEN FOR

| 아프세요? | a·p'ŭ·se·yo<br>Do you feel any pain? |
| --- | --- |
| 어디가 아프세요? | ŏ·di·ga a·p'ŭ·se·yo<br>Where does it hurt? |
| 이렇게 하면 아파요? | i·rŏ·k'é ha·myŏn a·p'a·yo<br>Does it hurt if I do this? |
| 열이 있나요? | yŏ·ri in·na·yo<br>Do you have a temperature? |
| 언제부터 이랬나요? | ŏn·je·bu·t'ŏ i·raen·na·yo<br>How long have you been like this? |
| 전에도 이런 적 있나요? | chŏ·ne·do i·rŏn·jŏ·gin·na·yo<br>Have you had this before? |
| 약 복용 중인가요? | yak po·gyong·jung in·ga·yo<br>Are you on medication? |
| 알레르기 있나요? | al·le·rŭ·gi in·na·yo<br>Are you allergic to anything? |

| | ...njured. | 전 다쳤어요 | chŏn ta·ch'ŏss·ŏ·yo |
| | ...'ve been vomiting. | 전 계속 토했어요 | chŏn kye·sok t'o·haess·ŏ·yo |
| | I have (a) ... | 저는 ... | chŏ·nŭn ... |

| | | | |
|---|---|---|---|
| asthma | | 천식이 있어요 | ch'ŏn·shi·gi iss·ŏ·yo |
| cold | | 감기에 걸렸어요 | kam·gi·é kŏl·lyŏss·ŏ·yo |
| constipation | | 변비가 있어요 | pyŏn·bi·ga iss·ŏ·yo |
| cough | | 기침을 해요 | ki·ch'i·mŭl hae·yo |
| diabetes | | 당뇨병이 있어요 | tang·nyo·byŏng·i iss·ŏ·yo |
| diarrhoea | | 설사를 해요 | sŏl·sa·rŭl hae·yo |
| fever | | 열이 나요 | yŏ·ri na·yo |
| headache | | 두통이 있어요 | tu·t'ong·i iss·ŏ·yo |
| nausea | | 메슥거려요 | me·sŭk·kŏ·ryŏ·yo |
| pain | | 통증이 있어요 | t'ong·jŭng·i iss·ŏ·yo |
| sore throat | | 목이 아파요 | mo·gi a·p'a·yo |

I feel ...

| | | | |
|---|---|---|---|
| dizzy | | 어지러워요. | ŏ·ji·rŏ·wŏ·yo |
| hot and cold | | 더운데 춥기도 해요. | tŏ·un·dé ch'up·ki·do hae·yo |
| nauseous | | 메슥거려요. | me·sŭk·kŏ·ryŏ·yo |
| shivery | | 덜덜 떨려요. | tŏl·tŏl ttŏl·lyŏ·yo |
| weak | | 힘이 없어요. | hi·mi ŏp·sŏ·yo |

# Women's Health

| | |
|---|---|
| Could I see a female doctor? | 여자 의사 있나요?<br>yŏ·ja ŭi·sa in·na·yo |
| I'm pregnant. | 전 임신 중이에요.<br>chŏn im·shin·jung i·e·yo |
| I think I'm pregnant. | 임신한 것 같아요.<br>im·shin han·gŏt ka·t'a·yo |
| I'm on the pill. | 피임약을 먹고 있어요.<br>p'i·im·nya·gŭl mŏk·ko iss·ŏ·yo |
| I haven't had my period for (eight) weeks. | (팔) 주 동안 생리가 없어요.<br>(p'al) ju·dong·an saeng·ni·ga ŏp·sŏ·yo |
| Do you have something for (period pain)? | (생리통) 약 있나요?<br>(saeng·ni·t'ong) yak in·na·yo |

## ◄ )) LISTEN FOR

| | |
|---|---|
| 섹스 하시나요? | sek·sŭ ha·shi·na·yo<br>Are you sexually active? |
| 피임 하시나요? | p'i·im ha·shi·na·yo<br>Are you using contraception? |
| 생리 중인가요? | saeng·ni·jung in·ga·yo<br>Are you menstruating? |
| 마지막 생리가 언제였나요? | ma·ji·mak saeng·ni·ga ŏn·jé yŏn·na·yo<br>When did you last have your period? |
| 임신 중인가요? | im·shin·jung in·ga·yo<br>Are you pregnant? |
| 임신하셨습니다. | im·shin ha·shŏss·sŭm·ni·da<br>You're pregnant. |

| I've noticed a lump here. | 여기 혹이 있어요.<br>yŏ·gi ho·gi iss·ŏ·yo |
| I have a urinary tract infection. | 요도염에 걸렸어요.<br>yo·do·yŏ·mé kŏl·lyŏss·ŏ·yo |
| I have a yeast infection. | 진균감염에<br>걸렸어요.<br>chin·gyun·ga·myŏ·mé<br>kŏl·lyŏss·ŏ·yo |
| I need contraception. | 피임을 하고 싶어요.<br>p'i·i·mŭl ha·go shi·p'ŏ·yo |
| I need the morning-after pill. | 사후피임약이 필요해요.<br>sa·hu·p'i·im·nya·gi p'i·ryo·hae·yo |
| I need a pregnancy test. | 임신 검사 하고 싶어요.<br>im·shin gŏm·sa ha·go shi·p'ŏ·yo |

## Allergies

| I have a skin allergy. | 전 피부 알레르기가 있어요.<br>chŏn p'i·bu al·le·rŭ·gi·ga iss·ŏ·yo |
| I'm allergic to ... | 전 ...에 알레르기가 있어요.<br>chŏn ...é al·le·rŭ·gi·ga iss·ŏ·yo |

| antibiotics | 항생제 | hang·saeng·jé |
| anti-<br>  inflammatories | 소염제 | so·yŏm·jé |
| aspirin | 아스피린 | a·sŭ·p'i·rin |
| bees | 벌 | pŏl |
| codeine | 코데인 | k'o·de·in |
| dairy products | 유제품 | yu·je·p'um |
| penicillin | 페니실린 | p'e·ni·shil·lin |
| pollen | 꽃가루 | ggok·ka·ru |
| sulphur-based<br>  drugs | 황화물이<br>들어간 약 | hwang·hwa·mu·ri<br>dŭ·rŏ·gan·nyak |

For food-related allergies, see **vegetarian & special meals** (p209).

 **LISTEN FOR**

| | |
|---|---|
| 오늘 뭘 드셨나요? | o·nŭl mwŏl dŭ·shŏn·na·yo<br>What did you eat today? |
| 담배 피우시나요? | tam·bae p'i·u·shi·na·yo<br>Do you smoke? |
| 술 드시나요? | sul dŭ·shi·na·yo<br>Do you drink? |
| 어제 술 드셨나요? | ŏ·jé sul dŭ·shŏn·na·yo<br>Did you drink last night? |
| 마약 하시나요? | ma·yak ha·shi·na·yo<br>Do you take drugs? |

## Alternative Treatments

| | |
|---|---|
| I don't use (Western medicine). | 전 (양약)을<br>안 써요.<br>chŏn (yang·yag)·ŭl<br>an·ssŏ·yo |
| Where can I find an Eastern medical clinic? | 한의원 어디에 있나요?<br>ha·ni·wŏn ŏ·di·é in·na·yo |
| Can I see someone who practises ...? | ... 찾을 수 있나요?<br>... ch'a·jŭl·su in·na·yo |

| | | |
|---|---|---|
| acupuncture | 침 놓는 분 | ch'im non·nŭn·bun |
| aromatherapy | 아로마테라피<br>하시는 분 | a·ro·ma t'e·ra·p'i<br>ha·shi·nŭn·bun |
| massage | 안마사 | an·ma·sa |
| moxibustion | 뜸 놓는 분 | ddŭm non·nŭn·bun |
| yoga | 요가<br>가르치시는 분 | yo·ga<br>ka·rŭ·ch'i·shi·nŭn·bun |

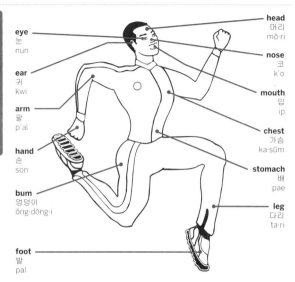

eye
눈
nun

ear
귀
kwi

arm
팔
p'al

hand
손
son

bum
엉덩이
ŏng·dŏng·i

foot
발
pal

head
머리
mŏ·ri

nose
코
k'o

mouth
입
ip

chest
가슴
ka·sŭm

stomach
배
pae

leg
다리
ta·ri

## Parts of the Body

| | |
|---|---|
| **My ... hurts.** | ...이/가 아파요.<br>...i/·ga a·p'a·yo |
| **I have a pain in my ...** | ...에 통증이 있어요.<br>...·é t'ong·jŭng·i iss·ŏ·yo |
| **I can't move my ...** | ...을/를 움직일 수가<br>없어요.<br>...·ŭl/·rŭl um·ji·gil·su·ga<br>ŏp·sŏ·yo |
| **I have a cramp in my ...** | ...에 경련이 났어요.<br>...·é kyŏng·nyŏ·ni nass·ŏ·yo |
| **My ... is swollen.** | ...이/가 부었어요.<br>...·i/·ga pu·ŏss·ŏ·yo |

# Pharmacist

| I need something for (a headache). | (두통) 약 주세요. |
| | (tu·t'ong) yak ju·se·yo |
| **Do I need a prescription for (antihistamines)?** | (항히스타민제) 사려면 처방전 필요한가요? |
| | (hang·hi·sŭ·t'a·min·jé) sa·ryŏ·myŏn ch'ŏ·bang·jŏn p'i·ryo han·ga·yo |
| **I have a prescription.** | 처방전 있어요. |
| | ch'ŏ·bang·jŏn iss·ŏ·yo |
| **How many times a day?** | 하루에 몇 번인가요? |
| | ha·ru·é myŏp·pŏn in·ga·yo |
| **Will it make me drowsy?** | 먹으면 졸릴까요? |
| | mŏ·gŭ·myŏn chol·lilk·ka·yo |

For more pharmaceutical items, see the **dictionary**.

# Dentist

| **I have a broken tooth.** | 이가 깨졌어요. |
| | i·ga kkae·jŏss·ŏ·yo |
| **I have a cavity.** | 충치가 있어요. |
| | ch'ung·ch'i·ga iss·ŏ·yo |

 **LISTEN FOR**

| 하루에 (세) 번 | ha·ru·é (se)·bŏn | (three) times a day |
| (네) 시간마다 | (ne) shi·gan·ma·da | every (four) hours |
| 식전 | shik·chŏn | (half an hour) |
| (삼십 분) | (sam·ship·pun) | before eating |
| 식후 | shi·k'u | (half an hour) |
| (삼십 분) | (sam·ship·pun) | after eating |
| 식간 | shik·kan | while eating |

### 🔊 LISTEN FOR

| | | |
|---|---|---|
| 아 하세요. | a ha·se·yo | Open wide. |
| 꽉 물어 보세요. | ggwak mu·rŏ·bo·se·yo | Bite down on this. |
| 움직이지 마세요. | um·ji·gi·ji ma·se·yo | Don't move. |
| 입 헹구세요. | ip heng·gu·se·yo | Rinse. |

| | |
|---|---|
| **I have a toothache.** | 이가 아파요.<br>i·ga a·p'a·yo |
| **One of my teeth is loose.** | 이가 흔들려요.<br>i·ga hŭn·dŭl·lyŏ·yo |
| **It keeps bleeding.** | 피가 안 멈춰요.<br>p'i·ga an·mŏm·ch'wŏ·yo |
| **I need an anaesthetic.** | 마취 해 주세요.<br>ma·ch'wi hae ju·se·yo |
| **I need a filling.** | 때워 주세요.<br>ddae·wŏ ju·se·yo |
| **I've lost a filling.** | 때운 데가<br>떨어졌어요.<br>ddae·un·de·ga<br>ddŏ·rŏ·jŏss·ŏ·yo |
| **My braces fell off.** | 교정기가<br>떨어졌어요.<br>kyo·jŏng·gi·ga<br>ddŏ·rŏ·jŏss·ŏ·yo |
| **My dentures are broken.** | 틀니가 깨졌어요.<br>t'ul·li·ga kkae·jŏss·ŏ·yo |
| **My gums hurt.** | 잇몸이 아파요.<br>in·mo·mi a·p'a·yo |
| **I don't want it extracted.** | 뽑지 마세요.<br>bbop·chi ma·se·yo |

# Food

# Eating Out

## KEY PHRASES

| | | |
|---|---|---|
| **Can you recommend a restaurant?** | 음식점 추천해 주시겠어요? | ŭm·shik·jŏm ch'u·ch'ŏn hae·ju·shi·gess·ŏ·yo |
| **A table for (two), please.** | (두) 명 자리 주세요. | (tu)·myŏng cha·ri ju·se·yo |
| **May we see the menu?** | 메뉴 볼 수 있나요? | me·nyu bol·su in·na·yo |
| **I'd like a beer, please.** | 맥주 주세요. | maek·chu ju·se·yo |
| **Please bring the bill.** | 계산서 가져다 주세요. | kye·san·sŏ ka·jŏ·da ju·se·yo |

## Basics

| | | |
|---|---|---|
| **breakfast** | 아침 | a·ch'im |
| **lunch** | 점심 | chŏm·shim |
| **dinner** | 저녁 | chŏ·nyŏk |
| **snack** | 간식 | kan·shik |
| **to eat** | 먹어요 (먹~) | mŏ·gŏ·yo (mŏk~) |
| **to drink** | 마셔요 (마시~) | ma·shŏ·yo (ma·shi~) |
| **I'd like ...** | ... 주세요. | ... ju·se·yo |

| | |
|---|---|
| **I'm starving!** | 배고파요!<br>pae·go·p'a·yo |

## Finding a Place to Eat

| | |
|---|---|
| **Where would you go for a celebration?** | 축하할 일이 있으면<br>어디가 좋아요?<br>ch'u·k'a·hal i·ri iss·ŭ·myŏn<br>ŏ·di·ga cho·a·yo |
| **Where would you go for a cheap meal?** | 저렴한 식사는<br>어디서 하나요?<br>chŏ·ryŏm·han shik·sa·nŭn<br>ŏ·di·sŏ ha·na·yo |
| **Where would you go for local specialities?** | 이 지방의 특별한<br>음식을 어디가 잘 하나요?<br>i·ji·bang·é t'ŭk·pyŏl·han<br>ŭm·shi·gŭl ŏ·di·ga chal ha·na·yo |
| **Can you recommend a bar/restaurant?** | 술집/음식점<br>추천해 주시겠어요?<br>sul·chip/ŭm·shik·jŏm<br>ch'u·ch'ŏn hae·ju·shi gŏss·ŏ·yo |
| **I'd like to reserve a table for (two) people.** | (두) 명 테이블 예약해 주세요.<br>(tu)·myŏng t'e·i·bŭl ye·ya·k'ae<br>ju·se·yo |

> **CULTURE TIP**
> **Meal Options**
> You can eat out well in Korea on any budget.
> Street stalls selling freshly made cheap kan·shik
> 간식 (snacks) can be found all over any city. Many offer
> light meals as well, with enclosed seating that's heated in
> winter. Small family-run restaurants offer full meals includ-
> ing side dishes, called pan·ch'an 반찬, at budget prices.
> Formal dining in foreign restaurant chains has become very
> popular, and many such establishments offer se·t'ŭ me·nyu
> 세트 메뉴 (set menus), which include a full meal from
> entrée to coffee and dessert.

**FOOD EATING OUT**

 **LISTEN FOR**

| | | |
|---|---|---|
| 끝났어요. | ggŭn·nass·ŏ·yo | We're closed. |
| 자리가 없어요. | cha·ri·ga ŏp·sŏ·yo | We're full. |
| 잠시만요. | cham·shi·man·nyo | One moment. |

| | |
|---|---|
| I'd like to reserve a table for (eight) o'clock. | (여덟) 시 테이블 예약해 주세요.<br>(yŏ·dŏl)·shi t'e·i·bŭl ye·ya·k'ae ju·se·yo |
| Are you still serving food? | 아직 음식 되나요?<br>a·jik ŭm·shik toé·na·yo |
| How long is the wait? | 얼마나 기다려야 되나요?<br>ŏl·ma·na ki·da·ryŏ·ya doé·na·yo |

## At the Restaurant

| | |
|---|---|
| A table for (two), please. | (두) 명 자리 주세요.<br>(tu)·myŏng cha·ri ju·se·yo |
| ✂ **For two, please.** | 두 명이요.    tu·myŏng·i·yo |
| We'd like the nonsmoking section, please. | 금연석 주세요.<br>kŭ·myŏn·sŏk chu·se·yo |
| We'd like the smoking section, please. | 흡연석 주세요.<br>hŭ·byŏn·sŏk ju·se·yo |
| What would you recommend? | 추천 해 주시겠어요?<br>ch'u·ch'ŏn hae·ju·shi·gess·ŏ·yo |
| Do you have an English menu? | 영어로 된 메뉴 있나요?<br>yŏng·ŏ·ro·doén me·nyu in·na·yo |
| Can we see the menu? | 메뉴 볼 수 있나요?<br>me·nyu bol·su in·na·yo |
| ✂ **Menu, please.** | 메뉴 주세요.    me·nyu chu·se·yo |

# Eating Out

## Can I see the menu, please?

메뉴 볼 수 있나요?
me·nyu bol·su in·na·yo

## What would you recommend for ...?

…로 뭘 추천하시겠어요?
...ro mwŏl ch'u·ch'ŏn ha·shi·gess·ŏ·yo

 **the main meal**
주요리
chu·yo·ri

 **dessert**
디저트
ti·jŏ·t'ŭ

 **drinks**
술
sul

## Can you bring me some ..., please?

… 가져다 주세요.
... ka·jŏ·da ju·se·yo

## I'd like the bill, please.

계산서 가져다주세요.
kye·san·sŏ ka·jŏ·da ju·se·yo

| | |
|---|---|
| **What comes with the set menu?** | 세트 시키면 뭐가 나오나요?<br>se·t'ŭ shi·k'i·myŏn mwŏ·ga na·o·na·yo |
| **I'll have what they're having.** | 저 분 들이랑 같은 걸로 주세요.<br>chŏ·bun·dŭ·ri·rang ka·t'ŭn·gŏl·lo ju·se·yo |
| **What's that called?** | 저거 이름이 뭔가요?<br>chŏ·gŏ i·rŭ·mi mwŏn·ga·yo |
| **What's in that dish?** | 저 음식에 뭐가 들어있나요?<br>chŏ·ŭm·shi·gé mwŏ·ga dŭ·rŏ·in·na·yo |
| **Does it take long to prepare?** | 나오는 데 오래 걸리나요?<br>na·o·nŭn·dé o·rae kŏl·li·na·yo |
| **Is this dish spicy?** | 이 음식 맵나요?<br>i·ŭm·shing·maem·na·yo |
| **I'd like some more of this side dish.** | 이 반찬 좀 더 주세요.<br>i·ban·ch'an chom tŏ ju·se·yo |
| **Is this drink refillable?** | 이 음료 리필 되나요?<br>i·ŭm·nyo ri·p'il doé·na·yo |
| **I'd like a refill.** | 리필 해 주세요.<br>ri·p'il hae·ju·se·yo |
| **Are these complimentary?** | 이거 공짜인가요?<br>i·gŏ kong·tcha in·ga·yo |
| **Could I please see the wine list?** | 와인 리스트 볼 수 있나요?<br>wa·in ri·sŭ·t'ŭ pol·su in·na·yo |

**CULTURE TIP**

**Ordering Food**
Foreign chains usually offer English-language menus and at least one staff member will speak English. Menus often come with pictures, or very realistic models of the food served are displayed in the window. Koreans don't mind if you ask a lot of questions or even point to someone else's meal.

| | | |
|---|---|---|
| **Can you recommend a good wine?** | 좋은 와인 추천해 주시겠어요? | cho·ŭn wa·in ch'u·ch'ŏn hae·ju·shi·gess·ŏ·yo |
| **I'd like (a/the) ..., please.** | ... 주세요. | ... ju·se·yo |

| | | |
|---|---|---|
| **one serving** | 일인분 | i·rin·bun |
| **two servings** | 이인분 | i·in·bun |
| **three servings** | 삼인분 | sa·min·bun |
| **children's menu** | 어린이 메뉴 | ŏ·ri·ni me·nyu |
| **drink menu** | 음료수 메뉴 | ŭm·nyo·su me·nyu |
| **half portion** | 반만 | pan·man |
| **huge portion** | 양 많은 것 | yang ma·nŭn·gŏt |
| **local speciality** | 이 지역의 유명한 음식 | i·ji·yŏ·gé yu·myŏng·han ŭm·shik |

## Requests

| | | |
|---|---|---|
| **Please bring (a/the) ...** | ... 가져다 주세요. | ... ka·jŏ·da ju·se·yo |

| | | |
|---|---|---|
| **chopsticks** | 젓가락 | chŏk·ka·rak |
| **fork** | 포크 | p'o·k'ŭ |
| **(wine)glass** | (와인) 잔 | (wa·in)·jan |
| **plates** | 개인 접시 | kae·in chŏp·shi |
| **knife** | 나이프 | na·i·p'ŭ |
| **serviette** | 냅킨 | naep·k'in |
| **spoon** | 숟가락 | suk·ka·rak |

FOOD  EATING OUT

◀)) **LISTEN FOR**

| | |
|---|---|
| 뭐 드릴까요? | mwŏ dŭ·rilk·ka·yo |
| | What can I get you? |
| … 좋아하세요? | … cho·a·ha·se·yo |
| | Do you like …? |
| … 맛있어요. | … ma·shiss·ŏ·yo |
| | I suggest the … |
| 여기 있습니다! | yŏ·gi iss·sŭm·ni·da |
| | Here you go! |
| 맛있게 드세요. | ma·shik·ké dŭ·se·yo |
| | Enjoy your meal. |

| | |
|---|---|
| **I'd like it with …** | … 넣어 주세요. |
| | … nŏ·ŏ ju·se·yo |
| **I'd like it without …** | … 넣지 마세요. |
| | … nŏ·ch'i ma·se·yo |

| | | |
|---|---|---|
| **cheese** | 치즈 | ch'i·jŭ |
| **chilli sauce** | 고추장 | ko·ch'u·jang |
| **garlic** | 마늘 | ma·nŭl |
| **ginger** | 생강 | saeng·gang |
| **ground pepper** | 후춧가루 | hu·ch'uk·ka·ru |
| **mayonnaise** | 마요네즈 | ma·yo·ne·jŭ |
| **mustard (Asian)** | 겨자 | kyŏ·ja |
| **nuts** | 땅콩 | ddang·k'ong |
| **oil** | 기름 | ki·rŭm |
| **red chillies** | 고추 | ko·ch'u |
| **red pepper powder** | 고춧가루 | ko·ch'uk·ka·ru |
| **salt** | 소금 | so·gŭm |
| **soy sauce** | 간장 | kan·jang |
| **vinegar** | 식초 | shik·ch'o |

## LOOK FOR

| | | |
|---|---|---|
| 애피타이저 | ae·p'i·t'a·i·jŏ | Appetisers |
| 앙트레 | ang·t'ŭ·ré | Entrées |
| 수프 | su·p'ŭ | Soups |
| 샐러드 | sael·lŏ·dŭ | Salads |
| 메인 코스 | me·in k'o·sŭ | Main Courses |
| 반찬 | pan·ch'an | Side Dishes |
| 후식 | hu·shik | Desserts |
| | | |
| 음료수 | ŭm·nyo·su | Drinks |
| 탄산음료 | t'an·san ŭm·nyo | Soft Drinks |
| 맥주 | maek·chu | Beers |
| 샴페인 | sham·p'e·in | Sparkling Wines |
| 화이트 와인 | hwa·i·t'ŭ wa·in | White Wines |
| 레드 와인 | re·dŭ wa·in | Red Wines |

For additional items, see the **menu decoder** (p212).

| | | |
|---|---|---|
| **Can you make it less spicy?** | 덜 맵게<br>해 주시겠어요?<br>tŏl maep·ké<br>hae·ju·shi·gess·ŏ·yo | |
| **I don't want it ...** | ... 마세요.<br>... ma·se·yo | |

| | | |
|---|---|---|
| **boiled** | 끓이지 | ggŭ·ri·ji |
| **broiled/grilled** | 굽지 | kup·chi |
| **deep-fried** | 튀기지 | t'wi·gi·ji |
| **fried** | 볶지 | pok·chi |
| **mashed** | 으깨지 | ŭk·kae·ji |

| I want it ... | | ... 주세요.<br>... ju·se·yo |
|---|---|---|
| boiled | 끓여 | ggŭ·ryŏ |
| broiled/grilled | 구워 | ku·wŏ |
| deep-fried | 튀겨 | t'wi·gyŏ |
| fried | 볶아 | pok·ka |
| mashed | 으깨 | ŭk·kae |
| medium | 미디엄으로 | mi·di·ŏ·mŭ·ro |
| rare | 레어로 | re·ŏ·ro |
| reheated | 다시 데워 | ta·shi de·wŏ |
| well done | 웰던으로 | wel·dŏ·nŭ·ro |
| without ... | ... 없이 | ... ŏp·shi |
| with the dressing<br>on the side | 드레싱이랑<br>같이 | tŭ·re·shing·i·rang<br>ka·ch'i |

For other specific meal requests, see **vegetarian & special meals**
(p209).

## Compliments & Complaints

| I love this dish. | 이거 맛있어요.<br>i·gŏ ma·shiss·ŏ·yo |
|---|---|
| I love the local cuisine. | 이 지역 음식이<br>맛있어요.<br>i·ji·yŏk ŭm·shi·gi<br>ma·shiss·ŏ·yo |
| That was delicious! | 맛있었어요!<br>ma·shiss·ŏss·ŏ·yo |
| I'm full. | 배불러요.<br>pae·bul·lŏ·yo |
| I didn't order this. | 이거 주문<br>안 했는데요.<br>i·gŏ ju·mun<br>an·haen·nŭn·de·yo |

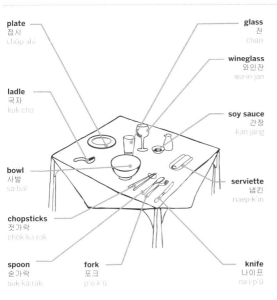

**plate**
접시
ch'ŏp·shi

**ladle**
국자
kuk·cha

**bowl**
사발
sa·bal

**chopsticks**
젓가락
chŏk·ka·rak

**spoon**
숟가락
suk·ka·rak

**fork**
포크
p'o·k'ŭ

**glass**
잔
chan

**wineglass**
와인잔
wa·in·jan

**soy sauce**
간장
kan·jang

**serviette**
냅킨
naep·k'in

**knife**
나이프
na·i·p'ŭ

This is ...

| | | |
|---|---|---|
| **burnt** | 탔어요. | t'ass·ŏ·yo |
| **cold** | 차가워요. | ch'a·ga·wŏ·yo |
| **(too) spicy** | (너무) 매워요. | (nŏ·mu) mae·wŏ·yo |
| **stale** | 싱싱하지 않아요. | shing·shing·ha·ji a·na·yo |
| **superb** | 최고예요. | ch'oé·go·ye·yo |

## Paying the Bill

| | | |
|---|---|---|
| **Please bring the bill.** | 계산서 가져다 주세요.<br>kye·san·sŏ ka·jŏ·da ju·se·yo | |
|  **Bill, please.** | 계산서 주세요. | kye·san·sŏ<br>chu·se·yo |
| **There's a mistake in the bill.** | 계산서가 이상해요.<br>kye·san·sŏ·ga i·sang·hae·yo | |

## Nonalcoholic Drinks

| | |
|---|---|
| **(a cup of) coffee** | 커피 (한 잔)<br>k'ŏ·p'i (han·jan) |
| **(a cup of) tea** | 차 (한 잔)<br>ch'a (han·jan) |
| **with (milk)** | (우유) 넣은<br>(u·yu) nŏ·ŭn |
| **without (sugar)** | (설탕) 뺀<br>(sŏl·t'ang) ppaen |
| **mineral water** | 생수<br>saeng·su |
| **orange juice** | 오렌지 주스<br>o·ren·ji jus·sŭ |
| **persimmon punch** | 수정과<br>su·jŏng·gwa |

### 🔍 LOOK FOR

| | | |
|---|---|---|
| 홍차 | hong·ch'a | black tea |
| 유자차 | yu·ja·ch'a | citron tea |
| 대추차 | tae·ch'u·ch'a | date tea |
| 생강차 | saeng·gang·ch'a | ginger tea |
| 녹차 | nok·ch'a | green tea |

## 🔍 LOOK FOR

| 블랙 | pŭl·laek | black |
| 무카페인 | mu·k'a·p'e·in | decaffeinated |
| 아이스 | a·i·sŭ | iced |
| 진한 | chin·han | strong |
| 약한 | ya·k'an | weak |
| 크림 넣은 | k'ŭ·rim nŏ·ŭn | with cream |
| 크림과 | k'ŭ·rim·gwa | with cream and |
| 설탕 넣은 | sŏl·t'ang nŏ·ŭn | sugar |

| soft drink | 탄산 음료<br>t'an·san ŭm·nyo |
|---|---|
| (boiled) water | (끓인) 물<br>(ggŭ·rin) mul |

## Alcoholic Drinks

| beer | 맥주<br>maek·chu |
|---|---|
| brandy | 브랜디<br>pŭ·raen·di |
| champagne | 샴페인<br>sham·p'e·in |
| cocktail | 칵테일<br>k'ak·t'e·il |
| glass of red wine | 레드 와인 한 잔<br>re·dŭ wa·in han·jan |
| glass of sparkling wine | 샴페인 한 잔<br>sham·p'e·in han·jan |
| glass of white wine | 화이트 와인 한 잔<br>hwa·i·t'ŭ wa·in han·jan |

**FOOD** **EATING OUT**

### LANGUAGE TIP

**'Alcohol' Suffix**
A helpful hint when poring over a Korean menu: lots of names for Korean alcoholic drinks end in ·ju/·chu 주 (based on the Chinese character for 'alcohol') – what precedes that is usually the other main ingredient.

| a shot of ... | ... 한 잔 |
|---|---|
| | ... han·jan |

| **gin** | 진 | chin |
|---|---|---|
| **rum** | 럼 | rŏm |
| **tequila** | 테킬라 | t'e·k'il·la |
| **vodka** | 보드카 | po·dŭ·k'a |
| **whisky** | 위스키 | wi·sŭ·k'i |

For additional items, see the **menu decoder** (p212), and the **dictionary**.

## In the Bar

| I'll buy you a drink. | 제가 살게요. |
|---|---|
| | che·ga salk·ke·yo |
| **Q** What would you like to drink? | 뭐 마시고 싶으세요? |
| | mwŏ ma·shi·go shi·p'ŭ·se·yo |
| **A** I'll have ... | ... 주세요. |
| | ... ju·se·yo |
| What side dish would you like to have? | 안주 뭐 드시겠어요? |
| | an·ju mwŏ dŭ·shi·gess·ŏ·yo |
| What kind of side dishes do you have? | 안주 뭐가 있나요? |
| | an·ju mwŏ·ga in·na·yo |

| | |
|---|---|
| **Do you serve meals here?** | 여기 식사도 되나요?<br>yŏ·gi shik·sa·do doé·na·yo |
| **Is food served here?** | 여기 식사 나오니요?<br>yŏ·gi shik·sa na·o·na·yo |
| **No ice, please.** | 얼음 빼고 주세요.<br>ŏ·rŭm ppae·go ju·se·yo |
| **It's my round.** | 제 차례예요.<br>ché ch'a·rye·ye·yo |
| **I'm next.** | 다음에 제가 살<br>차례예요.<br>ta·ŭ·mé che·ga sal<br>ch'a·rye·ye·yo |
| **You can get the next one.** | 다음 번에 사세요.<br>ta·ŭm·bŏ·né sa·se·yo |
| **Same again, please.** | 똑같은 걸로 주세요.<br>ddok·ka·t'ŭn·gŏl·lo ju·se·yo |

## Drinking Up

| | |
|---|---|
| **Cheers!** | 건배!<br>kŏn·bae |

**CULTURE TIP**

**Ordering Beer**

Beer is typically ordered by the bottle, mug or pitcher, which are ordered according to size. Rather than referring to the number of pints, litres or quarts, beer is ordered by shi·shi 시시 (millilitre, literally 'cc' for 'cubic centimetre').

| ... of beer | 맥주 ... | maek·chu ... |
|---|---|---|
| **half a litre (500mL)** | 오백 시시 | o·baek·shi·shi |
| **a litre (1000mL)** | 천 시시 | ch'ŏn·shi·shi |
| **one bottle** | 한 병 | han·byŏng |
| **two bottles** | 두 병 | tu·byŏng |
| **a pitcher** | 피처 한 개 | p'i·chŏ han·gae |

| Thanks, but I don't feel like it. | 고맙지만 오늘은<br>별로 내키지가 않네요.<br>ko·map·chi·man o·nŭ·rŭn<br>pyŏl·lo nae·k'i·ji·ga an·ne·yo |
| I don't usually drink much. | 보통 많이 안 마셔요.<br>po·t'ong ma·ni an·ma·shŏ·yo |
| I don't drink alcohol. | 전 술 안 마셔요.<br>chŏn sul an·ma·shŏ·yo |
| I'm tired, so I'd better get home. | 피곤해서 집에<br>가야겠어요.<br>p'i·gon·hae·sŏ chi·bé<br>ka·ya·gess·ŏ·yo |
| This is hitting the spot. | 정말 딱인데요.<br>chŏng·mal tta·gin·de·yo |
| I'm feeling drunk. | 저 취한 것 같아요.<br>chŏ ch'wi·han·gŏt ka·t'a·yo |
| I feel fantastic! | 환상적인 기분이에요.<br>hwan·sang·jŏ·gin ki·bu·ni·e·yo |
| I really, really love you. | 정말 정말<br>사랑해요.<br>chŏng·mal chŏng·mal<br>sa·rang·hae·yo |
| I think I've had one too many. | 저 약간 취한 것<br>같아요.<br>chŏ yak·kan ch'wi·han·gŏt<br>ka·t'a·yo |

 **CULTURE TIP**

**Paying for Drinks**

Drinking in Korea is a group activity, a chance to let loose with friends or colleagues. The bill is usually settled when the party is ready to leave, but there's also a trend towards paying as you go. Many bars still require a table of patrons to order an·ju 안주 ('side dishes' of snacks, French fries, fruit etc) as a kind of cover charge.

**LISTEN FOR**

| | |
|---|---|
| 뭐 드릴까요? | mwŏ dŭ·rilk·ka·yo<br>What are you having? |
| 많이 드신 것<br>같은데요. | ma·ni dŭ·shin·gŏt<br>ka·t'ŭn·de·yo<br>I think you've had enough. |
| 마지막 주문<br>받습니다. | ma·ji·mak chu·mun<br>pat·sŭm·ni·da<br>Last orders. |

| | |
|---|---|
| **I'm pissed.** | 저 취했어요.<br>chŏ ch'wi·haess·ŏ·yo |
| **I feel ill.** | 몸이 안 좋아요.<br>mo·mi an·jo·a·yo |
| **I think I'm going to throw up.** | 토할 것 같아요.<br>t'o·hal·gŏt ka·t'a·yo |
| **Please help me catch a taxi.** | 택시 잡는 것<br>도와 주세요.<br>t'aek·shi cham·nŭn·gŏt<br>to·wa ju·se·yo |
| **I don't think you should drive.** | 운전하시면<br>안 될 것 같아요.<br>un·jŏn·ha·shi·myŏn<br>an·doél·gŏt ka·t'a·yo |

# Self-Catering

## KEY PHRASES

| | | |
|---|---|---|
| **What's the local speciality?** | 지방 특산품에 뭐가 있나요? | chi·bang t'ŭk·san·p'u·mé mwŏ·ga in·na·yo |
| **Where can I find the ... section?** | ... 코너 어디 있나요? | ... k'o·nŏ ŏ·di in·na·yo |
| **I'd like some ...** | ... 조금 주세요. | ... cho·gŭm ju·se·yo |

## Buying Food

| | |
|---|---|
| **What's that?** | 저게 뭐예요? chŏ·gé mwŏ·ye·yo |
| **What's the local speciality?** | 지방 특산품에 뭐가 있나요? chi·bang t'ŭk·san·p'u·mé mwŏ·ga in·na·yo |
| **How much is (a kilo of kimchi)?** | (김치 일 킬로그램)에 얼마예요? (kim·ch'i il k'il·lo·gŭ·raem)·é ŏl·ma·ye·yo |
| **Can I taste it?** | 맛 볼 수 있나요? map·pol·su in·na·yo |
| **Can I have a bag, please?** | 봉투 주시겠어요? pong·t'u ju·shi·gess·ŏ·yo |
| **I don't need a bag, thanks.** | 봉투 없어도 돼요. pong·t'u ŏp·sŏ·do dwae·yo |

## 맛 볼 수 있나요?
map·pol·su in·na·yo
### *Can I taste it?*

I'd like ...      ... 주세요.
                   ... ju·se·yo

| | | |
|---|---|---|
| **(200) grams** | (이백) 그램 | (i·baek) kŭ·raem |
| **half a kilo** | 오백 그램 | o·baek kŭ·raem |
| **a kilo** | 일 킬로그램 | il k'il·lo·gŭ·raem |
| **(two) kilos** | (이) 킬로그램 | (i) k'il·lo·gŭ·raem |
| **a bottle** | 한 병 | han·byŏng |
| **a piece** | 한 개 | han·gae |
| **(three) pieces** | (세) 개 | (se)·gae |
| **a slice** | 한 쪽 | han·tchok |
| **(six) slices** | (여섯) 쪽 | (yŏ·sŏt)·tchok |
| **a can/tin** | 한 캔 | han·k'aen |
| **some ...** | ... 조금 | ... cho·gŭm |

| I'd like that/this one. | 저거/이거 주세요.<br>chŏ·gŏ/i·gŏ ju·se·yo |
| --- | --- |
| Do you have anything cheaper? | 더 싼 것 있나요?<br>tŏ·ssan·gŏt in·na·yo |
| Do you have other kinds? | 다른 것 있나요?<br>ta·rŭn·gŏt in·na·yo |
| Where can I find the ... section? | ... 코너 어디 있나요?<br>... k'o·nŏ ŏ·di in·na·yo |

| | | |
| --- | --- | --- |
| dairy | 유제품 | yu·je·p'um |
| fish | 생선 | saeng·sŏn |
| frozen goods | 냉동식품 | naeng·dong·shik·p'um |
| fruit and vegetable | 과일 야채 | kwa·il ya·ch'ae |
| health-food | 건강식품 | kŏn·gang shik·p'um |
| meat | 고기 | ko·gi |
| poultry | 닭 | tak |

For more food items, see the **menu decoder** (p212), and the **dictionary**.

## Cooking

| I need a ... | ...이/가 필요해요.<br>...i/·ga p'i·ryo·hae·yo |
| --- | --- |

| | | |
| --- | --- | --- |
| chopping board | 도마 | to·ma |
| frying pan | 프라이팬 | p'ŭ·ra·i·p'aen |
| knife | 나이프 | na·i·p'ŭ |
| saucepan | 냄비 | naem·bi |

For more cooking implements, see the **dictionary**.

# Vegetarian & Special Meals

**KEY PHRASES**

| | | |
|---|---|---|
| **Do you have vegetarian food?** | 채식주의 음식 있나요? | ch'ae·shik·chu·i ŭm·shik in·na·yo |
| **Could you prepare a meal without ...?** | ... 빼고 해 주시겠어요? | ... ppae·go hae·ju·shi·gess·ŏ·yo |
| **I'm allergic to ...** | 전 ... 알레르기가 있어요. | chŏn ... al·le·rŭ·gi·ga iss·ŏ·yo |

## Special Diets & Allergies

| I'm allergic to ... | 전 ... 알레르기가 있어요. |
|---|---|
| | chŏn ... al·le·rŭ·gi·ga iss·ŏ·yo |

| | | |
|---|---|---|
| **dairy produce** | 유제품 | yu·je·p'um |
| **eggs** | 계란 | kye·ran |
| **gelatine** | 젤라틴 | chel·la·t'in |
| **gluten** | 글루텐 | kŭl·lu·t'en |
| **honey** | 꿀 | ggul |
| **MSG** | 화학조미료 | hwa·hak·cho·mi·ryo |
| **nuts** | 견과류 | kyŏn·gwa·ryu |
| **peanuts** | 땅콩 | ddang·k'ong |
| **shellfish** | 조개 | cho·gae |

To explain your dietary restrictions with reference to religious beliefs, see **beliefs & culture** (p154).

**210**

 **LOOK FOR**

| 입구 | ip·ku | Entrance |
|------|-------|----------|
| 출구 | ch'ul·gu | Exit |
| 관계자 외 | kwan·gye·ja·oé | Authorised |
| 출입금지 | ch'u·rip·kŭm·ji | Personnel Only |
| 연중무휴 | yŏn·jung·mu·hyu | Open All Year |

| **Is there a vegetarian restaurant near here?** | 주위에 채식주의 음식점 있나요? chu·wi·é ch'ae·shik·chu·i ŭm·shik·chŏm in·na·yo |
|---|---|
| **I'm a vegan.** | 전 철저한 채식주의자예요. chŏn ch'ŏl·chŏ·han ch'ae·shik·chu·i·ja·ye·yo |
| **I'm a vegetarian.** | 전 채식주의자예요. chŏn ch'ae·shik·chu·i·ja·ye·yo |
| **I don't eat ...** | 전 ... 안 먹어요. chŏn ... an·mŏ·gŏ·yo |

## Ordering Food

| **Do you have any vegetarian dishes?** | 채식주의 음식 있나요? ch'ae·shik·chu·i ŭm·shik in·na·yo |
|---|---|
| **Do you have halal food?** | 할랄 음식 있나요? hal·lal ŭm·shik in·na·yo |
| **Do you have kosher food?** | 유대인 음식 있나요? yu·dae·in ŭm·shik in·na·yo |
| **Is it cooked in/with ...?** | ... 들어 가나요? ... dŭ·rŏ ga·na·yo |

**Could you prepare a meal without ...?**

... 빼고
해 주시겠어요?
... ppao·go
hae·ju·shi·gess·ŏ·yo

| | | |
|---|---|---|
| **butter** | 버터 | bŏ·t'ŏ |
| **chicken** | 닭고기 | tak·ko·gi |
| **fish (stock)** | 생선 (국물) | saeng·sŏn (gung·mul) |
| **ham** | 햄 | haem |
| **meat** | 고기 | ko·gi |
| **meat stock** | 육수 | yuk·su |
| **oil** | 기름 | ki·rŭm |
| **pork** | 돼지고기 | twae·ji·go·gi |
| **red meat** | 쇠고기 | soé·go·gi |
| **seafood** | 해물 | hae·mul |

**Is this ...?**

이거 ...?
i·gŏ ...

| | | |
|---|---|---|
| **decaffeinated** | 무카페인인가요 | mu·k'a·p'e·in in·ga·yo |
| **free of animal produce** | 고기<br>안 들었나요 | ko·gi<br>an·dŭ·rŏn·na·yo |
| **free-range** | 방목했나요 | pang·mo·k'aen·na·yo |
| **genetically modified** | 유전자 변형<br>식품인가요 | yu·jŏn·ja byŏn·hyŏng<br>shik·p'u·min·ga·yo |
| **low-fat** | 저지방인가요 | chŏ·ji·bang in·ga·yo |
| **low in sugar** | 설탕 조금<br>들었나요 | sŏl·t'ang cho·gŭm<br>dŭ·rŏn·na·yo |
| **low in salt** | 저염도인가요 | chŏ·yŏm·do·in·ga·yo |
| **salt-free** | 무염인가요 | mu·yŏ·min·ga·yo |
| **organic** | 유기농인가요 | yu·gi·nong in·ga·yo |

FOOD VEGETARIAN & SPECIAL MEALS

# Menu
## ~ DECODER ~
음식 사전

These Korean dishes and ingredients are listed in alphabetical order according to their pronunciation, so you can easily understand what's on offer and ask for what takes your fancy when you're eating out.

## ~ A ~

**a·bo·k'a·do** 아보카도 avocado
**a·ch'im** 아침 breakfast
**ae·ho·bak** 애호박 courgette • squash • zucchini
**aek·sang k'ǔ·rim** 액상 크림 cream
**ae·p'i·t'a·i·jŏ** 애피타이저 appetiser
**a·gwi·tchim** 아귀찜 steamed spicy angler fish
**a·i·sǔ k'ŏ·p'i** 아이스 커피 iced coffee
**a·i·sǔ·k'ǔ·rim** 아이스크림 ice cream
**a·mon·dǔ** 아몬드 almonds
**ang·t'ǔ·ré** 앙트레 entrée
**an·shim·gu·i** 안심 구이 grilled tenderloin
**a·sǔ·p'a·ra·gŏ·sǔ** 아스파라거스 asparagus

## ~ B ~

**bbang** 빵 bread
**bul·go·gi** 불고기 marinated beef or pork grilled at the table & eaten with lettuce & other vegetables

## ~ C ~

**ch'a** 차 tea
**cha·du** 자두 plums
**chaem** 잼 jam

**ch'ae·shik bwi·p'é** 채식 뷔페 vegetarian buffet
**ch'ae·shik·chu·i·ja** 채식주의자 vegetarian
**cha·jang·myŏn** 자장면 noodles in black-bean sauce
**ch'am·ch'i** 참치 tuna
**ch'am·ch'i ch'o·bap** 참치 초밥 tuna sushi
**ch'am·gi·rǔm** 참기름 sesame oil
**cha·moé** 참외 honeydew melon
**chan·ch'i·guk·su** 잔치 국수 thin noodles, usually in a broth made from anchovies & zucchini
**chang·ŏ·gu·i** 장어 구이 grilled eel
**chap·ch'ae** 잡채 transparent noodles stir-fried in sesame oil with strips of egg, meat & vegetables
**che·ri** 체리 cherries
**ch'i·jǔ** 치즈 cheese
**ch'i·jǔ kim·bap** 치즈 김밥 rice-and-seaweed roll with cheese
**ch'il·myŏn·jo** 칠면조 turkey
**chin** 진 gin
**cho·gae** 조개 shellfish • scallop • razor clam
**cho·gak** 조각 slice
**ch'o·k'ol·lik·k'e·i·k'ǔ** 초콜릿 케이크 chocolate cake

ch'o·k'ol·lit 초콜릿 chocolate
chok·pal 족발 steamed pork hocks
chŏk·p'o·do 적포도 red grapes
chŏk·p'o·dŏ·ju 적포도주 red wine
chŏm·shim 점심 lunch
chŏn·bok·chuk 전복죽 rice porridge with abalone
ch'ŏn·do pok·sung·a 천도 복숭아 nectarine
ch'ong·gak·kim·ch'i 총각김치 pickled radish seasoned with garlic & red chilli
ch'ŏng·ŏ 청어 herring
chŏng·ŏ·ri 정어리 sardine
ch'ŏng·p'o·do 청포도 white grapes
chŏng·su·gi·mul 정수기 물 filtered water
chŏ·nyŏk 저녁 dinner
cho·ri·doén 조리 된 cooked
cho·rin 졸인 braised
chŏ·rin 절인 pickled
chŏ·rin ya·ch'ae 절인 야채 pickled vegetables
chuk 죽 boiled rice
chŭng·nyu·su 증류수 distilled water
ch'u·ŏ·t'ang 추어탕 mudfish soup
chu·yo·ri 주요리 main course

## ~ D ~

ddal·gi 딸기 strawberries
ddang·k'ong 땅콩 peanuts
ddŏk 떡 rice cakes
ddŏk·pok·ki 떡볶이 rice cakes cooked in red pepper paste
ddŭ·gŏ·un ŭm·nyo 뜨거운 음료 hot drinks

## ~ G ~

ggak·tu·gi 깍두기 pickled cubed radish seasoned with garlic & red chilli
ggo·ch'i 꼬치 Korean-style shish kebabs
ggo·ri·gom·t'ang 꼬리곰탕 oxtail soup

ggul 꿀 honey
ggŭ·rin 끓인 boiled
ggwŏng·baek·suk 꿩백숙 pheasant stew

## ~ H ~

hae·ba·ra·gi 해바라기 sunflower
hae·jang·guk 해장국 'sunrise soup' – a hangover remedy consisting of boiled bones, chopped radish, radish leaves, cabbage, green onions & fresh blood direct from the slaughterhouse
haem 햄 ham
haem·bŏ·gŏ 햄버거 hamburger
hae·mul 해물 seafood
hae·mul bok·kŭm·bap 해물 볶음밥 fried rice with seafood
hae·mul·t'ang 해물탕 spicy assorted seafood soup
hae·san·mul ya·ch'ae t'wi·gim 해산물 야채 튀김 seafood & vegetables fried in batter
ham·hŭng·naeng·myŏn 함흥냉면 North Korean cold noodles
han·gwa 한과 traditional whole-grain cookies
han·jŏng·shik 한정식 banquet of traditional meats, seafood & vegetables
hat·to·gŭ 핫도그 corn dog • hot dog
he·i·jŭl·lŏt 헤이즐넛 hazelnuts
hin·k'ong 흰 콩 white tofu beans
ho·bak·jŏn 호박전 fried squash slices
hŏ·bŭ 허브 herbs
hŏ·bŭ·t'i 허브티 herbal tea
ho·du 호두 walnuts
ho·du·gwa·ja 호두과자 red bean paste in a walnut-flavoured pastry
hoé 회 sashimi without the rice
hoé·dŏp·pap 회덮밥 raw fish on rice
hoé·naeng·myŏn 회냉면 cold buckwheat noodles with raw fish in hot sauce
hong·ch'a 홍차 black tea

**D**

**MENU DECODER**

**I**

**hong·hap** 홍합 mussels

**hong·hap·pap** 홍합밥 rice with mussels (& side dishes)

**hop·pang** 호빵 large steamed buns stuffed with sweet red beans, mincemeat or minced vegetables

**hot·tŏk** 호떡 pitta bread with a cinnamon & honey filling

**hu·ch'u** 후추 black pepper

**hu·ch'uk·ka·ru** 후춧가루 ground pepper

**hŭ·gyŏm·so jung·t'ang** 흑염소 중탕 goat soup

**hun·jé** 훈제 smoked

**hu·shik** 후식 dessert

**hwa·i·t'ŭ wa·in** 화이트 와인 white wine

~ **I** ~

**in·sam** 인삼 ginseng

**in·sam·ch'a** 인삼차 ginseng tea

**in·sam·ju** 인삼주 ginseng liquor

**in·sŭ·t'ŏn·t'ŭ k'ŏ·p'i** 인스턴트 커피 instant coffee

~ **J** ~

**jjamp·pong** 짬뽕 spicy seafood noodle soup of Chinese origin

**jjan** 짠 salty

**jjim·dak** 찜닭 spicy chicken pieces with noodles

**jjin** 찐 steamed

**jjin·man·du** 찐만두 steamed dumplings

**jji·nok·su·su** 찐 옥수수 corn on the cob

**jjinp·pang** 찐빵 giant steamed bun with sweet bean paste

**jus·sŭ** 주스 juice

~ **K** ~

**ka·jae** 가재 crayfish

**ka·ji** 가지 aubergine • eggplant

**k'ak·t'e·il** 칵테일 cocktail

**kal·bi** 갈비 ribs

**kal·bi·gu·i** 갈비 구이 grilled ribs

**kal·bi·t'ang** 갈비탕 short rib stew – ribs are cooked with pyogo mushrooms, carrots, gingko nuts & jujubes in a sauce featuring soy sauce, green onions, garlic, pepper, sesame seeds, pear juice & ginger juice

**kal·bi·tchim** 갈비찜 steamed short ribs

**k'al·guk·su** 칼국수 thick handmade noodles in thick broth

**kam** 감 persimmon

**kam·ja** 감자 potatoes

**kam·ja·bok·kŭm** 감자 볶음 fried potatoes

**kam·ja·jŏn** 감자전 potato pancake

**kam·ja·t'ang** 감자탕 spicy soup with meat & potatoes

**kam·ja·t'wi·gim** 감자 튀김 chips • French fries

**kan** 간 liver

**kang·nang·k'ong** 강낭콩 kidney beans

**ka·ni·doén** 간이 된 salted

**kan·jang** 간장 soy sauce

**kan·shik** 간식 snack

**k'a·p'u·ch'i·no** 카푸치노 cappuccino

**k'a·ré** 카레 curry

**ké** 게 crab

**k'e·ch'ŏp** 케첩 ketchup

**k'e·i·k'ŭ** 케이크 cake

**ke·jang** 게장 pickled raw crab served with rice

**ke·tchim** 게찜 steamed crab

**kim** 김 seaweed

**kim·bap** 김밥 rice rolled in seaweed

**kim·ch'i** 김치 kimchi – Korean national dish of pickled cabbage with ground red pepper; has hundreds of varieties (eg with cucumbers, radishes or other vegetables, and in a nonspicy version)

**kim·ch'i·bok·kŭm·bap** 김치 볶음밥 fried rice with kimchi

**kim·ch'i·man·du** 김치 만두 kimchi dumplings

**kim·ch'i·tchi·gae** 김치 찌개 kimchi stew

**k'i·wi** 키위 kiwi fruit

**ko·ch'u** 고추 red chillies • red pepper

**ko·ch'u·jang** 고추장 chilli sauce • red pepper paste

**ko·ch'uk·ka·ru** 고춧가루 chilli pepper • red pepper powder

**ko·dŭng·ŏ·gu·i** 고등어 구이 grilled mackerel

**ko·gi** 고기 meat

**ko·gu·ma** 고구마 sweet potato

**k'o·k'o·a** 코코아 cocoa

**k'o·k'o·nŏt** 코코넛 coconut

**kol·baeng·i mu·ch'im** 골뱅이 무침 seasoned river snails with mixed vegetables

**k'ol·li·p'ül·la·wŏ** 콜리플라워 cauliflower

**kŏ·mŭn·k'ong** 검은 콩 black beans

**ko·myŏng** 고명 garnish

**k'ong** 콩 beans

**k'ong·guk·su** 콩국수 noodles in cold soy milk soup

**k'ong·na·mul** 콩나물 bean sprouts

**k'ong·na·mul·guk** 콩나물국 bean sprout soup

**k'ong·nyu** 콩류 legumes

**kŏn·jo** 건조 dried

**kŏn·p'o·do** 건포도 raisins

**kop·ch'ang·gu·i** 곱창 구이 grilled intestines (typically pork) cooked on a metal plate over charcoal & served with a light bean paste sauce & chopped green onions

**kop·ch'ang jŏn·gol** 곱창 전골 tripe hotpot

**k'ŏ·p'i** 커피 coffee

**k'ŏ·sŭ·t'ŏ·dŭ** 커스터드 custard

**kuk·su** 국수 noodles

**kul** 굴 oyster

**kul·so·sŭ** 굴소스 oyster sauce

**k'ŭ·rae·k'ŏ** 크래커 cracker

**k'ŭ·rim·gwa sŏl·t'ang nŏ·ŭn k'ŏ·p'i** 크림과 설탕 넣은 커피 coffee with cream & sugar

**k'ŭ·rim nŏ·ŭn k'ŏ·p'i** 크림 넣은 커피 coffee with cream

**k'ŭ·ru·a·sang** 크루아상 croissant

**ku un** 구운 baked • broiled • grilled • roasted

**ku·un·gam·ja** 구운 감자 plain roasted potatoes

**kwa·il** 과일 fruit

**kwa·il jus·sŭ** 과일 주스 fruit juice

**kwang·ŏ·hoé** 광어회 raw halibut

**kwi·ri** 귀리 oats

**kye·ran** 계란 egg

**kye·ranp·pang** 계란빵 small cake with egg inside

**kye·ran sael·lŏ·dŭ** 계란 샐러드 egg salad

**kye·ran·tchim** 계란찜 steamed egg

**kyŏ·ja** 겨자 mustard (Korean-style)

**kyŏn·gwa·ryu** 견과류 nuts

**kyul** 귤 mandarin • tangerine

### ~ M ~

**maek·chu** 맥주 beer

**mae·shil·chu** 매실주 green plum wine

**mae·un** 매운 hot (spicy)

**mae·un·t'ang** 매운탕 spicy fish soup

**ma·ga·rin** 마가린 margarine

**mak·kŏl·li** 막걸리 fermented/unstrained rice wine • a milky liquor with a low alcohol content

**mak·kuk·su** 막국수 buckwheat noodles with vegetables, meat & chicken broth

**mal·lin kwa·il** 말린 과일 dried fruit

**ma·mŏl·le·i·dŭ** 마멀레이드 marmalade

**man·du** 만두 small dumplings filled with mincemeat, seafood, vegetables & herbs

**man·du·guk·su** 만두 국수 dumpling & noodle soup

**man·duk·kuk** 만둣국 soup with meat-filled dumplings

**man·du·t'wi·gim** 만두 튀김 fried dumplings

**N**

**mang·go** 망고 mango
**man·ju** 만쥬 freshly baked minicakes filled with custard
**ma·nŭl** 마늘 garlic
**ma·rŭn o·jing·ŏ** 마른 오징어 dried squid – at street stalls, this is roasted over a bed of pebbles
**mat·t'ang** 맛탕 honey-coated & roasted sweet potatoes
**ma·yo·ne·jŭ** 마요네즈 mayonnaise
**me·ch'u·ri·al** 메추리알 quail eggs
**me·in k'o·sŭ** 메인 코스 main course
**mel·lon** 멜론 melon
**me·mil·ju** 메밀주 liquor flavoured with buckwheat flowers
**met·tu·gi·bok·kŭm** 메뚜기 볶음 fried grasshoppers
**met·twae·ji** 멧돼지 wild pig
**mi·di·ŏm** 미디엄 medium (of meat)
**mil** 밀 wheat
**mil·ka·ru** 밀가루 flour
**mi·so** 미소 see **toén·jang**
**mi·t'ŭ·bol** 미트볼 meatballs
**mi·yŏk** 미역 thin strips of dried seaweed
**mi·yŏk·kuk** 미역국 brown seaweed soup
**mo·dum·hoé** 모둠회 mixed raw fish platter
**mo·dum saeng·sŏn ch'o·bap** 모둠 생선 초밥 assorted sushi
**mo·gwa** 모과 Chinese quince
**mŏ·sŭ·t'ŏ·dŭ** 머스터드 mustard (Western-style)
**mu** 무 radish
**mu·hwa·gwa** 무화과 fig
**muk** 묵 jellied acorn purée
**mu·k'a·pe·in k'ŏ·p'i** 무카페인 커피 decaffeinated coffee
**mul** 물 water
**mul·kim·ch'i** 물김치 cold nonspicy kimchi floating in cool water
**mul·laeng·myŏn** 물냉면 cold buckwheat noodles in an icy, sweetish broth, garnished with shredded vegetables & half a hard-boiled egg

**myŏl·ch'i** 멸치 anchovies
**myŏl·ch'i·bok·kŭm** 멸치 볶음 anchovies stir-fried with garlic, ginger, soy sauce, corn syrup & cooking wine, then deep-fried

## ~ N ~

**nae·jang** 내장 giblets (meat)
**nak·chi** 낙지 octopus
**nak·chi·bok·kŭm** 낙지 볶음 octopus or baby octopus chopped up in a mixture of red pepper paste & soy sauce, then stir-fried with onions, chilli & green onions
**nak·chi·jŏn·gol** 낙지 전골 octopus hotpot
**noé** 뇌 brains
**nok·ch'a** 녹차 green tea
**nok·tu bin·daet·tŏk** 녹두 빈대떡 mung bean pancake
**nŭl·gŭn ho·bak** 늙은 호박 pumpkin
**nu·rung·ji** 누룽지 crunchy scorched rice snack

## ~ O ~

**o·gok·pap** 오곡밥 five-grain rice, usually consisting of glutinous & regular rice, glutinous sorghum, glutinous millet, dried black beans & dried sweet beans
**o·gol·gyé** 오골계 black chicken
**o·i** 오이 cucumber
**o·i·so·ba·gi** 오이소박이 pickled stuffed cucumber seasoned with garlic & red chilli
**o·jing·ŏ** 오징어 cuttlefish • squid
**o·jing·ŏ·dŏp·pap** 오징어 덮밥 rice topped with cuttlefish roasted in hot pepper paste
**o·jing·ŏ sun·dae** 오징어 순대 stuffed squid
**ok·su·su** 옥수수 corn
**ok·su·su·ch'a** 옥수수차 roasted corn tea
**ol·li·bŭ** 올리브 olive

ol·li·bŭ o·il 올리브 오일 olive oil

ŏ·muk 어묵 pressed fish & seafood cakes in broth

ŏ·mul·let 오믈넷 omelette

o·mŭ·ra·i·sŭ 오므라이스 omelette with rice

o·ren·ji 오렌지 orange

o·ren·ji jus·sŭ 오렌지 주스 orange juice

o·ri 오리 duck

o·ri·gu·i 오리 구이 roast duck

o·ri·t'ang 오리탕 duck soup

ŏ·rŭm 얼음 ice

~ P ~

p'a 파 leek

pa·bi·k'yu 바비큐 barbecue

pa·dak·ka·jae 바다가재 lobster

pae 배 pear

pae·ch'u 배추 cabbage (Chinese)

pae·ch'u kim·ch'i 배추김치 pickled cabbage seasoned with garlic & red chilli

paek·kim·ch'i 백김치 pickled white cabbage – non-spicy & with a sour taste

paek·p'o·do·ju 백 포도주 white wine

p'aen·k'e·i·k'ŭ 팬케이크 pancakes

p'a·i 파이 pie

p'a·i·nae·p'ŭl 파인애플 pineapple

p'a·jŏn 파전 green onion pancake

pa·k'a 박하 mint

pam 밤 chestnuts

pa·na·na 바나나 banana

pan·ch'an 반찬 side dishes

pan·su·k'an 반숙한 soft-boiled

pap 밥 steamed rice

p'ap·ping·su 팥빙수 red bean parfait

p'a·sŭl·li 파슬리 parsley

p'a·sŭ·t'a 파스타 pasta

p'at 팥 red bean paste

p'e·i·k'ŏn 베이컨 bacon

p'e·i·sŭ·t'ŭ·ri 페이스트리 pastry

pi·bim·bap 비빔밥 rice, vegetables & meat topped with an egg

pi·bim·naeng·myŏn 비빔냉면 cold buckwheat noodles with vegetables & meat in hot sauce

p'i·ja 피자 pizza

p'i·k'ŭl 피클 pickles

p'i·mang 피망 capsicum • paprika

pi·sŭ·k'it 비스킷 biscuit

p'i·sŭ·t'a·ch'i·o 피스타치오 pistachio

pi·t'ŭp·pu·ri 비트 뿌리 beetroot

p'o·do 포도 grapes

p'o·do·jus·sŭ 포도 주스 grape juice

p'o·do·na·mu 포도나무 vine

po·dŭ·k'a 보드카 vodka

po·gŏ 복어 blowfish • puffer fish

pok·kŭm·bap 볶음밥 fried rice

pok·kŭm·na·myŏn 볶음 라면 fried ramen noodles

pok·kŭn 볶은 sautéed

pok·kŭnt·tang·k'ong 볶은 땅콩 roasted nuts

pok·sung·a 복숭아 peach

pŏn·de·gi 번데기 silkworm larvae snack

po·ri·bap 보리밥 boiled/steamed rice with steamed barley

po·ri·ch'a 보리차 barley tea

po·shin·t'ang 보신탕 dog-meat soup

pŏ·sŏp·pap 버섯밥 rice with mushrooms

pŏ·sŏt 버섯 mushrooms

pŏ·sŏt·chŏn·gol 버섯 전골 mushroom hotpot

po·ssam 보쌈 steamed pork & cabbage

pŏ·t'ŏ 버터 butter

pu·dae·tchi·gae 부대 찌개 ham-and-everything stew

p'uk·ko·ch'u 풋고추 green pepper

pul·go·gi 불고기 marinated beef or pork grilled at the table & eaten with lettuce & other vegetables

pŭl·laek k'ŏ·p'i 블랙 커피 black coffee

pul·tak 불닭 very spicy chicken

pung·ŏp·pang 붕어빵 fish-shaped cake with red bean filling

pŭ·raen·di 브랜디 brandy

**p'ŭ·ri·ma** 프리마 creamer (for coffee)
**pŭ·ro·k'ol·li** 브로콜리 broccoli
**pwi·p'é** 뷔페 buffet

## ~ R ~

**ra·im** 라임 lime
**ra·jŭ·be·ri** 라즈베리 raspberries
**ra·myŏn** 라면 instant ramen noodles served in a hot chilli soup
**re·dŭ wa·in** 레드 와인 red wine
**re·mon** 레몬 lemon
**re·mo·ne·i·dŭ** 레모네이드 lemonade
**ren·jŭ·k'ong** 렌즈콩 lentils
**re·ŏ** 레어 rare (of meat)
**rolp·pang** 롤빵 bread roll
**rŏm** 럼 rum

## ~ S ~

**sael·lŏ·dŭ** 샐러드 salad
**saen·dŭ·wi·ch'i** 샌드위치 sandwich
**saeng** 생 raw
**saeng·gang** 생강 ginger
**saeng·gang·ch'a** 생강차 ginger tea
**saeng·gwa·il jus·sŭ** 생과일 주스 freshly squeezed fruit juice
**saeng·maek·chu** 생맥주 draught beer
**saeng·sŏn** 생선 fish
**saeng·sŏn ch'o·bap** 생선 초밥 sushi
**saeng·sŏn·gu·i** 생선 구이 broiled & salted fish • grilled fish
**saeng·sŏn·hoé** 생선회 raw fish
**saeng·sŏn t'wi·gim** 생선 튀김 seasoned fish dipped in batter & fried
**saeng·su** 생수 mineral spring water
**sae·u** 새우 shrimp
**sae·u·gu·i** 새우 구이 grilled prawns
**sae·u·t'wi·gim** 새우 튀김 prawn pieces dipped in batter & deep-fried
**sa·gwa** 사과 apple
**sal·gu** 살구 apricot
**sal·la·mi so·shi·ji** 살라미 소시지 salami
**sal·mŭn** 삶은 boiled
**sal·sa** 살사 salsa

**sam·gak·kim·bap** 삼각 김밥 triangular sushi
**sam·gye·t'ang** 삼계탕 a small whole chicken stuffed with glutinous rice, red dates, garlic & ginseng boiled in broth
**sam·gyŏp·sal** 삼겹살 barbecued bacon-type pork
**san·ch'ae·bi·bim·bap** 산채비빔밥 rice, mountain vegetables & meat topped with an egg
**san·ch'ae·jŏng·shik** 산채 정식 banquet of mountain vegetables
**sang·ŏ** 상어 shark
**san·nak·chi** 산낙지 live baby octopus
**sa·wŏ·k'ŭ·rim** 사워크림 sour cream
**sel·lŏ·ri** 셀러리 celery
**sha·bŭ·sha·bŭ** 샤브샤브 beef & vegetable casserole
**sham·p'e·in** 샴페인 champagne • sparkling wine
**sha·rŭ·do·né** 샤르도네 chardonnay
**shi·gol·bap·sang** 시골 밥상 countryside-style meal
**shi·gŭm·ch'i** 시금치 spinach
**shi·gŭm·ch'i mu·ch'im** 시금치 무침 whole spinach cut into pieces & seasoned with soy sauce, sesame oil & a touch of sugar
**shik·ch'o** 식초 vinegar
**shi·k'yé** 식혜 dessert of sweet rice • rice punch with grains of rice
**shin·sŏl·lo** 신선로 'fairy stew' – a special-occasion dish of specially arranged meatballs, fried egg slivers, fried fish fillets, mushrooms, fried liver, pre-cooked carrots, gingko nuts, walnuts & pine nuts
**shin·sŏn·han** 신선한 fresh
**shi·ri·ŏl** 시리얼 cereal
**so·bul·go·gi** 소불고기 marinated beef grilled at the table & eaten with lettuce & other vegetables
**soé·gal·bi** 쇠갈비 barbecued beef ribs
**soé·go·gi** 쇠고기 beef

**soé·go·gi ssam** 쇠고기 쌈 barbecued beef slices & lettuce wrap (with side dishes)

**soé·go·gi guk** 쇠고기 국 beef soup

**soé·go·gi guk·pap** 쇠고기 국밥 beef & rice soup

**soé·go·gi kim·bap** 쇠고기 김밥 rice-and-seaweed roll with beef

**so·gal·bi·tang** 소갈비탕 beef ribs soup

**so·gal·bi·tchim** 소갈비 찜 barbecued beef rib stew

**so·gŭl ch'ae·un** 속을 채운 stuffed

**so·gŭm** 소금 salt

**so·ju** 소주 traditional Korean liquor generally made from sweet potatoes (similar to vodka, but less potent)

**sŏl·t'ang** 설탕 sugar

**song·a·ji·go·gi** 송아지 고기 veal

**sŏng·nyu** 석류 pomegranate

**song·p'yŏn** 송편 crescent-shaped rice-flour cakes stuffed with beans, chestnuts or sesame seeds & steamed on a layer of pine needles – associated with Chusok (Harvest Moon Festival)

**sŏn·jik·kuk** 선짓국 rice with ox-blood soup

**so·shi·ji** 소시지 pork sausage

**so·sŭ** 소스 sauce

**ssal·gwa·ja** 쌀과자 rice crackers

**ssam·bap** 쌈밥 rice with side dishes & leaf wraps

**su·bak** 수박 watermelon

**su·je·bi** 수제비 dough flakes in shellfish broth

**su·jŏng·gwa** 수정과 persimmon punch with cinnamon flavouring

**sŭ·k'ŭ·raem·bŭl·dŭ e·gŭ** 스크램블드 에그 scrambled eggs

**sul** 술 alcoholic drink

**sun·dae** 순대 noodle & vegetable sausage

**sun·du·bu·tchi·gae** 순두부 찌개 spicy uncurdled tofu stew

**sung·nyung** 숭늉 burnt-rice tea

**su·p'u** 수프 soup

**sŭ·t'e·i·k'ŭ** 스테이크 steak

## ~ T ~

**t'a·ba·sŭ·k'o so·sŭ** 타바스코 소스 tabasco sauce

**tae·ch'u** 대추 jujube (red date)

**tae·ch'u·ch'a** 대추차 jujube tea

**tae·ch'u·sul** 대추술 red date liquor

**tae·gu** 대구 cod

**tae·ha** 대하 prawn

**tae·hap·cho·gae** 대합조개 clams

**ta·jin·go·gi** 다진 고기 mincemeat

**tak·kal·bi** 닭갈비 spicy chicken pieces, cabbage, vegetables & finger-sized pressed rice cakes that are grilled at your table

**tak·ko·ch'i** 닭꼬치 spicy grilled chicken on skewers

**tak·ko·gi** 닭고기 chicken

**tak·ku·i** 닭구이 roasted chicken

**tak·kuk** 닭국 chicken stew

**tak·pa·bi·k'yu** 닭 바비큐 barbecued chicken

**tak pok·kŭm·t'ang** 닭 볶음탕 a spicy mix of chicken pieces, transparent noodles, potatoes & vegetables

**tak·t'wi·gim** 닭 튀김 fried chicken

**t'al·chi u·yu** 탈지 우유 skim milk

**tan** 단 sweet

**tang·gŭn** 당근 carrot

**t'ang·su·yuk** 탕수육 sweet & sour pork

**tan·mu·ji** 단무지 pickled daikon radish

**t'an·san ŭm·nyo** 탄산음료 soft drink

**tchi·gae** 찌개 stew

**te·ch'in** 데친 poached

**t'e·k'il·la** 테킬라 tequila

**tŏ·dŏk·ku·i** 더덕 구이 grilled toduk (a mountain herb) root seasoned with a red pepper sauce, sesame oil & sugar

**toén·jang** 된장 soybean paste

**toén·jang·tchi·gae** 된장 찌개 soybean paste stew with tofu, vegetables, some meat & tiny shellfish

**to·ga·ni·t'ang** 도가니탕 cow knee-caps soup

**tol·sop·pap** 돌솥밥 hotpot rice

**U**

**tol·sop·pi·bim·bap** 돌솥 비빔밥 rice, vegetables & meat topped with an egg & cooked in a stone hotpot

**t'o·ma·t'o** 토마토 tomatoes

**t'o·ma·t'o so·sŭ** 토마토 소스 tomato sauce

**tong·dong·ju** 동동주 clear rice wine

**tong·gŭ·rang·ttaeng** 동그랑땡 large mincemeat patty

**t'ong·milp·pang** 통밀빵 wholemeal bread

**tonk·ka·sŭ** 돈가스 pork cutlet with rice & salad

**to·nŏt** 도넛 doughnuts

**to·ra·ji mu·ch'im** 도라지 무침 a red-coloured salad of raw bellflower roots dressed with salt, vinegar, red pepper powder, sesame seeds & oil

**t'o·sŭ·t'ŭ** 토스트 fried sandwich

**to·t'o·ri·muk** 도토리 묵 acorn jelly

**tu·bu** 두부 tofu

**tu·bu·jo·rim** 두부 조림 sliced tofu marinated in soy sauce, red pepper powder, garlic, green onions & hot green pepper, then fried or steamed

**tu·bu·tchi·gae** 두부 찌개 spicy tofu stew with soybean paste & kimchi

**tŭng·shim·gu·i** 등심 구이 grilled sirloin

**tu·yu** 두유 soy milk

**twae·ji ba·bi·k'yu** 돼지 바비큐 barbecued pork

**twae·ji·bul·go·gi** 돼지불고기 marinated pork grilled at the table & eaten with lettuce & other vegetables

**twae·ji·gal·bi ba·bi·k'yu** 돼지 갈비 바비큐 barbecued pork ribs

**twae·ji·go·gi** 돼지고기 pork

**t'wi·gin** 튀긴 deep-fried

**~ U ~**

**ŭk·kaen** 으깬 mashed

**ŭm·nyo·su** 음료수 drink

**ŭn·haeng** 은행 gingko nuts

**u·yu** 우유 milk

**~ W ~**

**wa·in** 와인 wine

**wan·du·k'ong** 완두콩 peas

**wan·su·gé** 완숙의 hard-boiled

**wa·p'ŭl** 와플 waffles

**wel·dŏn** 웰던 well-done (of meat)

**wi·sŭ·k'i** 위스키 whisky

**~ Y ~**

**ya·ch'ae** 야채 vegetables

**ya·ch'ae'·t'wi·gim** 야채튀김 deep-fried vegetables in tempura

**yak·shik** 약식 flavoured glutinous rice mixed with honey, dates & chestnuts

**yang·bae·ch'u** 양배추 cabbage (Western)

**yang·go·gi** 양고기 lamb • mutton

**yang·p'a** 양파 onion

**yang·sang·ch'u** 양상추 lettuce

**yo·gu·rŭ·t'ŭ** 요구르트 yogurt

**yŏl·mu·naeng·myŏn** 열무 냉면 cold noodles with radish kimchi soup

**yŏn·hoé** 연회 banquet

**yŏ·nŏ** 연어 salmon

**yŏt** 엿 strips of toffee sliced off a huge slab & served on a stick

**yu·ja·ch'a** 유자차 citron tea

**yuk·kae·jang** 육개장 boiled beef entrails seasoned with red pepper powder & cooked again in beef broth with vegetables

**yu·k'oé** 육회 seasoned raw beef

**yul·mu·ch'a** 율무차 'Job's tears' tea – a hot drink that has a nutty flavour, made from the powdered seeds of the 'Job's tears' tropical grass

# Dictionary

## ENGLISH to KOREAN
영어 – 한국어

Words in this dictionary are marked as nouns n, adjectives a, adverbs adv, verbs v, pronouns pron or prepositions prep for clarity where required. The abbreviations sg (singular), pl (plural), inf (informal) and pol (polite) are also used where applicable. Korean verbs are given in their polite form (ending in ~yo ~요). The verb stem is repeated between brackets after the verb. For more information, see **grammar**.

## A

**aboard** 타고 t'a·go
**abortion** 낙태 nak·t'ae
**about ...** ...에 대하여 ...é dae·ha·yŏ
**above ...** ... 위에 ... wi·é
**abroad** 외국에 oé·gu·gé
**accept** 받아들여요 (받아들이~)
pa·da·dŭ·ryŏ·yo (pa·da·dŭ·ri~)
**accident** 사고 sa·go
**accommodation** 숙박 suk·pak
**account (bill)** n 계산서 kye·san·sŏ
**across ...** ... 맞은 편에 ...
ma·jŭn p'yŏ·né
**actor** 배우 pae·u
**acupuncture** 침 ch'im
**adaptor** 어댑터 ŏ·daep·t'ŏ
**addiction** 중독 chung·dok
**address** n 주소 chu·so
**administration** 관리 kwal·li
**administrator** 관리자 kwal·li·ja
**admission (price)** 입장료 ip·jang·nyo
**admit (let in)** 허락해요 (허락하~)
hŏ·ra·k'ae·yo (hŏ·ra·k'a~)
**adult** n 성인 sŏng·in

**advertisement** 광고 kwang·go
**advice** 조언 cho·ŏn
**aeroplane** 비행기 pi·haeng·gi
**after ...** ... 후에 ... hu·é
**afternoon** 오후 o·hu
**again** 다시 ta·shi
**against ...** ...에 반대하여
...é pan·dae·ha·yŏ
**age** n inf/pol 나이/연세 na·i/yŏn·sé
**ago** 전에 jŏ·né
**agree** 동의해요 (동의하~)
tong·i·hae·yo (tong·i·ha~)
**agriculture** 농사 nong·sa
**ahead** 앞 쪽에 ap·tcho·gé
**AIDS** 에이즈 é·i·jŭ
**air** n 공기 kong·gi
**air-conditioned** 냉방 중
naeng·bang·jung
**air conditioning** 냉방 naeng·bang
**airline** 항공사 hang·gong·sa
**airmail** 항공 우편 hang·gong u·p'yŏn
**airplane** 비행기 pi·haeng·gi
**airport** 공항 kong·hang
**airport tax** 공항세 kong·hang·sé
**aisle (on plane)** 통로 t'ong·no

**B**

**alarm clock** 알람 시계 al·lam shi·gyé
**alcohol** 술 sul
**all** 모든 mo·dûn
**allergic to ...** ...에 알레르기가 있는
...é al·le·rû·gi·ga in·nûn
**allergy** 알레르기 al·le·rû·gi
**almond** 아몬드 a·mon·dû
**almost** 거의 kŏ·i
**alone** 홀로 hol·lo
**already** 벌써 pŏl·ssŏ
**also** 또한 ddo·han
**altitude** 고도 ko·do
**always** 언제나 ŏn·je·na
**ambassador** 대사 tae·sa
**ambulance** 구급차 ku·gûp·ch'a
**amusement park** 유원지 yu·wŏn·ji
**anaemia** 빈혈 pin·hyŏl
**anchovy** 멸치 myŏl·ch'i
**ancient** a 고대의 ko·dae·ûi
**and** 그리고 kû·ri·go
**angry** 화난 hwa·nan
**animal** 동물 tong·mul
**ankle** 발목 pal·mok
**another** 또 하나의 ddo ha·na·é
**answer** n 대답 tae·dap
**answer** v 대답해요 (대답하~)
tae·da·p'ae·yo (tae·da·p'a~)
**ant** 개미 kae·mi
**antibiotics** 항생제 hang·saeng·jé
**antihistamines** 항히스타민제
hang·hi·sû·t'a·min·jé
**antinuclear movement** 반핵 운동
pan·haek un·dong
**antique** n 골동품 kol·dong·p'um
**antiseptic** n 소독약 so·dong·nyak
**any** 무엇이든 mu·ŏ·shi·dûn
**apartment** 아파트 a·p'a·t'û
**appendicitis** 맹장염
maeng·jang·nyŏm
**appendix (body)** 맹장 maeng·jang
**apple** 사과 sa·gwa
**appointment** 약속 yak·sok
**apricot** 살구 sal·gu
**aquarium** 수족관 su·jok·kwan
**archaeology** 고고학 ko·go·hak
**architect** 건축가 kŏn·ch'uk·ka
**architecture** 건축 kŏn·ch'uk

**argue** 논쟁해요 (논쟁하~)
non·jaeng·hae·yo (non·jaeng·ha~)
**arm (body)** 팔 p'al
**arrest** 체포해요 (체포하~)
ch'e·p'o·hae·yo (ch'e·p'o·ha~)
**arrivals** 도착 to·ch'ak
**arrive** 도착해요 (도착하~)
to·ch'a·k'ae·yo (to·ch'a·k'a~)
**art** 미술 mi·sul
**art gallery** 미술관 mi·sul·gwan
**artist (painter)** 화가 hwa·ga
**ashtray** 재떨이 chaet·tŏ·ri
**ask (a question)** 물어봐요 (물어보~)
mu·rŏ·bwa·yo (mu·rŏ·bo~)
**ask (for something)** 부탁해요
(부탁하~) pu·t'a·k'ae·yo (pu·t'a·k'a~)
**asparagus** 아스파라거스
a·sû·p'a·ra·gŏ·sû
**aspirin** 아스피린 a·sû·p'i·rin
**asthma** 천식 ch'ŏn·shik
**at ...** ...에서 ...e·sŏ
**athletics** 운동 un·dong
**atmosphere** 분위기 pu·nwi·gi
**attraction** 매력 mae·ryŏk
**aubergine** 가지 ka·ji
**aunt (maternal)** 이모 i·mo
**aunt (paternal)** 고모 ko·mo
**Australia** 호주 ho·ju
**ATM** 현금인출기 hyŏn·gû·min·ch'ul·gi
**autumn** 가을 ka·ûl
**avenue** 대로 tae·ro
**avocado** 아보카도 a·bo·k'a·do
**awful** 형편 없는
hyŏng·p'yŏn ŏm·nûn

**B**

**B&W film** 흑백 필름 hûk·paek·p'il·lûm
**baby** 아기 a·gi
**baby food** 유아식 yu·a·shik
**babysitter** 육아 도우미 yu·ga·do·u·mi
**back (body)** 허리 hŏ·ri
**back (position)** 뒤쪽 twi·tchok
**backpack** 배낭 pae·nang
**bacon** 베이컨 pe·i·k'ŏn
**bad** 나쁜 nap·pûn
**bag** 가방 ka·bang
**baggage** 짐/수하물 chim/su·ha·mul

**baggage allowance** 수하물 허용량
su·ha·mul hŏ·yong·nyang
**baggage claim** 수하물 수취대
su·ha·mul su·ch'wi·dae
**bakery** 빵집 bbang·tchip
**balance (account)** 잔액 cha·naek
**balcony** 발코니 pal·k'o·ni
**ball (sport)** 공 kong
**ballet** 발레 pal·le
**banana** 바나나 pa·na·na
**band (music)** 밴드 paen·dŭ
**bandage** 붕대 pung·dae
**Band-Aid** 반창고 pan·ch'ang·go
**bank** n 은행 ŭn·haeng
**bank account** 은행 계좌 ŭn·haeng
kye·jwa
**banknote** 지폐 chi·p'yé
**banquet** 연회 yŏn·hoé
**bar** n 술집 sul·chip
**barbecue** 바비큐 pa·bi·k'yu
**barber shop** 이발소 i·bal·so
**baseball** 야구 ya·gu
**basket** 바구니 pa·gu·ni
**basketball** 농구 nong·gu
**bath** n 목욕 mo·gyok
**bathing suit** 수영복 su·yŏng·bok
**bathroom** 욕실 yok·shil
**battery** 배터리 bae·t'ŏ·ri
**bay** 만 man
**be ...** ...이에요/예요 ...i·e·yo/·ye·yo
**beach (for swimming)** 해수욕장
hae·su·yok·chang
**bean** 콩 k'ong
**bean sprouts** 콩나물 k'ong·na·mul
**beautician** 미용사 mi·yong·sa
**beautiful** 아름다운 a·rŭm·da·un
**beauty salon** 미용실 mi·yong·shil
**because** 왜냐하면 wae·nya·ha·myŏn
**bed** 침대 ch'im·dae
**bedding** 이부자리 i·bu·ja·ri
**bedroom** 침실 ch'im·shil
**bed sheet** 침대 시트 ch'im·dae shi·t'ŭ
**bee** 벌 pŏl
**beef** 쇠고기 soé·go·gi
**beer** 맥주 maek·chu
**beetroot** 비트 뿌리 pi·t'ŭp·pu·ri

**begin** 시작해요 (시작하~)
shi·ja·k'ae·yo (shi·ja·k'a~)
**before ...** ... 전에 ... jŏ·né
**beggar** 거지 kŏ·ji
**behind ...** ... 뒤에 ... dwi·é
**below ...** ... 아래 ... a·rae
**beside ...** ... 옆에 ... yŏ·p'é
**best** 최고의 ch'oé·go·é
**bet** n 내기 nae·gi
**bet** v 내기해요 (내기하~)
nae·gi·hae·yo (nae·gi·ha~)
**better** 더 나은 tŏ·na·ŭn
**between ...** ... 사이의 ... sa·i·é
**bicycle** 자전거 cha·jŏn·gŏ
**big** 큰 k'ŭn
**bigger** 더 큰 tŏ·k'ŭn
**biggest** 제일 큰 che·il·k'ŭn
**bike** 자전거 cha·jŏn·gŏ
**bike chain** 자전거 체인 cha·jŏn·gŏ
ch'e·in
**bike lock** 자전거 자물쇠 cha·jŏn·gŏ
cha·mul·soé
**bike path** 자전거 도로 cha·jŏn·gŏ
do·ro
**bike shop** 자전거 매장 cha·jŏn·gŏ
mae·jang
**bill (restaurant)** n 계산서 kye·san·sŏ
**billiards** 당구 tang·gu
**billion** 십억 shi·bŏk
**binoculars** 쌍안경 ssang·an·gyŏng
**bird** 새 sae
**birth certificate** 출생증명서
ch'ul·saeng·jŭng·myŏng·sŏ
**birthday** 생일 saeng·il
**biscuit** 비스킷 pi·sŭ·k'it
**bite (insect/mammal)** n 물림 mul·lim
**bitter** 쓴 ssŭn
**black** 검은 kŏ·mŭn
**bladder** 방광 pang·gwang
**blanket** 담요 tam·nyo
**blind** a 시각 장애의 shi·gak
chang·ae·ŭi
**blister** n 물집 mul·chip
**blocked** 막힌 ma·k'in
**blood** 혈액 hyŏ·raek
**blood group** 혈액형 hyŏ·rae·k'yŏng
**blood pressure** 혈압 hyŏ·rap

**C**

**blood test** 혈액 검사 hyŏ·raek·kŏm·sa
**blue** 파란 p'a·ran
**board (plane, ship)** v 타요 (타~) t'a·yo (t'a~)
**boarding house** 하숙집 ha·suk·chip
**boarding pass** 탑승권 t'ap·sŭng·kwŏn
**boat** 배 pae
**body** 몸 mom
**boiled** 끓인 ggŭ·rin
**bone** 뼈 bbyŏ
**book** n 책 ch'aek
**book (make a booking)** v 예약해요 (예약하~) ye·ya·k'ae·yo (ye·ya·k'a~)
**booked out** 매진 mae·jin
**bookshop** 서점 sŏ·jŏm
**boot (footwear)** 부츠 pu·ch'ŭ
**border (national)** n 국경 kuk·kyŏng
**bored** 심심한 shim·shim·han
**boring** 재미없는 chae·mi·ŏm·nŭn
**borrow** 빌려요 (빌리~) pil·lyŏ·yo (pil·li~)
**botanic garden** 수목원 su·mo·gwŏn
**both** 둘 다 tul·da
**bottle** 병 pyŏng
**bottle opener** 병따개 pyŏngt·ta·gae
**bottom (body)** 엉덩이 ŏng·dŏng·i
**bottom (position)** 바닥 pa·dak
**boutique (fashion)** 의류 매장 ŭi·ryu mae·jang
**bowl (plate)** n 사발 sa·bal
**box** n 상자 sang·ja
**boxing** 권투 kwŏn·t'u
**boy** 남자 아이 nam·ja·a·i
**boyfriend** 남자 친구 nam·ja ch'in·gu
**bra** 브래지어 pŭ·rae·ji·ŏ
**brakes** 브레이크 pŭ·re·i·k'ŭ
**brassware** 놋쇠 제품 nos·soé je·p'um
**brave** 용감한 yong·gam·han
**bread** 빵 bbang
**break** v 깨뜨려요 (깨뜨리~) ggaet·tŭ·ryŏ·yo (ggaet·tŭ·ri~)
**break down** 고장나요 (고장나~) ko·jang·na·yo (ko·jang·na~)
**breakfast** 아침 a·ch'im
**breast (body)** 가슴 ka·sŭm
**breathe** 숨 쉬어요 (숨 쉬~) sum·shi·ŏ·yo (sum·shi~)

**bribe** n 뇌물 noé·mul
**bridge (structure)** n 다리 ta·ri
**briefcase** 서류 가방 sŏ·ryu·ga·bang
**bring** 가지고 와요 (가지고 오~) ka·ji·go·wa·yo (ka·ji·go·o~)
**brochure** 소책자 so·ch'aek·cha
**broken** 깨진 ggae·jin
**broken down** 고장난 ko·jang·nan
**bronchitis** 기관지염 ki·gwan·ji·yŏm
**brother** 형제 hyŏng·je
**brown** 갈색의 kal·sae·gé
**bruise** n 멍 mŏng
**brush** n 솔 sol
**bucket** 양동이 yang·dong·i
**budget** n 예산 ye·san
**buffet** 뷔페 pwi·p'é
**bug** n 벌레 pŏl·le
**build** 지어요 (짓~) chi·ŏ·yo (chit~)
**building** 빌딩 pil·ding
**bumbag** 여행 복대 yŏ·haeng·bok·tae
**burn** n 화상 hwa·sang
**burnt** 탄 t'an
**bus** 버스 bŏ·sŭ
**business** n 사업 sa·ŏp
**business class** 비즈니스석 pi·jŭ·ni·sŭ·sŏk
**businessperson** 사업가 sa·ŏp·ka
**business trip** 출장 ch'ul·chang
**busker** 길거리 공연자 kil·gŏ·ri kong·yŏn·ga
**bus station** 버스 터미널 bŏ·sŭ t'ŏ·mi·nŏl
**bus stop** 버스 정류장 bŏ·sŭ chŏng·nyu·jang
**busy (person)** 바쁜 pap·pŭn
**busy (phone)** 통화중 t'ong·hwa·jung
**but** 하지만 ha·ji·man
**butcher's shop** 정육점 chŏng·yuk·chŏm
**butter** n 버터 pŏ·t'ŏ
**button** n 단추 tan·ch'u
**buy** 사요 (사~) sa·yo (sa~)

**C**

**cafe** 카페 k'a·pé
**cake** 케이크 k'e·i·k'ŭ
**calculator** 계산기 kye·san·gi

**calendar** 달력 tal·lyŏk
**call (phone)** v 전화해요 (전화 하~)
chŏn·hwa·hae·yo (chŏn·hwa·ha~)
**calligraphy** 서예 sŏ·ye
**camera** 카메라 k'a·me·ra
**camera shop** 카메라 가게 k'a·me·ra
·ka·ge
**camp** v 야영해요 (야영하~)
ya·yŏng·hae·yo (ya·yŏng·ha~)
**camping store** 야영용품점
ya·yŏng·yong·p'um·jŏm
**campsite** 야영장 ya·yŏng·jang
**can** n 캔 k'aen
**can (be able)** 할 수 있어요
(할 수 있~) hal·su·iss·ŏ·yo
(hal·su·iss~)
**can (have permission)** 해도 돼요
(해도 되~) hae·do dwae·yo (hae·do
doé~)
**Canada** 캐나다 k'ae·na·da
**cancel** 취소해요 (취소하~)
ch'wi·so·hae·yo (ch'wi·so·ha~)
**cancer** 암 am
**candle** 초 ch'o
**candy** 사탕 sa·t'ang
**can opener** 캔따개 k'aen·t·ta·gae
**capsicum** 고추 ko·ch'u
**car** 차 ch'a
**cardiac arrest** 심장마비
shim·jang·ma·bi
**cards (playing)** 카드 k'a·dŭ
**care (for someone)** 아껴요 (아끼~)
ak·kyŏ·yo (ak·ki~)
**car hire** 렌트카 ren·t'ŭ·k'a
**car park** 주차장 chu·ch'a·jang
**carpenter** 목수 mok·su
**carpet** 카펫 k'a·p'et
**car registration** 자동차 등록증
cha·dong·ch'a dŭng·nok·chŭng
**carrot** 당근 tang·gŭn
**carry** 날라요 (나르~) nal·la·yo
(na·rŭ~)
**carton** 팩 p'aek
**cash** n 현금 hyŏn·gŭm
**cash (a cheque)** v 현금으로 바꿔
요 (현금으로 바꾸~) hyŏn·gŭ·mŭ·ro
pak·kwŏ·yo (hyŏn·gŭ·mŭ·ro pak·ku~)

**cash register** 금전 등록기 kŭm·jŏn
dŭng·nok·ki
**casino** 카지노 k'a·ji·no
**cassette** 카세트 k'a·se·t'ŭ
**castle** 성 sŏng
**cat** 고양이 ko·yang·i
**cathedral** 성당 sŏng·dang
**cauliflower** 콜리플라워
k'ol·li·p'ŭl·la·wŏ
**cave** n 동굴 tong·gul
**cavity (dental)** 충치 ch'ung·ch'i
**CD** 시디 shi·di
**celebration** 축하 ch'u·k'a
**celery** 셀러리 sel·lŏ·ri
**cell phone** 휴대폰 hyu·dae·p'on
**cemetery** 묘지 myo·ji
**centimetre** 센티미터 sen·t'i·mi·t'ŏ
**centre** n 중앙 chung·ang
**ceramics** 도자기 to·ja·gi
**cereal (breakfast)** 시리얼 shi·ri·ŏl
**ceremony** 의식 ŭi·shik
**certificate** 증명서 chŭng·myŏng·sŏ
**chain** n 체인 ch'e·in
**chair** n 의자 ŭi·ja
**chairlift (skiing)** 리프트 ri·p'ŭ·t'ŭ
**championships** 선수권 대회
sŏn·suk·kwŏn dae·hoé
**chance** n 기회 ki·hoé
**change** n 변화 pyŏn·hwa
**change (coins)** n 잔돈 chan·don
**change (money)** v 환전해요 (환전하
~) hwan·jŏn·hae·yo (hwan·jŏn·ha~)
**changing room** 탈의실 t'a·ri·shil
**chapel** 예배당 ye·bae·dang
**charming** 매력적인
mae ryŏk·chŏ·gin
**chat up** 말 걸어요 (말 걸~)
mal kŏ·rŏ·yo (mal kŏl~)
**cheap** 싼 ssan
**cheat** n 속임수 so·gim·su
**cheat** v 속여요 (속이~) so·gyŏ·yo
(so·gi~)
**check (banking)** n 수표 su·p'yo
**check (bill)** n 계산서 kye·san·sŏ
**check** v 점검해요 (점검하~)
chŏm·gŏm·hae·yo (chŏm·gŏm ha~)
**check-in (desk)** 체크 인 ch'e·k'ŭ·in

**C**

checkpoint 검문소 kŏm·mun·so
cheese 치즈 ch'i·jŭ
chef 요리사 yo·ri·sa
chemist (pharmacist) 약사 yak·sa
chemist (pharmacy) 약국 yak·kuk
cheque (banking) 수표 su·p'yo
cherry 체리 ch'e·ri
chess 체스 ch'e·sŭ
chessboard 체스판 ch'e·sŭ·p'an
chest (body) 가슴 ka·sŭm
chestnut 밤 pam
chewing gum 껌 ggŏm
chicken (animal) 닭 tak
chicken (meat) 닭고기 tak·ko·gi
chicken pox 수두 su·du
child 어린이 ŏ·ri·ni
child-minding service 아이 돌보기
a·i·dol·bo·gi
children (general) 어린이 ŏ·ri·ni
children (offspring) 자녀 cha·nyŏ
child seat 어린이용 좌석 ŏ·ri·ni·yong
chwa·sŏk
chilli 고추 ko·ch'u
China 중국 chung·guk
chiropractor 척추 지압사 ch'ŏk·ch'u
chi·ap·sa
chocolate 초콜릿 ch'o·k'ol·lit
choose 선택해요 (선택하~)
sŏn·t'ae·k'ae·yo (sŏn·t'ae·k'a~)
chopping board 도마 to·ma
chopsticks 젓가락 chŏk·ka·rak
church 교회 kyo·hoé
cigar 시가 shi·ga
cigarette 담배 tam·bae
cigarette lighter 라이터 ra·i·t'ŏ
cinema 영화관 yŏng·hwa·gwan
circus 서커스 sŏ·k'ŏ·sŭ
citizenship 시민권 shi·mink·kwŏn
city 도시 to·shi
city centre 시내 shi·nae
civil rights 시민권 shi·mink·kwŏn
class (category) n 종류 chong·nyu
class (school) 수업 su·ŏp
classical 고전 ko·jŏn
class system 계급 제도
kye·gŭp·che·do
clean a 깨끗한 ggaek·kŭ·t'an

clean v 청소해요 (청소하~)
ch'ŏng·so·hae·yo (ch'ŏng·so·ha~)
cleaning 청소 ch'ŏng·so
client 고객 ko·gaek
cliff 절벽 chŏl·byŏk
climb v 올라요 (오르~) ol·la·yo (o·rŭ~)
cloakroom 휴대품 보관소
hyu·dae·p'um bo·gwan·so
clock n 시계 shi·gyé
close a 가까운 kak·ka·un
close v 닫아요 (닫~) ta·da·yo (tad~)
closed 휴무 hyu·mu
clothesline 빨랫줄 bbal·laet·chul
clothing 옷 ot
clothing store 옷가게 ok·ka·gé
cloud n 구름 ku·rŭm
cloudy 구름이 많은 ku·rŭ·mi ma·nŭn
clutch (car) 클러치 k'ŭl·lŏ·ch'i
coach (trainer) n 코치 k'o·ch'i
coach v 가르쳐요 (가르치~)
ka·rŭ·ch'ŏ·yo (ka·rŭ·ch'i~)
coast n 해안 hae·an
coat n 코트 k'o·t'ŭ
cockroach 바퀴벌레 pa·k'wi·bŏl·lé
cod 대구 tae·gu
coffee 커피 k'ŏ·p'i
coins 동전 tong·jŏn
cold (flu) n 감기 kam·gi
cold (to senses) a 차가운 ch'a·ga·un
cold (weather) a 추운 ch'u·un
colleague 동료 tong·nyo
collect call 수신자 부담 통화
su·shin·ja bu·dam t'ong·hwa
college 대학 tae·hak
colour n 색깔 saek·kal
colour film 컬러 필름 k'ŏl·lŏ p'il·lŭm
comb n 빗 pit
come 와요 (오~) wa·yo (o~)
comedy 코메디 k'o·me·di
comfortable 편안한 p'yŏ·nan·han
commission 수수료 su·su·ryo
communion 영성체 yŏng·sŏng·ch'é
communism 공산주의 kong·san·ju·i
communist n 공산주의자
kong·san·ju·i·ja
companion 동료 tong·nyo
company (firm) 회사 hoé·sa

compass 나침반 na·ch'im·ban

complain 불평해요 (불평하~)
pul·p'yŏng·hae·yo (pul·p'yŏng·ha~)

complaint 불편 pul·p'yŏng

complimentary (free) 공짜 kong·tcha

computer 컴퓨터 k'ŏm·p'yu·t'ŏ

computer game 컴퓨터 게임
k'ŏm·p'yu·t'ŏ ge·im

concert 콘서트 k'on·sŏ·t'ŭ

concussion 진동 chin·dong

conditioner (hair) 컨디셔너
k'ŏn·di·shŏ·nŏ

condom 콘돔 k'on·dom

conference 회의 hoé·i

confession (religious) 고해성사
ko·hae·sŏng·sa

confirm (a booking) 확인해요 (확인
하~) hwa·gin·hae·yo (hwa·gin·ha~)

conjunctivitis 결막염
kyŏl·mang·nyŏm

connection (transport) n 환승
hwan·sŭng

conservative a 보수적인 po·su·jŏ·gin

constipation 변비 pyŏn·bi

consulate 영사관 yŏng·sa·gwan

contact lenses 콘택트 렌즈
k'on·t'aek·t'ŭ ren·jŭ

contact lens solution 콘택트 렌즈
용액 k'on·t'aek·t'ŭ ren·jŭ yong·aek

contraceptives 피임 p'i·im

contract n 계약서 kye·yak·sŏ

convenience store 편의점 p'yŏ·ni·jŏm

convent 수도원 su·do·wŏn

cook n 요리사 yo·ri·sa

cook v 요리해요 (요리하~)
yo·ri·hae·yo (yo·ri·ha·)

cookie 과자 kwa·ja

cooking 요리 yo·ri

cool (groovy) 멋진 mŏt·chin

cool (temperature) 시원한
shi·wŏn·han

corkscrew 코르크 따개 k'o·rŭ·k'ŭ
tta·gae

corn 옥수수 ok·su·su

corner n 모퉁이 mo·t'ung·i

corrupt a 부패한 pu·p'ae·han

corruption 부패 pu·p'ae

cost n 비용 pi·yong

cost v 들어요 (들~) tŭ·rŏ·yo (tŭl~)

cotton (fabric) n 면 myŏn

cotton balls 솜 som

cough n 기침 ki·ch'im

cough v 기침 해요 (기침 하~)
ki·ch'im hae·yo (ki·ch'im ha~)

cough medicine 기침약
ki·ch'im·nyak

count v 세요 (세~) se·yo (se~)

country 나라 na·ra

countryside 시골 shi·gol

coupon 쿠폰 k'u·p'on

courgette 애호박 ae·ho·bak

court (legal) 법정 pŏp·chŏng

court (tennis) 코트 k'o·t'ŭ

cover charge 팁 t'ip

cow 젖소 chŏt·so

crab 게 ké

cracker 크래커 k'ŭ·rae·k'ŏ

crafts 공예품 kong·ye·p'um

crash n 충돌 ch'ung·dol

crazy 미친 mi·ch'in

cream (food) 액상 크림 aek·sang
k'ŭ·rim

cream (lotion) 크림 k'ŭ·rim

credit card 신용카드 shi·nyong·k'a·dŭ

croissant 크루아상 k'ŭ·ru·a·sang

crop (riding) n 채찍 ch'ae·tchik

cross (religious) n 십자가 ship·cha·ga

crossing (pedestrian) 건널목
kŏn·nŏl·mok

crowded 붐비는 pum·bi·nŭn

cucumber 오이 o·i

cup 컵 k'ŏp

cupboard 찬장 ch'an·tchang

currency exchange 환율 hwa·nyul

current (electricity) 전류 chŏl·lyu

current affairs 시사 shi·sa

curry 카레 k'a·ré

custom 풍습 p'ung·sŭp

customs 세관 se·gwan

cut n 삭제 sak·ché

cut v 잘라요 (자르~) chal·la·yo
(cha·rŭ~)

cutlery 수저와 포크 su·jŏ·wa p'o·k'ŭ

CV 이력서 i·ryŏk·sŏ

**D**

cycle (ride) v 자전거를 타요
(자전거를 타~) cha·jŏn·gŏ·rŭl t'a·yo
(cha·jŏn·gŏ·rŭl t'a~)
cycling 사이클 sa·i·k'ŭl
cyclist 사이클 선수 sa·i·k'ŭl sŏn·su
cystitis 방광염 pang·gwang·nyŏm

**D**

dad 아빠 ap·pa
daily adv 매일 mae·il
dairy products 유제품 yu·je·p'um
dance n 춤 ch'um
dance v 춤 취요 (춤 추~)
ch'um·ch'wŏ·yo (ch'um·ch'u~)
dangerous 위험한 wi·hŏm·han
dark 어두운 ŏ·du·un
date (appointment) 약속 yak·sok
date (day) 날짜 nal·tcha
date (fruit) 대추 tae·ch'u
date (romantic) 데이트 te·i·t'ŭ
date of birth 생년월일
saeng·nyŏn·wŏ·ril
daughter 딸 ddal
dawn 새벽 sae·byŏk
day 하루 ha·ru
daytime 낮 nat
dead 죽은 chu·gŭn
deaf 귀가 먼 kwi·ga·mŏn
decide 결정해요 (결정하~)
kyŏl·chŏng·hae·yo (kyŏl·chŏng·ha~)
deep 깊은 ki·p'ŭn
deer 사슴 sa·sŭm
deforestation 삼림 벌채 sam·nim
pŏl·ch'ae
degrees (temperature) 도 do
delay n 지연 chi·yŏn
delicatessen 식품점 shik·p'um·jŏm
deliver 배달해요 (배달하~)
pae·dal·hae·yo (pae·dal·ha~)
demilitarized zone (DMZ)
비무장지대 pi·mu·jang·ji·dae
democracy 민주주의 min·ju·ju·i
Democratic People's Republic
of Korea 조선인민공화국 cho·sŏn
in·min kong·hwa·guk
demonstration (display) 시연 shi·yŏn
demonstration (rally) 시위 shi·wi

dental floss 치실 ch'i·shil
dentist 치과의사 ch'i·kwa ŭi·sa
deodorant 데오드란트 te·o·dŭ·ran·t'ŭ
depart 떠나요 (떠나~) ddŏ·na·yo
(ddŏ·na~)
department store 백화점
pae·k'wa·jŏm
departure 출발 ch'ul·bal
departure hall 출국장 ch'ul·guk·chang
deposit n 보증금 po·jŭng·gŭm
derailleur 변속 장치 pyŏn·sok
chang·ch'i
descendent 후손 hu·son
desert n 사막 sa·mak
design n 디자인 ti·ja·in
dessert 후식 hu·shik
destination 목적지 mok·chŏk·chi
details 자세한 내용 cha·se·han
nae·yong
diabetes 당뇨병 tang·nyo·byŏng
dial tone 발신음 pal·shi·nŭm
diaper 기저귀 ki·jŏ·gwi
diaphragm (contraceptive) 페서리
p'e·sŏ·ri
diarrhoea 설사 sŏl·sa
diary 일기 il·gi
dice 주사위 chu·sa·wi
dictionary 사전 sa·jŏn
die 죽어요 (죽~) chu·gŏ·yo (chug~)
diet (to lose weight) n 다이어트
ta·i·ŏ·t'ŭ
different 다른 ta·rŭn
difficult 어려운 ŏ·ryŏ·un
digital a 디지털 ti·ji·t'ŏl
dinner 저녁 chŏ·nyŏk
direct a 직접적인 chik·chŏp·chŏ·gin
direct-dial 직통 전화 chik·t'ong
jŏn·hwa
direction 방향 pang·hyang
director 지휘자 chi·hwi·ja
dirty 더러운 tŏ·rŏ·un
disabled person 장애인 chang·ae·in
disco 디스코 ti·sŭ·k'o
discount n 할인 ha·rin
discrimination 차별 ch'a·byŏl
disease 병 pyŏng
dish n 접시 chŏp·shi

disk (CD-ROM) 시디 shi·di
diving 다이빙 ta·i·bing
diving equipment 다이빙 용품 ta·i·bing yong·p'um
divorced 이혼한 i·hon·han
dizzy 어지러운 ŏ·ji·rŏ·un
do 해요 (하~) hae·yo (ha~)
doctor 의사 ŭi·sa
doctor of Eastern medicine 한의사 ha·ni·sa
dog 개 kae
doll 인형 in·hyŏng
dollar 달러 tal·lŏ
door 문 mun
dope (illicit drugs) 마약 ma·yak
double a 두 배의 tu·bae·é
double bed 더블 베드 tŏ·bŭl be·dŭ
double room 더블 룸 tŏ·bŭl·lum
doughnut 도넛 to·nŏt
down 아래로 a·rae·ro
downhill 내리막 nae·ri·mak
drama 드라마 tŭ·ra·ma
draught beer 생맥주 saeng·maek·chu
dream n 꿈 ggum
dress n 드레스 tŭ·re·sŭ
dried 말린 mal·lin
dried fruit 말린 과일 mal·lin kwa·il
drink n 음료수 ŭm·nyo·su
drink v 마셔요 (마시~) ma·shŏ·yo (ma·shi~)
drink (alcoholic) 술 sul
drinking fountain 급수대 kŭp·su·dae
drive v 운전해요 (운전하~) un·jŏn·hae·yo (un·jŏn·ha~)
drivers licence 운전면허증 un·jŏn myŏn·hŏ·jŭng
drug (medication) n 약 yak
drug addiction 마약 중독 ma·yak·chung·dok
drug dealer 마약상 ma·yak·sang
drugs (illicit) 마약 ma·yak
drug trafficking 마약 밀매 ma·yang·mil·mae
drug user 마약 사용자 ma·yak sa·yong·ja
drum (instrument) n 드럼 tŭ·rŏm
drunk 술 취한 sul·ch'wi·han

dry a 마른 ma·rŭn
dry v 말려요 (말리~) mal·lyŏ·yo (mal·li~)
duck n 오리 o·ri
dummy (pacifier) 노리개젖꼭지 no·ri·gae jŏk·kok·chi
dumplings 만두 man·du
duty-free 면세 myŏn·sé
DVD 디브이디 di·bŭ·i·di
dynasty 왕조 wang·jo

## E

each 각각의 kak·ka·gé
ear 귀 kwi
early adv 이른 i·rŭn
earn 벌어요 (벌~) pŏ·rŏ·yo (pŏl~)
earplugs 귀마개 kwi·ma·gae
earrings 귀고리 kwi·go·ri
earth 땅 ddang
earthquake 지진 chi·jin
east n 동쪽 tong·tchok
Eastern medical clinic 한의원 ha·ni·wŏn
Eastern medicine 한약 ha·nyak
easy 쉬운 shi·un
eat 먹어요 (먹~) mŏ·gŏ·yo (mŏg~)
economy class 이코노미석 i·k'o·no·mi·sŏk
eczema 습진 sŭp·chin
education 교육 kyo·yuk
eel 뱀장어 paem·jang·ŏ
egg 계란 kye·ran
eggplant 가지 ka·ji
election 선거 sŏn·gŏ
electrical store 전파사 chŏn·p'a·sa
electrician 전기 기사 chŏn·gi ki·sa
electricity 전기 chŏn·gi
electronics 전자제품 chŏn·ja·je·p'um
elevator 엘리베이터 el·li·be·i·t'ŏ
email n 이메일 i·me·il
embarrassed 창피한 ch'ang·p'i·han
embassy 대사관 tae·sa·gwan
embroidery 자수품 cha·su·p'um
emergency 응급 상황 ŭng·gŭp sang·hwang
emergency exit 비상구 pi·sang·gu
emotional 감정적인 kam·jŏng·jŏ·gin

**F**

**employee** 직원 chi·gwŏn
**employer** 고용인 ko·yong·in
**empty** a 빈 pin
**end** n 끝 ggŭt
**end** v 끝나요 (끝나~) gŭn·na·yo (gŭn·na~)
**endangered species** 멸종 위기의 종 myŏl·chong wi·gi·ŭi chong
**engaged (phone)** 통화 중인 t'ong·hwa·jung·in
**engaged (to be married)** 약혼한 ya·k'on·han
**engagement (to marry)** 약혼 ya·k'on
**engine** 엔진 en·jin
**engineer** n 엔지니어 en·ji·n·i·ŏ
**engineering** 공학 kong·hak
**England** 영국 yŏng·guk
**English (language)** 영어 yŏng·ŏ
**enjoy (oneself)** 즐겨요 (즐기~) chŭl·gyŏ·yo (chŭl·gi~)
**enough** 충분한 ch'ung·bun·han
**enter** 들어가요 (들어가~) tŭ·rŏ·ga·yo (tŭ·rŏ·ga~)
**entrance** 입구 ip·ku
**entry** n 입장 ip·chang
**envelope** n 봉투 pong·t'u
**environment** 환경 hwan·gyŏng
**epilepsy** 간질 kan·jil
**equality** 평등 p'yŏng·dŭng
**equipment** 장비 chang·bi
**escalator** 에스컬레이터 e·sŭ·k'ŏl·le·i·t'ŏ
**estate agency** 부동산 pu·dong·san
**euro** 유로 yu·ro
**Europe** 유럽 yu·rŏp
**euthanasia** 안락사 al·lak·sa
**evening** 저녁 chŏ·nyŏk
**every** a 모든 mo·dŭn
**everyone** 모두 mo·du
**everything** 전부 chŏn·bu
**exactly** 정확히 chŏng·hwa·k'i
**example** 예 yé
**excellent** 뛰어난 ddwi·ŏ·nan
**excess baggage** 초과 수하물 ch'o·gwa su·ha·mul
**exchange** n 교환 kyo·hwan

**exchange** v 교환해요 (교환하~) kyo·hwan·hae·yo (kyo·hwan·ha~)
**exchange rate** 환율 hwa·nyul
**excluded** 제외된 che·oé·doén
**exhaust (car)** 매연 mae·yŏn
**exhibition** 전시회 chŏn·shi·hoé
**exit** n 출구 ch'ul·gu
**expensive** 비싼 piss·an
**experience** n 경험 kyŏng·hŏm
**exploitation** 이용 i·yong
**express** a 고속의 ko·so·gé
**express mail** 빠른 우편 bba·rŭn u·p'yŏn
**extension (visa)** (비자) 연장 (pi·ja) yŏn·jang
**eye** 눈 nun
**eye drops** 안약 a·nyak

**F**

**fabric** 천 ch'ŏn
**face** n 얼굴 ŏl·gul
**face cloth** 세수 수건 se·su su·gŏn
**factory** 공장 kong·jang
**factory worker** 공장 직원 kong·jang ji·gwŏn
**fall (autumn)** n 가을 ka·ŭl
**fall (down)** v 떨어져요 (떨어지~) ddŏ·rŏ·jŏ·yo (ddŏ·rŏ·ji~)
**family** 가족 ka·jok
**family name** 성 sŏng
**famous** 유명한 yu·myŏng·han
**fan (hand-held)** 부채 pu·ch'ae
**fan (machine)** 선풍기 sŏn·p'ung·gi
**fan (politics/sport)** 팬 p'aen
**fan belt** 팬 벨트 p'aen·bel·t'ŭ
**far** adv 멀리 mŏl·li
**fare** n 요금 yo·gŭm
**farm** n 농장 nong·jang
**farmer** 농부 nong·bu
**fashion** n 패션 p'ae·shŏn
**fat** a 뚱뚱한 ddungt·tung·han
**father** 아버지 a·bŏ·ji
**father-in-law (husband's father)** 시아버지 shi·a·bŏ·ji
**father-in-law (wife's father)** 장인어른 chang·i·nŏ·rŭn
**faucet** 수도꼭지 su·dok·kok·chi

**(someone's) fault** n 잘못 chal·mot

**faulty** 불량인 pul·lyang·in

**feed** 먹여요 (먹이~) mŏ·gyŏ·yo (mŏ·gi~)

**feel (touch)** v 느껴요 (느끼~) nŭk·kyŏ·yo (nŭk·ki~)

**feelings** 감정 kam·jŏng

**female** a 여성의 yŏ·sŏng·é

**fence** n 담장 tam·jang

**ferry** n 페리 p'e·ri

**festival** 축제 ch'uk·ché

**fever** 열 yŏl

**few** 몇 개 myŏk·kae

**fiancé** 약혼자 ya·k'on·ja

**fiancée** 약혼녀 ya·k'on·nyŏ

**fiction** 소설 so·sŏl

**fig** 무화과 mu·hwa·gwa

**fight** v 싸워요 (싸우~) ssa·wŏ·yo (ssa·u~)

**fill** 채워요 (채우~) ch'ae·wŏ·yo (ch'ae·u~)

**film (cinema)** 영화 yŏng·hwa

**film (for camera)** 필름 p'il·lŭm

**film speed** 필름 감도 p'il·lŭm kam·do

**filtered** 걸러진 kŏl·lŏ·jin

**find** 찾아요 (찾~) ch'a·ja·yo (ch'aj~)

**fine** n 벌금 pŏl·gŭm

**fine** a 좋은 cho·ŭn

**finger** 손가락 son·ga·rak

**finish** n 끝 ggŭt

**finish** v 마쳐요 (마치~) ma·chŏ·yo (ma·ch'i~)

**fire** n 불 pul

**firewood** 장작 chang·jak

**first** a 첫 ch'ŏt

**first** adv 처음으로 ch'ŏ·ŭ·mŭ·ro

**first-aid kit** 구급 상자 ku·gŭp·sang·ja

**first class** 퍼스트 클래스 p'ŏ·sŭ·t'ŭ k'ŭl·lae·sŭ

**first name** 이름 i·rŭm

**fish (animal)** 물고기 mul·go·gi

**fish (food)** 생선 saeng·sŏn

**fishing** 낚시 nakk·shi

**fishmonger** 생선 장수 saeng·sŏn jang·su

**fish shop** 생선 가게 saeng·sŏn ka·gé

**flag** n 깃발 kip·pal

**flash (camera)** 플래시 p'ŭl·lae·shi

**flashlight** 손전등 son·jŏn·dŭng

**flat (apartment)** n 아파트 a·p'a·t'ŭ

**flat** a 평평한 p'yŏng·p'yŏng·han

**flea** 벼룩 pyŏ·ruk

**fleamarket** 벼룩 시장 pyŏ·ruk shi·jang

**flight** 비행 pi·haeng

**flood** n 홍수 hong·su

**floor** n 바닥 pa·dak

**floor (storey)** 층 ch'ŭng

**florist** 꽃집 ggot·chip

**flour** 밀가루 milk·ka·ru

**flower** n 꽃 ggot

**flu** 독감 tok·kam

**fly** n 파리 p'a·ri

**fly** v 날아요 (날~) na·ra·yo (nal~)

**foggy** 안개 낀 an·gaek·kin

**folk music** 민속 음악 min·sok ŭ·mak

**folk village** 민속촌 min·sok·ch'on

**follow** 따라가요 (따라가~) dda·ra·ga·yo (dda·ra·ga~)

**food** 음식 ŭm·shik

**food court** 푸드 코트 p'u·dŭ k'o·t'ŭ

**food poisoning** 식중독 shik·chung·dok

**food shop** 슈퍼 shu·p'ŏ

**foot (body)** 발 pal

**football (soccer)** 축구 ch'uk·ku

**footpath** 보도 po·do

**foreign** 외국의 oé·gu·gé

**foreigner** 외국인 oé·gu·gin

**forest** 숲 sup

**forever** 영원히 yŏng·wŏn·hi

**forget** 잊어요 (잊~) i·jŏ·yo (ij~)

**forgive** 용서해요 (용서하~) yong·sŏ·hae·yo (yong·sŏ·ha~)

**fork** 포크 p'o·k'ŭ

**fortnight** 이 주일 i·ju·il

**fortress** 요새 yo·sae

**fortune-teller** 점쟁이 chŏm·jaeng·i

**fortune-telling** 점 chŏm

**foul (soccer)** n 파울 p'a·ul

**fountain** 분수 pun·su

**foyer** 휴게실 hyu·ge·shil

**fragile** 깨지기 쉬운 ggae·ji·gi shi·un

**France** 프랑스 p'ŭ·rang·sŭ

**free (available)** a 한가한 han·ga·han

**free (gratis)** a 공짜의 kong·tcha·é
**free (not bound)** a 자유로운 cha·yu·ro·un
**freeze** 얼려요 (얼려~) ŏl·lyŏ·yo (ŏl·li~)
**fresh** 신선한 shin·sŏn·han
**fridge** 냉장고 naeng·jang·go
**fried** 튀긴 t'wi·gin
**friend** 친구 ch'in·gu
**from ...** ...에서 ...e·sŏ
**frost** 서리 sŏ·ri
**frozen food** 냉동 식품 naeng·dong shik·p'um
**fruit** 과일 kwa·il
**fruit juice** 과일 주스 kwa·il jus·sŭ
**fry** 튀겨요 (튀기~) t'wi·gyŏ·yo (t'wi·gi~)
**frying pan** 프라이팬 p'ŭ·ra·i·p'aen
**full** 가득 찬 ka·dŭk·ch'an
**full-time** 전 시간의 chŏn·shi·ga·né
**fun** a 재미있는 chae·mi·in·nŭn
**funeral** 장례식 chang·nye·shik
**funny** 우스운 u·sŭ·un
**furniture** 가구 ka·gu
**future** n 미래 mi·rae

**G**

**game (sport)** 경기 kyŏng·gi
**garage** 차고 ch'a·go
**garbage** 쓰레기 ssŭ·re·gi
**garbage can** 쓰레기통 ssŭ·re·gi·t'ong
**garden** n 정원 chŏng·wŏn
**gardener** 정원사 chŏng·wŏn·sa
**gardening** 정원 가꾸기 chŏng·wŏn kak·ku·gi
**garlic** 마늘 ma·nŭl
**gas (for cooking)** 가스 ka·sŭ
**gas (petrol)** 휘발유 hwi·bal·yu
**gas cartridge** 부탄 가스통 bu·t'an·ga·sŭ·t'ong
**gastroenteritis** 위장염 wi·jang·nyŏm
**gate (airport, etc)** 문 mun
**gauze** 거즈 kŏ·jŭ
**gay (homosexual)** n 동성애자 tong·sŏng·ae·ja
**gearbox** 변속장치 pyŏn·sok chang·ch'i
**Germany** 독일 to·gil

**get** 얻어요 (얻~) ŏ·dŏ·yo (ŏd~)
**get off (bus, train)** 내려요 (내리~) nae·ryŏ·yo (nae·ri~)
**gift** 선물 sŏn·mul
**gig** 공연장 kyong·yŏn·jang
**ginger** 생강 saeng·gang
**gingko nut** 은행 ŭn·haeng
**ginseng** 인삼 in·sam
**girl** 여자 아이 yŏ·ja·a·i
**girlfriend** 여자 친구 yŏ·ja ch'in·gu
**give** 줘요 (주~) chwŏ·yo (chu~)
**given name** 이름 i·rŭm
**glandular fever** 선열 sŏ·nyŏl
**glass (drinking)** 잔 chan
**glasses (spectacles)** 안경 an·gyŏng
**gloves (clothing)** 장갑 chang·gap
**gloves (latex)** 고무 장갑 ko·mu jang·gap
**glue** n 풀 p'ul
**go** 가요 (가~) ka·yo (ka~)
**goal (sport)** 골 kol
**goalkeeper** 골키퍼 kol·k'i·pŏ
**goat** 염소 yŏm·so
**god (general)** 신 shin
**goggles (skiing)** 스키 고글 sŭ·k'i·go·gŭl
**goggles (swimming)** 물안경 mu·ran·gyŏng
**gold** n 금 kŭm
**golf** 골프 kol·p'ŭ
**golf ball** 골프공 kol·p'ŭ·gong
**golf course** 골프장 kol·p'ŭ·jang
**good** 좋은 cho·ŭn
**go out** 나가요 (나가~) na·ga·yo (na·ga~)
**gorge** 골짜기 kol·tcha·gi
**go shopping** 쇼핑해요 (쇼핑하~) sho·p'ing·hae·yo (sho·p'ing·ha~)
**government** 정부 chŏng·bu
**gram** 그램 kŭ·raem
**granddaughter** 손녀 son·nyŏ
**grandfather** 할아버지 ha·ra·bŏ·ji
**grandmother** 할머니 hal·mŏ·ni
**grandson** 손자 son·ja
**grass (lawn)** 잔디 chan·di
**grateful** 감사해요 (감사하~) kam·sa·hae·yo (kam·sa·ha~)

grave n 무덤 mu·döm
great (fantastic) 좋은 cho·ün
green 초록색 ch'o·rok·saek
greengrocer 청과상 chöng·gwa·sang
grey 회색의 hoe·sae·gë
grilled 구운 ku·un
grocery 슈퍼 shu·p'ö
grow 자라요 (자라~) cha·ra·yo
(cha·ra~)
guarantee n 보증 po·jüng
guess v 추측해요 (추측하~)
ch'u·chü·k'ae·yo (ch'u·chü·k'a~)
guesthouse 민박집 min·bak·chip
guide (audio) 음성 안내 üm·söng
an·nae
guide (person) 가이드 ka·i·dü
guidebook 가이드 책자 ka·i·dü
ch'aek·cha
guide dog 맹인 안내견 maeng·in
an·nae·gyön
guided tour 가이드 투어 ka·i·dü t'u·ö
guilt 유죄 yu·joé
guitar 기타 ki·t'a
gum (chewing) 껌 ggöm
gum (of mouth) 잇몸 in·mom
gun 총 ch'ong
gym (gymnasium) 체육관
ch'e·yuk·kwan
gym (health club) 헬스장 hel·sü·jang
gymnastics 체조 ch'e·jo
gynaecologist 산부인과
san·bu·ink·kwa

## H

hair 머리 mö·ri
hairbrush 빗 pit
haircut 헤어 커트 he·ö·k'ö·t'ü
hairdressing salon 미용실
mi·yong·shil
halal a 할랄 hal·lal
half n 반 ban
hallucination 환각 hwan·gak
ham 햄 haem
hamburger 햄버거 haem·bö·gö
hammer n 망치 mang·ch'i
hammock 그물 침대 kü·mul ch'im·dae
hand 손 son

handbag 핸드백 haen·dü·baek
handball 핸드볼 haen·dü·bol
handicraft 수공예품 su·gong·ye·p'um
handkerchief 손수건 con·cu·gön
handlebars 핸들 haen·dül
handmade 수제 su·jé
handsome 잘생긴 chal·saeng·gin
happy 행복한 haeng·bo·k'an
harassment 희롱 hi·rong
harbour n 항구 hang·gu
hard (difficult) 어려운 ö·ryö·un
hard (not soft) 단단한 tan·dan·han
hardware store 철물점
ch'öl·mul·chöm
hat 모자 mo·ja
have 가져요 (갖~) ka·jö·yo (kaj~)
have a cold 감기 걸렸어요
(감기 걸리~) kam·gi köl·lyöss·ö·yo
(kam·gi köl·li~)
have fun 즐거워요 (즐겁~)
chül·gö·wö·yo (chül·göp~)
hay fever 건초열 kön·ch'o·yöl
hazelnut 헤이즐넛 he·i·jül·löt
he inf 그 kü
he pol 그분 kü·bun
head 머리 mö·ri
headache 두통 tu·t'ong
headlights 헤드라이트 he·dü·ra·i·t'ü
health 건강 kön·gang
hear 들어요 (듣~) tü·rö·yo (tüt~)
hearing aid 보청기 po·ch'öng·gi
heart 심장 shim·jang
heart attack 심장 마비 shim·jang
ma·bi
heart condition 심장 상태 shim·jang
sang·t'ae
heat n 열 yöl
heated 데운 te·un
heater 히터 hi·t'ö
heating 난방 nan·bang
heavy (weight) 무거운 mu·gö·un
helmet 헬멧 hel·met
help n 도움 to·um
help v 도와줘요 (도와주~)
to·wa·jwö·yo (to·wa·ju~)
hepatitis 간염 ka·nyöm
her (possessive) 그녀의 kü·nyö·é

**herb** 허브 hŏ·bŭ
**here** 여기 yŏ·gi
**hermitage** 암자 am·ja
**herring** 청어 ch'ŏng·ŏ
**high (height)** 높은 no·p'ŭn
**highchair** 어린이용 높은 의자 ŏ·ri·ni·yong no·p'ŭn ŭi·ja
**high school** 고등학교 ko·dŭng·hak·kyo
**high tide** 만조 man·jo
**highway** 고속도로 ko·sok·to·ro
**hike** v 등산해요 (등산하~) tŭng·san·hae·yo (tŭng·san·ha~)
**hiking** 등산 tŭng·san
**hiking boots** 등산화 tŭng·san·hwa
**hiking route** 등산로 tŭng·san·no
**hill** 언덕 ŏn·dŏk
**hire** v 고용해요 (고용하~) ko·yong·hae·yo (ko·yong·ha~)
**his** 그의 kŭ·ŭi
**historical** 역사상의 yŏk·sa·sang·é
**history** 역사 yŏk·sa
**HIV** 에이즈 바이러스 e·i·jŭ ba·i·rŏ·sŭ
**hockey** 하키 ha·k'i
**holiday** n 휴일 hyu·il
**home** 집 chip
**homeless people** 노숙자 no·suk·cha
**homemaker** 가정 주부 ka·jŏng·ju·bu
**homesick** 고향이 그리운 ko·hyang·i gŭ·ri·un
**homosexual** n 동성애자 tong·sŏng·ae·ja
**honey** 꿀 ggul
**honeymoon** 신혼 여행 shin·hon yŏ·haeng
**horoscope** 별자리 점 pyŏl·cha·ri·jŏm
**horse** 말 mal
**horse racing** 경마 kyŏng·ma
**horse riding** 승마 sŭng·ma
**hospital** 병원 pyŏng·won
**hospitality** 환대 hwan·dae
**hostel** 호스텔 ho·sŭ·t'el
**hot (to the touch)** 뜨거운 ddŭ·gŏ·un
**hot (weather)** 더운 tŏ·un
**hot dog** 핫도그 hat·to·gŭ
**hotel** 호텔 ho·t'el
**hot spring** 온천 on·ch'ŏn
**hot water** 온수 on·su

**hot water bottle** 보온병 po·on·byŏng
**hour** 시간 shi·gan
**house** n 집 chip
**housework** 집안일 chi·ban·nil
**how** 어떻게 ŏt·tŏ·k'e
**how many** 몇 개 myŏk·kae
**hug** n 포옹 p'o·ong
**huge** 거대한 kŏ·dae·han
**human rights** 인권 ink·kwŏn
**hungry** 배고픈 pae·go·p'ŭn
**hunting** 사냥 sa·nyang
**hurt** v 아파요 (아프~) a·p'a·yo (a·p'ŭ~)
**husband** 남편 nam·p'yŏn

**I**

**I** inf/pol 나/ 저 na/chŏ
**ice** 얼음 ŏ·rŭm
**ice axe** 아이스바일 a·i·sŭ·ba·il
**ice cream** 아이스크림 a·i·sŭ·k'ŭ·rim
**identification** 신원 확인 shin·wŏn hwa·gin
**identification card (ID)** 신분증 shin·bun·tchŭng
**idiot** n 바보 pa·bo
**if** 만약 ma·nyak
**ill** 아픈 a·p'ŭn
**immigration** 출입국 ch'u·rip·kuk
**important** 중요한 chung·yo·han
**impossible** 불가능한 pul·ga·nŭng·han
**in ...** ... 안에 ... a·né
**(be) in a hurry** v 급해요 (급하~) kŭ·p'ae·yo (kŭ·p'a~)
**included** 포함된 p'o·ham·doen
**income tax** 소득세 so·dŭk·sé
**independence** 독립 tong·nip
**India** 인도 in·do
**indicator** 깜빡이 ggamp·pa·gi
**indigestion** 소화불량 so·hwa·bul·lyang
**indoor** a 실내의 shil·lae·é
**industry** 산업 sa·nŏp
**infection** 감염 ka·myŏm
**inflammation** 염증 yŏm·tchŭng
**influenza** 독감 tok·kam
**information** 안내 an·nae
**in front of ...** ... 앞에 ... a·p'é
**ingredient** 재료 chae·ryo

**inhaler (for asthma)** (천식환자용) 흡입기 (chŏn·shik hwan·ja·yong) hŭ·bip·ki

**inject** 주사해요 (주사히 ) chu·sa·hae·yo (chu·sa·ha~)

**injection** 주사 chu·sa

**injured** 다친 ta·ch'in

**injury** 부상 pu·sang

**inner tube** 튜브 t'yu·bŭ

**innocent** a 순진한 sun·jin·han

**insect** 벌레 pŏl·lé

**insect repellent** 방충제 pang·ch'ung·jé

**inside** adv 안에 a·né

**instructor** 강사 kang·sa

**insurance** 보험 po·hŏm

**interesting** 흥미로운 hŭng·mi·ro·un

**intermission** 휴식 시간 hyu·shik shi·gan

**international** 국제적인 kuk·che·jŏ·gin

**internet** 인터넷 in·t'ŏ·net

**internet cafe** PC방 p'i·shi·bang

**interpreter** 통역사 t'ong·yŏk·sa

**interview** n 면접 myŏn·jŏp

**invite** 초대해요 (초대하~) ch'o·dae·hae·yo (ch'o·dae·ha~)

**Ireland** 아일랜드 a·il·laen·dŭ

**iron (for clothes)** n 다리미질 ta·ri·mi·jil

**island** 섬 sŏm

**Israel** 이스라엘 i·sŭ·ra·el

**it** 그것 kŭ·gŏt

**Italy** 이탈리아 i·t'al·li·a

**itchy** 가려운 ka·ryŏ·un

**itinerary** 여행 일정 yŏ·haeng il·chŏng

**IUD** 자궁내 피임장치 cha·gung·nae p'i·im·jang·ch'i

## J

**jacket** 재킷 chae·k'it

**jail** n 교도소 kyo·do·so

**jam** n 짬 chaem

**Japan** 일본 il·bon

**jar** 항아리 hang·a·ri

**jaw** 턱 t'ŏk

**jealous** 질투하는 chil·t'u·ha·nŭn

**jeans** 청바지 ch'ŏng·ba·ji

**jeep** 지프차 chi·p'ŭ·ch'a

**jet lag** 시차증 shi·ch'a·jŭng

**jewellery** 보석 po·sŏk

**job** n 일 il

**joke** n 농담 nong·dam

**journalist** 기자 ki·ja

**journey** n 여행 yŏ·haeng

**judge** n 판사 p'an·sa

**juice** n 주스 jus·sŭ

**jump** v 뛰어올라요 (뛰어오르~) ddwi·ŏ·ol·la·yo (ddwi·ŏ·o·rŭ~)

**jumper (sweater)** 스웨터 sŭ·we·t'ŏ

## K

**karaoke** 노래방 no·rae·bang

**ketchup** 케첩 k'e·ch'ŏp

**key (door, etc)** 열쇠 yŏl·soé

**keyboard** 키보드 k'i·bo·dŭ

**kick** v 차요 (차~) ch'a·yo (ch'a~)

**kidney** 신장 shin·jang

**kill** 죽여요 (죽이~) chu·gyŏ·yo (chu·gi~)

**kilogram** 킬로그램 k'il·lo·gŭ·raem

**kilometre** 킬로미터 k'il·lo·mi·t'ŏ

**kind (nice)** 친절한 ch'in·jŏl·han

**kindergarten** 유치원 yu·ch'i·wŏn

**king** 왕 wang

**kiosk** 신문 가판대 shin·mun ga·p'an·dae

**kiss** n 키스 k'i·sŭ

**kiss** v 키스해요 (키스하~) k'i·sŭ·hae·yo (k'i·sŭ·ha~)

**kitchen** 주방 chu·bang

**knee** 무릎 mu·rŭp

**knife** n 칼 k'al

**know** 알아요 (알~) a·ra·yo (al~)

**Korea** 한국 han·guk

**Korean** a 한국의 han·gu·gé

**Korean (language)** n 한국어 han·gu·gŏ

## L

**labourer** 노동자 no·dong·ja

**lace (fabric)** n 레이스 re·i·sŭ

**lacquerware** 칠기 ch'il·gi

**lake** 호수 ho·su

**lamb (meat)** 양고기 yang·go·gi
**land** n 땅 ddang
**landlord** 집주인 chip·chu·in
**language** 언어 ŏ·nŏ
**laptop** 노트북 no·t'ŭ·buk
**large** 거대한 kŏ·dae·han
**last (final)** 마지막 ma·ji·mak
**last (previous)** 지난 chi·nan
**late** adv 늦게 nŭk·ke
**later** 다음에 ta·ŭ·me
**laugh** v 웃어요 (웃~) u·sŏ·yo (us~)
**launderette** 빨래방 bbal·lae·bang
**laundry (clothes)** 빨래 bbal·lae
**laundry (room)** 세탁실 se·t'ak·shil
**law (legislation)** 법 pŏp
**law (profession/study)** 법학 pŏ·p'ak
**lawyer** 변호사 pyŏn·ho·sa
**laxative** 배변촉진제 pae·byŏn·ch'ok·chin·je
**lazy** 게으른 ke·ŭ·rŭn
**leader** 지도자 chi·do·ja
**leaf** n 잎 ip
**learn** 배워요 (배우~) pae·wŏ·yo (pae·u~)
**leather** n 가죽 ka·juk
**lecturer** 강사 kang·sa
**ledge** 선반 sŏn·ban
**leeks** 파 p'a
**left (direction)** 왼쪽 oён·tchok
**left luggage** 분실 수하물 pun·shil su·ha·mul
**left-luggage office** 분실 수하물 보관소 pun·shil su·ha·mul po·gwan·so
**left-wing** 좌익 chwa·ik
**leg (body)** 다리 ta·ri
**legal** 합법의 hap·pŏ·bé
**legislation** 법률 제정 pŏm·nyul che·jŏng
**legume** 콩류 k'ong·nyu
**lemon** 레몬 re·mon
**lemonade** 레모네이드 re·mo·ne·i·dŭ
**lens (camera)** 렌즈 ren·jŭ
**lentil** 렌즈콩 ren·jŭ·k'ong
**lesbian** 레즈비언 re·jŭ·bi·ŏn
**less** 보다 적은 po·da chŏ·gŭn
**letter (mail)** 편지 p'yŏn·ji
**lettuce** 양상추 yang·sang·ch'u

**liar** 거짓말쟁이 kŏ·jin·mal·chaeng·i
**library** 도서관 to·sŏ·gwan
**lice** 이 i
**licence** n 면허 myŏn·hŏ
**license plate number** 자동차번호 cha·dong·ch'a·bŏn·ho
**lie (not stand)** 누워요 (눕~) nu·wŏ·yo (nup~)
**lie (not tell the truth)** v 거짓말해요 (거짓말하~) kŏ·jin·mal·hae·yo (kŏ·jin·mal·ha~)
**life** 인생 in·saeng
**life jacket** 구명 조끼 ku·myŏng·jok·ki
**lifeboat** 구명선 ku·myŏng·sŏn
**lift (elevator)** 엘리베이터 el·li·be·i·t'ŏ
**light (brightness)** n 빛 pit
**light (colour)** 밝은 pal·gŭn
**light (weight)** 가벼운 ka·byŏ·un
**light bulb** 전구 chŏn·gu
**lighthouse** 등대 tŭng·dae
**lighter (cigarette)** 라이터 ra·i·t'ŏ
**light meter** 조명 측정기 cho·myŏng ch'ŭk·jŏng·gi
**like** v 좋아해요 (좋아하~) cho·a·hae·yo (cho·a·ha~)
**lime** 라임 ra·im
**linen (material)** 리넨 ri·nen
**linen (sheets)** 리넨천 ri·nen·ch'ŏn
**linguist** 언어학자 ŏ·nŏ·hak·cha
**lip balm** 립밤 rip·pam
**lips** 입술 ip·sul
**lipstick** 립스틱 rip·sŭ·t'ik
**liquor store** 주류 판매점 chu·ryu p'an·mae·jŏm
**listen** 들어요 (듣~) tŭ·rŏ·yo (tŭt~)
**little (quantity)** n 조금 cho·gŭm
**little (size)** a 작은 cha·gŭn
**live** v 살아요 (살~) sa·ra·yo (sal~)
**liver** 간 kan
**lizard** 도마뱀 to·ma·baem
**local** a 지방의 chi·bang·é
**location** 위치 wi·ch'i
**lock** n 자물쇠 cha·mul·soé
**lock** v 잠궈요 (잠그~) cham·gwŏ·yo (cham·gŭ~)
**locked** 잠긴 cham·gin
**lollies** 막대 사탕 mak·tae sa·t'ang

long 긴 kin
look v 봐요 (보~) pwa·yo (po~)
look after 돌봐요 (돌보~) tol·bwa·yo (tol·bo~)
look for 찾아요 (찾~) ch'a·ja yo (ch'aj~)
lookout 전망대 chŏn·mang·dae
loose change 푼돈 p'un·don
lose 잃어버렸어요 (잃어버리~) i·rŏ·bŏ·ryŏss·ŏ·yo (i·rŏ·bŏ·ri~)
lost 잃어버린 i·rŏ·bŏ·rin
lost-property office 분실물 센터 pun·shil·mul sen·t'ŏ
loud 소리가 큰 so·ri·ga k'ŭn
love n 사랑 sa·rang
love v 사랑해요 (사랑하~) sa·rang·hae yo (sa·rang·ha~)
lover 애인 ae·in
low 낮은 na·jŭn
low tide 간조 kan·jo
lubricant 윤활제 yun·hwal·che
luck 행운 haeng·un
lucky 운 좋은 un cho·ŭn
luggage 짐/수하물 chim/su·ha·mul
luggage locker 짐 보관함 chim po·gwan·ham
luggage tag 수하물 꼬리표 su·ha·mul kko·ri·p'yo
lump 혹 hok
Lunar New Year 설날 sŏl·lal
lunch 점심 chŏm·shim
lung 폐 p'ye
luxury 사치 sa·ch'i

# M

machine 기계 ki·gyé
magazine 잡지 chap·chi
mail (letters) n 편지 p'yŏn·ji
mail (postal system) n 우편 u·p'yŏn
mail v 부쳐요 (부치~) pu·ch'ŏ·yo (pu·ch'i~)
mailbox 우체통 u·ch'e·t'ong
main a 주된 chu·doén
main road 주요 도로 chu·yo·do·ro
make 만들어요 (만들~) nan·dŭ·rŏ·yo (man·dŭl~)
make-up n 화장 hwa·jang

mall (shopping) 쇼핑몰 sho·p'ing·mol
mammography 유방조영술 yu·bang·jo·yŏng·sul
man n 남자 nam·ja
manager 매니저 mae·ni·jŏ
mandarin 귤 kyul
mango 망고 mang·go
manual worker 육체 노동자 yuk·ch'é no·dong·ja
many 많은 ma·nŭn
map (of country) 지도 chi·do
map (of neighbourhood) 약도 yak·to
margarine 마가린 ma·ga·rin
marital status 결혼 상태 kyŏl·hon sang·t'ae
market (indoor) n 대형 할인점 tae·hyŏng ha·rin·jŏm
market (outdoor) n 시장 shi·jang
marriage 결혼 kyŏl·hon
married 결혼한 kyŏl·hon·han
marry 결혼해요 (결혼하~) kyŏl·hon·hae·yo (kyŏl·hon·ha~)
martial arts 무술 mu·sul
mask n 탈 t'al
massage n 안마 an·ma
masseur/masseuse 안마사 an·ma·sa
mat (sleeping) 요 yo
match (sport) 경기 kyŏng·gi
matches (for lighting) 성냥 sŏng·nyang
mattress 매트리스 mae·t'ŭ·ri·sŭ
maybe 아마 a·ma
mayonnaise 마요네즈 ma·yo·ne·jŭ
mayor 시장 shi·jang
meal 식사 shik·sa
measles 홍역 hong·yŏk
meat 고기 ko·gi
mechanic n 정비사 chŏng·bi·sa
media 미디어 mi·di·ŏ
medicine (medication) 약 yak
medicine (profession/study) 의학 ŭi·hak
meditation 명상 myŏng·sang
meet 만나요 (만나~) man·na·yo (man·na~)
melon 멜론 mel·lon
member 회원 hoé·wŏn

**M**

memorial n 기념물 ki·nyŏm·mul
memory card/stick 메모리 카드/스틱 me·mo·ri k'a·dŭ/sŭ·t'ik
menstruation 생리 saeng·ni
menu 메뉴 me·nyu
message 메시지 me·shi·ji
metal 금속 kŭm·sok
metre 미터 mi·t'ŏ
metro (train) 지하철 chi·ha·ch'ŏl
metro station 지하철역 chi·ha·ch'ŏl·yŏk
microwave oven 전자레인지 chŏn·ja·re·in·ji
midday 정오 chŏng·o
midnight 자정 cha·jŏng
migraine 편두통 p'yŏn·du·t'ong
military n 군대 kun·dae
military police 헌병 hŏn·byŏng
military service 군복무 kun·bong·mu
milk 우유 u·yu
millimetre 밀리미터 mil·li·mi·t'ŏ
mind n 마음 ma·ŭm
mineral water 생수 saeng·su
minute n 분 pun
mirror n 거울 kŏ·ul
miscarriage 유산 yu·san
miss (feel absence of) 그리워해요 (그리워해~) kŭ·ri·wŏ·hae·yo (kŭ·ri·wŏ·ha~)
miss (not catch train, etc) 놓쳐요 (놓치~) no·ch'ŏ·yo (no·ch'i~)
mistake n 실수 shil·su
mix v 섞어요 (섞~) sŏk·kŏ·yo (sŏkk~)
mobile phone 휴대폰 hyu·dae·p'on
modem 모뎀 mo·dem
modern 현대의 hyŏn·dae·é
moisturiser 보습제 po·sŭp·ché
monarchy 군주제 kun·ju·jé
monastery 수도원 su·do·wŏn
money 돈 ton
Mongolia 몽고 mong·go
monk (Buddhist) 스님 sŭ·nim
monk (Catholic) 수사 su·sa
monkey 원숭이 wŏn·sung·i
monsoon 장마 chang·ma
month 달 tal
monument 기념비 ki·nyŏm·bi

moon 달 tal
more 더 많은 tŏ·ma·nŭn
morning 아침 a·ch'im
morning sickness 입덧 ip·tŏt
mosque 이슬람 사원 i·sŭl·lam·sa·wŏn
mosquito 모기 mo·gi
mosquito coil 모기향 mo·gi·hyang
mosquito net 모기장 mo·gi·jang
motel 모텔/여관 mo·t'el/yŏ·gwan
mother 어머니 ŏ·mŏ·ni
mother-in-law (husband's mother) 시어머니 shi·ŏ·mŏ·ni
mother-in-law (wife's mother) 장모님 chang·mo·nim
motorbike 모터사이클 mo·t'ŏ·sa·i·k'ŭl
motorboat 모터보트 mo·t'ŏ·bo·t'ŭ
motorway (tollway) 고속도로 ko·sok·to·ro
mountain 산 san
mountain bike 산악 자전거 sa·nak cha·jŏn·gŏ
mountaineering 등산 tŭng·san
mountain pass 산길 san·gil
mountain path 등산로 tŭng·san·no
mountain range 산맥 san·maek
mouse 쥐 chwi
mouth 입 ip
movie 영화 yŏng·hwa
mud 진흙 chin·hŭk
mum 엄마 ŏm·ma
mumps 이하선염 i·ha·sŏ·nyŏm
mural 벽화 pyŏ·k'wa
murder n 살인 sa·rin
murder v 살인해요 (살인하~) sa·rin·hae·yo (sa·rin·ha~)
muscle 근육 kŭ·nyuk
museum (art) 미술관 mi·sul·gwan
museum (other) 박물관 pang·mul·gwan
mushroom 버섯 pŏ·sŏt
music 음악 ŭ·mak
musician 음악가 ŭ·mak·ka
music shop 음반 매장 ŭm·ban mae·jang
mussel 홍합 hong·hap

**mute** a 무언의 mu·ŏn·é
**mutton** 양고기 yang·go·gi
**my** inf/pol 나의/저의 na·é/chŏ·é

## N

**nail clippers** 손톱깎이 son·top kkak·ki
**(first) name** n inf 이름 i·rŭm
**(full) name** n pol 성명 sŏng·myŏng
**napkin** 냅킨 naep·k'in
**nappy** 기저귀 ki·jŏ·gwi
**nappy rash** 기저귀 발진 ki·jŏ·gwi bal·chin
**nationality (citizenship)** 국적 kuk·chŏk
**nationality (ethnicity)** 민족 min·jok
**national park** 국립 공원 kung·nip·kong·won
**nature** 자연 cha·yŏn
**nature reserve** 자연 보호 지역 cha·yŏn bo·ho ji·yŏk
**nausea** 메스꺼움 me·sŭk·kŏ·um
**near ...** prep ... 가까이 ... kak·ka·i
**nearest** 제일 가까운 che·il kak·ka·un
**necessary** 필요한 p'i·ryo·han
**neck** 목 mok
**necklace** 목걸이 mok·kŏ·ri
**nectarine** 천도 복숭아 ch'ŏn·do pok·sung·a
**need** v 필요해요 (필요하~) p'i·ryo·hae·yo (p'i·ryo·ha~)
**needle (sewing)** 바늘 pa·nŭl
**needle (syringe)** 주사바늘 chu·sa·ba·nŭl
**negative** a 부정적인 pu·jŏng·jŏ·gin
**negatives (photos)** 네거티브 ne·gŏ·t'i·bŭ
**neighbourhood** 동네 tong·né
**neither** adv 어느 것도 아닌 ŏ·nŭ·gŏt·to a·nin
**net** 그물 kŭ·mul
**Netherlands** 네덜란드 ne·dŏl·lan·dŭ
**network (phone)** 통신사 t'ong·shin·sa
**new** 새로운 sae·ro·un
**news** 뉴스 nyu·sŭ
**newsagency** 통신사 t'ong·shin·sa
**newspaper** 신문 shin·mun

**newsstand** 신문가판대 shin·mun·ga·p'an·dae
**New Zealand** 뉴질랜드 nyu·jil·laen·dŭ
**next (following)** 다음 ta·ŭm
**next to ...** ... 다음에 ... da·ŭ·mé
**nice** 좋은 cho·ŭn
**nickname** 별명 pyŏl·myŏng
**night** 밤 pam
**no** 아니요 a·ni·yo
**noisy** 시끄러운 shik·kŭ·rŏ·un
**nonsmoking area** 금연 구역 kŭ·myŏn gu·yŏk
**noodles** 국수 kuk·su
**noon** 정오 chŏng·o
**north** n 북쪽 puk·tchok
**North Korea** 북한 pu·k'an
**nose** 코 k'o
**not** 안 an
**notebook** 공책 kong·ch'aek
**now** 지금 chi·gŭm
**nuclear energy** 핵 에너지 hae·ge·nŏ·ji
**nuclear testing** 핵 실험 haek·shil·hŏm
**nuclear waste** 핵 폐기물 haek·p'ye·gi·mul
**number** n 숫자 sut·cha
**numberplate** 번호판 bŏn ho p'an
**nun (Buddhist)** 여승 yŏ·sŭng
**nun (Catholic)** 수녀 su·nyŏ
**nurse** n 간호사 kan·ho·sa
**nut (food)** 견과류 kyŏn·gwa·ryu

## O

**oats** 귀리 kwi·ri
**ocean** 바다 pa·da
**octopus** 낙지 nak·chi
**off (power)** 꺼짐 ggŏ·jim
**off (spoilt)** 상한 sang·han
**offence** 위반 wi·ban
**office** 사무실 sa·mu·shil
**office worker** 회사원 hoé·sa·wŏn
**often** 자주 cha·ju
**oil (cooking)** 기름 ki·rŭm
**oil (petrol)** 휘발유 hwi·bal·yu
**old (people)** 늙은 nŭl·gŭn
**old (things)** 오래된 o·rae·doén
**olive** 올리브 ol·li·bŭ
**olive oil** 올리브유 ol·li·bŭ·yu

**P**

**on** prep 위에 wi·é
**on (power)** 켜짐 k'yŏ·jim
**once** 한 번 han·bŏn
**one-way (road)** 일방통행 il·bang
t'ong·haeng
**one-way ticket** 편도 표 p'yŏn·do p'yo
**onion** 양파 yang·p'a
**only ...** ...만 ...man
**on time** 정각에 chŏng·ga·gé
**open (shop)** a 영업 중 yŏng·ŏp·chung
**open** v 열어요 (열~) yŏ·rŏ·yo (yŏl~)
**opening hours** 영업 시간 yŏng·ŏp
shi·gan
**opera house** 오페라 극장 o·p'e·ra
gŭk·chang
**operation (medical)** 수술 su·sul
**operator (telephone)** 교환원
kyo·hwan·wŏn
**opinion** 의견 ŭi·gyŏn
**opposite** prep 반대편에
pan·dae·p'yŏ·né
**optometrist** 안경사 an·gyŏng·sa
**or** 아니면 a·ni·myŏn
**orange (fruit)** n 오렌지 o·ren·ji
**orange (colour)** a 주황색
chu·hwang·saek
**orchestra** 오케스트라 o·k'e·sŭ·t'ŭ·ra
**order** n 주문 chu·mun
**order** v 주문해요 (주문하~)
chu·mun·hae·yo (chu·mun·ha~)
**ordinary** 보통 po·t'ong
**organic food** 유기농 식품 yu·gi·nong
shik·p'um
**original** a 진짜의 chin·tcha·é
**other** 다른 ta·rŭn
**our** 우리의 u·ri·é
**outdoor** a 실외 shi·loé
**out of order** 고장 난 ko·jang·nan
**outside** adv 밖에서 pak·ke·sŏ
**ovarian cyst** 난소 낭종 nan·so
nan·jong
**ovary** 난소 nan·so
**oven** 오븐 o·bŭn
**overcoat** 외투 oé·t'u
**overdose** n 과량 투여 kwa·ryang t'u·yŏ
**overnight** adv 밤새 pam·sae
**overseas** n 해외 hae·oé

**owe** 빚져요 (빚지~) pit·chŏ·yo
(pit·chi~)
**owner** 주인 chu·in
**ox** 황소 hwang·so
**oxygen** 산소 san·so
**oyster** 굴 kul

**P**

**pacemaker** 심장 박동 조절 장치
shim·jang bak·tong cho·jŏl chang·ch'i
**pacifier (dummy)** 노리개 젖꼭지
no·ri·gae chŏk·kok·chi
**package** n 소포 so·p'o
**packet (general)** 꾸러미 ggu·rŏ·mi
**padlock** 자물쇠 cha·mul·soé
**page** n 페이지 p'e·i·ji
**pagoda** 탑 t'ap
**pain** n 고통 ko·t'ong
**painful** 괴로운 koé·ro·un
**painkiller** 진통제 chin·t'ong·jé
**painter (artist)** 화가 hwa·ga
**painting (a work)** 그림 그리기
kŭ·rim kŭ·ri·gi
**painting (the art)** 회화 hoé·hwa
**pair (couple)** n 한 쌍 han·ssang
**palace** 궁전 kung·jŏn
**pan** 프라이팬 p'ŭ·ra·i·p'aen
**pants (trousers)** 바지 pa·ji
**pantyhose** 팬티스타킹
p'aen·t'i·sŭ·t'a·k'ing
**panty liners** 팬티라이너
p'aen·t'i·ra·i·nŏ
**paper** n 종이 chong·i
**paper lanterns** 연등 yŏn·dŭng
**papers (documents)** 서류 sŏ·ryu
**paperwork** 문서 업무 mun·sŏ ŏm·mu
**pap smear** 자궁암 세포 검사
cha·gung·am se·p'o gŏm·sa
**paraplegic** n 하반신 마비 환자
ha·ban·shin ma·bi hwan·ja
**parcel** n 소포 so·p'o
**parents** 부모님 pu·mo·nim
**park** n 공원 kong·wŏn
**park (a car)** v 주차해요 (주차하~)
chu·ch'a·hae·yo (chu·ch'a·ha~)
**parking structure** 주차 빌딩
chu·ch'a bil·ding
**parliament** 국회 ku·k'oé

**part (component)** n 부분 pu·bun

**part-time** 시간제의 shi·gan·je·é

**party (politics)** 정당 chŏng·dang

**pass (go by)** 지나가요 (지나가~) chi·na·ga·yo (chi·na·ga~)

**pass (kick/throw)** v 차요 (차~) ch'a·yo (ch'a~)

**passenger** 승객 sŭng·gaek

**passport** 여권 yŏk·kwŏn

**passport number** 여권번호 yŏk·kwŏn·bŏn·ho

**past** n 과거 kwa·gŏ

**path** 길 kil

**patient** n 환자 hwan·ja

**pay** v 돈 내요 (돈 내~) ton·nae·yo (ton·nae~)

**payment** 지불 chi·bul

**pea** 완두콩 wan·du·k'ong

**peace** 평화 p'yŏng·hwa

**peach** 복숭아 pok·sung·a

**peak (mountain)** 봉우리 pong·u·ri

**peanut** 땅콩 ddang·k'ong

**pear** 배 pae

**pedal** n 페달 p'e·dal

**pedestrian** n 보행자 po·haeng·ja

**pedestrian crossing** 건널목 kŏn·nŏl·mok

**pedestrian overpass** 육교 yuk·kyo

**pedestrian underpass** 지하도 chi·ha·do

**pen (ballpoint)** 볼펜 pol·p'en

**pencil** 연필 yŏn·p'il

**pensioner** 연금 생활자 yŏn·gŭm saeng·hwal·cha

**people** 사람들 sa·ram·dŭl

**per (day)** (하루)당 (ha·ru)·dang

**per cent** 퍼센트 p'ŏ·sen·t'ŭ

**perfect** a 완벽한 wan·byŏ·k'an

**performance** 공연 kong·yŏn

**perfume** 향수 hyang·su

**period pain** 생리통 saeng·ni·t'ong

**permission** 허가 hŏ·ga

**permit** n 허가증 hŏ·ga·tchŭng

**person** 사람 sa·ram

**personality** 성격 sŏng·gyŏk

**petrol** 휘발유 hwi·bal·yu

**petrol station** 주유소 chu·yu·so

**pharmacist** 약사 yak·sa

**pharmacy** 약국 yak·kuk

**phone book** 전화번호부 chŏn·hwa·bŏn·ho·bu

**phone box** 전화박스 chŏn·hwa·bak·sŭ

**phonecard** 전화카드 chŏn·hwa·k'a·dŭ

**photo** 사진 sa·jin

**photograph** v 사진 찍어요 (사진 찍~) sa·jin tchi·gŏ·yo (sa·jin tchig~)

**photographer** 사진작가 sa·jin·chak·ka

**photography** 사진술 sa·jin·sul

**phrasebook** 회화책 hoe·hwa·ch'aek

**piano** 피아노 p'i·a·no

**pickled** 절인 chŏ·rin

**pickles** 피클 p'i·k'ŭl

**picnic** n 소풍 so·p'ung

**pie** 파이 p'a·i

**piece** n 조각 cho·gak

**pig** 돼지 twae·ji

**pilgrimage** 성지 순례 sŏng·ji sul·lye

**(the) pill** 경구 피임약 kyŏng·gu p'i·im·nyak

**pill (medicine)** 알약 al·lyak

**pillow** 베개 pe·gae

**pillowcase** 베갯잇 pe·gaen·nit

**pineapple** 파인애플 p'a·i·nae·p'ŭl

**pink** 분홍색 pun·hong·saek

**pistachio** 피스타치오 p'i·sŭ·t'a·ch'i·o

**place** n 장소 chang·so

**place of birth** 출생지 ch'ul·saeng·ji

**plane** 비행기 pi·haeng·gi

**planet** 행성 haeng·sŏng

**plant** n 식물 shing·mul

**plastic** n 플라스틱 p'ŭl·la·sŭ·t'ik

**plate** 접시 chŏp·shi

**plateau** 고원 ko·wŏn

**platform** 승강장 sŭng·gang·jang

**play (theatre)** n 연극 yŏn·gŭk

**play (game)** 해요 (하~) hae·yo (ha~)

**play (instrument)** 연주해요 (연주하~) yŏn·ju·hae·yo (yŏn·ju·ha~)

**plug (bath)** n 마개 ma·gae

**plug (electricity)** n 플러그 p'ŭl·lŏ·gŭ

**plum** 자두 cha·du

**plumber** 배관공 pae·gwan·gong

**poaching (illegal hunting)** 밀렵 mil·lyŏp

242

**P**

**pocket** n 주머니 chu·mŏ·ni
**pocket knife** 주머닐칼 chu·mŏ·ni·k'al
**poetry** 시 shi
**point** v 가리켜요 (가리키~) ka·ri·k'yŏ·yo (ka·ri·k'i~)
**poisonous** 유독한 yu·do·k'an
**police** 경찰 kyŏng·ch'al
**police officer** 경찰관 kyŏng·ch'al·gwan
**police station** 경찰서 kyŏng·ch'al·sŏ
**policy** 정책 chŏng·ch'aek
**politician** 정치인 chŏng·ch'i·in
**politics** 정치 chŏng·ch'i
**pollen** 꽃가루 ggok·ka·ru
**pollution** 오염 o·yŏm
**pool (game)** 포켓볼 p'o·k'ep·pol
**pool (swimming)** 수영장 su·yŏng·jang
**poor (wealth)** 가난한 ka·nan·han
**popular** 인기 좋은 in·gi cho·ŭn
**pork** 돼지고기 twae·ji·go·gi
**port (river/sea)** 항구 hang·gu
**positive** a 긍정적인 kŭng·jŏng·jŏ·gin
**possible** 가능한 ka·nŭng·han
**post (letter)** v 편지 부쳐요 (편지 부치~) p'yŏn·ji bu·ch'ŏ·yo (p'yŏn·ji bu·ch'i~)
**postcard** 엽서 yŏp·sŏ
**postcode** 우편번호 u·p'yŏn·bŏn·ho
**poster** 포스터 p'o·sŭ·t'ŏ
**post office** 우체국 u·ch'e·guk
**pot (ceramics)** 항아리 hang·a·ri
**pot (cooking)** 냄비 naem·bi
**potato** 감자 kam·ja
**pottery** 도자기 to·ja·gi
**pound** 파운드 p'a·un·dŭ
**poverty** 가난 ka·nan
**powder** n 가루 ka·ru
**powdered formula** 가루형 이유식 ka·ru·hyŏng·i·yu·shik
**powdered milk** 분유 pu·nyu
**power** n 힘 him
**prawn** 대하 tae·ha
**prayer** 기도 ki·do
**prayer book** 기도서 ki·do·sŏ
**prefer** 더 좋아해요 (더 좋아하~) tŏ·jo·a·hae·yo (tŏ·jo·a·ha~)

**pregnancy test kit** 임신 진단 키트 im·shin·jin·dan·k'i·t'ŭ
**pregnant** 임신 중인 im·shin·jung·in
**premenstrual tension** 생리전 증후군 saeng·ni·jŏn·chŭng·hu·gun
**prepare** 준비해요 (준비하~) chun·bi·hae·yo (chun·bi·ha~)
**prescription** 처방전 ch'ŏ·bang·jŏn
**present (gift)** n 선물 sŏn·mul
**present (time)** n 현재 hyŏn·jae
**president (company)** 사장 sa·jang
**president (nation)** 대통령 tae·t'ong·nyŏng
**pressure (tyre)** n 공기압 kong·gi·ap
**pretty** 예쁜 yep·pŭn
**prevent** 막아요 (막~) ma·ga·yo (mag~)
**price** n 가격 ka·gyŏk
**priest (Buddhist)** 스님 sŭ·nim
**priest (Catholic)** 신부님 shin·bu·nim
**prime minister** 수상 su·sang
**printer (computer)** 프린터 p'ŭ·rin·t'ŏ
**prison** 교도소 kyo·do·so
**prisoner** 죄수 choé·su
**private** 사적인 sa·jŏ·gin
**produce** v 생산해요 (생산하~) saeng·san·hae·yo (saeng·san·ha~)
**profession** 직업 chi·gŏp
**professor** 교수 kyo·su
**profit** n 이윤 i·yun
**projector** 프로젝터 p'ŭ·ro·jek·t'ŏ
**promise** v 약속해요 (약속하~) yak·so·k'ae·yo (yak·so·k'a~)
**prostitute** n 매춘부 mae·ch'un·bu
**protect** 보호해요 (보호하~) po·ho·hae·yo (po·ho·ha~)
**protest** n 시위 shi·wi
**protest** v 항의해요 (항의하~) hang·i·hae·yo (hang·i·ha~)
**province** 도 to
**provisions** 식량 shing·nyang
**pub** 맥주집 maek·chu·jip
**public phone** 공중 전화 kong·jung·jŏn·hwa
**public toilet** 공중 화장실 kong·jung·hwa·jang·shil

DICTIONARY

**pull** v 당겨요 (당기~) tang·gyŏ·yo (tang·gi~)

**pump** n 펌프 p'ŏm·p'ŭ

**pumpkin** 늙은 호박 nŭl·gŭn ho·bak

**puncture** n 펑크 p'ŏng·k'u

**pure** 순수한 sun·su·han

**purple** 보라색 po·ra·saek

**purse** 핸드백 haen·dŭ·baek

**push** v 밀어요 (밀~) mi·rŏ·yo (mil~)

**put** 놓아요 (놓~) no·a·yo (no~)

**Pyongyang** 평양 p'yŏng·yang

## Q

**quadriplegic** n 사지 마비 환자 sa·ji ma·bi hwan·ja

**qualifications** 자격 cha·gyŏk

**quality** n 질 chil

**quarantine** 검역 kŏ·myŏk

**quarrel** n 말싸움 mal·ssa·um

**quarter** n 사 분의 일 sa·bu·ne·il

**queen** 여왕 yŏ·wang

**question** n 질문 chil·mun

**queue** n 줄 chul

**quick** 빠른 bba·rŭn

**quiet** 조용한 cho·yong·han

**quilt** 퀼트 k'wil·t'ŭ

**quit** 그만둬요 (그만두~) kŭ·man·dwŏ·yo (ku·man·du~)

## R

**rabbit** 토끼 t'ok·ki

**race (sport)** n 경주 kyŏng·ju

**racetrack** 경마장 kyŏng·ma·jang

**racing bike** 경주용 자전거 kyŏng·ju·yong cha·jŏn·gŏ

**racism** 인종 차별 주의 in·jong ch'a·byŏl·chu·i

**racquet** 라켓 ra·k'et

**radiator** 라디에이터 ra·di·e·i·t'ŏ

**radio** n 라디오 ra·di·o

**radish** 무 mu

**railway** 철도 ch'ŏl·do

**railway station** 기차역 ki·ch'a·yŏk

**rain** n 비 pi

**raincoat** 우비 u·bi

**rainy season** 장마 chang·ma

**raisin** 건포도 kŏn·p'o·do

**rally (protest)** n 집회 chi·p'oé

**rape** n 강간 kang·gan

**rare (uncommon)** 희귀한 hi·gwi·han

**rash** 발진 pal·chin

**raspberry** 라즈베리 ra·jŭ·be·ri

**rat** 쥐 chwi

**raw** 날 nal

**razor** 면도기 myŏn·do·gi

**razor blade** 면도날 myŏn·do·nal

**read** 읽어요 (읽~) il·gŏ·yo (ilg~)

**reading** 독서 tok·sŏ

**ready** a 준비된 chun·bi·doén

**real estate agency** 부동산 pu·dong·san

**realistic** 현실적인 hyŏn·shil·chŏ·gin

**rear (location)** a 뒤쪽의 twi·tcho·gé

**reason** n 이유 i·yu

**receipt** n 영수증 yŏng·su·jŭng

**receive** 받아요 (받~) pa·da·yo (pad~)

**recently** 요즘 yo·jŭm

**recommend** 추천해요 (추천하~) ch'u·ch'ŏn·hae·yo (ch'u·ch'ŏn·ha~)

**record** v 기록해요 (기록하~) ki·ro·k'ae·yo (ki·ro·k'a~)

**recording** 기록 ki·rok

**recycle** 재활용해요 (재활용하~) chae·hwa·ryong·hae·yo (chae·hwa·ryong·ha~)

**red** 빨간 bbal·gan

**referee** n 심판 shim·p'an

**reference** n 참조 ch'am·jo

**refill** n 리필 ri·p'il

**refrigerator** 냉장고 naeng·jang·go

**refugee** 난민 nan·min

**refund** n 환불 hwan·bul

**refuse** 거절해요 (거절하~) kŏ·jŏl·hae·yo (kŏ·jŏl·ha~)

**regional** 지방의 chi·bang·é

**registered mail** 등기우편 tŭng·gi·u·p'yŏn

**rehydration salts** 수분 보충용 소금 su·bun bo·ch'ung·yong so·gŭm

**relationship** 관계 kwan·gyé

**relax** 긴장 풀어요 (긴장 풀~) kin·jang p'u·rŏ·yo (kin·jang p'ul~)

**relic** 유물 yu·mul

**S**

**religion** 종교 chong·gyo
**religious** 종교적인 chong·gyo·jŏ·gin
**remember** 기억해요 (기억하~) ki·ŏ·k'ae·yo (ki·ŏ·k'a~)
**remote** a 먼 mŏn
**remote control** 리모컨 ri·mo·k'ŏn
**rent** n 집세 chip·sé
**rent** v 빌려요 (빌리~) pil·lyŏ·yo (pil·li~)
**repair** v 수리해요 (수리하~) su·ri·hae·yo (su·ri·ha~)
**repeat** v 반복해요 (반복하~) pan·bo·k'ae·yo (pan·bo·k'a~)
**republic** 공화국 kong·hwa·guk
**Republic of Korea** 대한민국 tae·han min·guk
**reservation (booking)** 예약 ye·yak
**reserve** v 예약해요 (예약하~) ye·ya·k'ae·yo (ye·ya·k'a~)
**resort** n 휴양지 hyu·yang·ji
**rest** v 쉬어요 (쉬~) shi·ŏ·yo (shi~)
**restaurant** 식당 shik·tang
**résumé (CV)** 이력서 i·ryŏk·sŏ
**retired** 은퇴한 ŭn·t'oe·han
**return (give back)** v 돌려줘요 (돌려주~) tol·lyŏ·jwŏ·yo (tol·lyŏ·ju~)
**return (go back)** v 돌아가요 (돌아가~) to·ra·ga·yo (to·ra·ga~)
**return ticket** 왕복 표 wang·bok p'yo
**review** n 비평 pi·p'yŏng
**rhythm** 박자 pak·cha
**rib (body)** 갈비뼈 kal·bip·pyŏ
**ribs (food)** 갈비 kal·bi
**rice (as grain)** 쌀 ssal
**rice (cooked)** 밥 pap
**rich (wealthy)** 부유한 pu·yu·han
**ride** n 탈 것 t'al·gŏt
**ride (bike, horse)** v 타요 (타~) t'a·yo (t'a~)
**right (correct)** 옳은 o·rŭn
**right (direction)** 오른쪽 o·rŭn·tchok
**right-wing** 우익 u·ik
**ring (jewellery)** n 반지 pan·ji
**ring (phone)** v 전화해요 (전화하~) chŏn·hwa·hae·yo (chŏn·hwa·ha~)
**rip-off** n 바가지 pa·ga·ji
**risk** n 위험 wi·hŏm
**river** 강 kang

**riverside** n 강변 kang·byŏn
**road** 도로 to·ro
**road map** 도로지도 to·ro·ji·do
**roasted** 구운 ku·un
**rob** 훔쳐요 (훔치~) hum·ch'ŏ·yo (hum·ch'i~)
**rock** n 바위 pa·wi
**rock (music)** 록 음악 ro·gŭ·mak
**rock climbing** 암벽 등반 am·byŏk tŭng·ban
**rock group** 록 그룹 rok·kŭ·rup
**roll (bread)** 롤빵 rolp·pang
**romantic** a 낭만적인 nang·man·jŏ·gin
**room** n 방 pang
**room number** 방 번호 pang·bŏn·ho
**rope** n 줄 chul
**rose** 장미 chang·mi
**round** a 동그란 tong·gŭ·ran
**roundabout** 원형 교차로 wŏn·hyŏng kyo·ch'a·ro
**route** n 경로 kyŏng·no
**rowing** 배 젓기 pae·jŏk·ki
**rubbish** 쓰레기 ssŭ·re·gi
**rubella** 풍진 p'ung·jin
**rucksack** 배낭 pae·nang
**rug** 깔개 ggal·gae
**ruins** 옛터 yet·t'ŏ
**rule** n 규칙 kyu·ch'ik
**run** v 뛰어요 (뛰~) ddwi·ŏ·yo (ddwi~)
**running** 달리기 tal·li·gi
**runny nose** 콧물 k'on·mul
**Russia** 러시아 rŏ·shi·a

**S**

**sad** 슬픈 sŭl·p'ŭn
**saddle** 안장 an·jang
**safe** n 안전 an·jŏn
**safe** a 안전한 an·jŏn·han
**safe sex** 콘돔 사용하는 섹스 k'on·dom sa·yong·ha·nŭn sek·sŭ
**saint** n 성인 sŏng·in
**salad** 샐러드 sael·lŏ·dŭ
**salami** 살라미 소시지 sal·la·mi so·shi·ji
**salary** 봉급 pong·gŭp
**sale** n 세일 se·il
**sales assistant** 판매원 p'an·mae·wŏn
**salmon** 연어 yŏ·nŏ

**salt** n 소금 so·gŭm
**salty** 짠 jjan
**same** 같은 ka·t'ŭn
**sand** 모래 mo·rae
**sandals** 샌들 saen·dŭl
**sandwich** 샌드위치 saen·dŭ·wi·ch'i
**sanitary napkin** 생리대 saeng·ni·dae
**sardine** 정어리 chŏng·ŏ·ri
**sauce** n 소스 so·sŭ
**saucepan** 냄비 naem·bi
**sauna** 사우나 sa·u·na
**sausage** 소시지 so·shi·ji
**say** 말해요 (말하~) mal·hae·yo
(mal·ha~)
**scalp** 두피 tu·p'i
**scarf** 스카프 sŭ·k'a·p'ŭ
**school** 학교 hak·kyo
**science** 과학 kwa·hak
**scientist** 과학자 kwa·hak·cha
**scissors** 가위 ka·wi
**score** 득점해요 (득점하~)
tŭk·chŏm·hae·yo (tŭk·chŏm·ha~)
**scoreboard** 득점판 tŭk·chŏm·p'an
**sculpture** 조각 cho·gak
**sea** 바다 pa·da
**seafood** 해물 hae·mul
**seasick** 뱃멀미하는
paen·mŏl·mi·ha·nŭn
**seaside** n 해변 hae·byŏn
**season** n 계절 kye·jŏl
**seat (place)** n 자리 cha·ri
**seatbelt** 안전벨트 an·jŏn·bel·t'ŭ
**second** n 초 ch'o
**second** a 둘째 tul·tchae
**second class** n 이등 i·dŭng
**secondhand** 중고의 chung·go·é
**secondhand shop** 중고품점
chung·go·p'um·jŏm
**secretary** 비서 pi·sŏ
**see** 봐요 (보~) pwa·yo (po~)
**self-employed** 자영업 하는
cha·yŏng·ŏ·p'a·nŭn
**selfish** 이기적인 i·gi·jŏ·gin
**sell** 팔아요 (팔~) p'a·ra·yo (p'al~)
**send** 보내요 (보내~) po·nae·yo
(po·nae~)
**sensible** 현명한 hyŏn·myŏng·han

**sensual** 관능적인 kwan·nŭng·jŏ·gin
**Seoul** 서울 sŏ·ul
**separate** a 따로따로의
dda·ro·tta·ro·é
**serious** 심각한 shim·ga·k'an
**service** n 서비스 sŏ·bi·sŭ
**service charge** 팁 t'ip
**service station** 주유소 chu·yu·so
**serviette** 냅킨 naep·k'in
**several** 몇 개의 myŏk·kae·é
**sew** 바느질해요 (바느질하~)
pa·nŭ·jil·hae·yo (pa·nŭ·jil·ha~)
**sex (gender)** 성별 sŏng·byŏl
**sex (intercourse)** 섹스 sek·sŭ
**sexism** 성 차별 sŏng·ch'a·byŏl
**sexy** 섹시한 sek·shi·han
**shade** n 그늘 kŭ·nŭl
**shadow** n 그림자 kŭ·rim·ja
**shaman** 무당 mu·dang
**shamanism** 무속신앙
mu·sok·shi·nang
**shampoo** 샴푸 sham·p'u
**shape** n 모양 mo·yang
**share (accommodation)** v
방 같이 써요 (방 같이 쓰~) pang
ka·ch'i ssŏ·yo (pang ka·ch'i ssŭ~)
**share (with)** v 나눠요 (나누~)
na·nwŏ·yo (na·nu~)
**shark** 상어 sang·ŏ
**shave** v 면도해요 (면도하~)
myŏn·do·hae·yo (myŏn·do·ha~)
**shaving cream** 면도 크림 myŏn·do
k'ŭ·rim
**she** inf 그녀 kŭ·nyŏ
**she** pol 그분 kŭ·bun
**sheep** 양 yang
**sheet (bed)** 시트 shi·t'ŭ
**shelf** 선반 sŏn·ban
**shiatsu** 지압 chi·ap
**shingles (illness)** 대상포진
tae·sang·p'o·jin
**ship** n 배 pae
**shirt** 셔츠 shŏ·ch'ŭ
**shoes** 신발 shin·bal
**shoelace** 신발끈 shin·balk·kun
**shoe shop** 신발 가게 shin·bal ka·gé
**shoot** 쏴요 (쏘~) sswa·yo (sso~)

S

**shop** n 가게 ka·gé
**shop** v 쇼핑해요 (쇼핑하~)
sho·p'ing·hae·yo (sho p'ing·ha~)
**shoplifter** 가게 좀도둑 ka·gé
chom·do·duk
**shopping** 쇼핑 sho·p'ing
**short (height)** 작은 cha·gŭn
**short (length)** 짧은 jjal·bŭn
**shortage** 부족 pu·jok
**shorts** 반바지 pan·ba·ji
**shoulder** 어깨 ŏk·kae
**shout** v 소리질러요 (소리지르~)
so·ri·jil·lŏ·yo (so·ri ji·rŭ~)
**show** n 쇼 sho
**show** v 보여줘요 (보여주~)
po·yŏ·jwŏ·yo (po·yŏ·ju~)
**shower** n 샤워 sha·wŏ
**shrimp** 새우 sae·u
**shrine** 사당 sa·dang
**shut** a 닫긴 tak·kin
**shy** 수줍은 su·ju·bŭn
**sick** 아픈 a·p'ŭn
**sickness** 병 pyŏng
**side** 옆면 yŏm·myŏn
**side dish** 반찬 pan·ch'an
**sign** n 간판 kan·p'an
**sign** v 서명해요 (서명하~)
sŏ·myŏng·hae·yo (sŏ·myŏng·ha~)
**signature** 서명 sŏ·myŏng
**sign language** 수화 su·hwa
**silk** n 비단 pi·dan
**silver** n 은 ŭn
**similar** 비슷한 pi·sŭ·t'an
**simple** 간단한 kan·dan·han
**since (time)** 부터 bu·t'ŏ
**sing** 노래불러요 (노래부르~)
pul·lŏ·yo (no·rae pu·rŭ~)
**singer** 가수 ka·su
**single (person)** 싱글 shing·gŭl
**single room** 싱글 룸 shing·gŭl·lum
**sister** 자매 cha·mae
**sit** 앉아요 (앉~) an·ja·yo (anj~)
**size (clothes, shoes)** n 치수 ch'i·su
**size (general)** 크기 k'ŭ·gi
**skate** v 스케이트 타요 (스케이트 타~)
sŭ·k'e·i·t'ŭ·t'a·yo (sŭ·k'e·i·t'ŭ t'a~)
**ski** n 스키 sŭ·k'i

**ski** v 스키 타요 (스키 타~)
sŭ·k'i·t'a·yo (sŭ·k'i·t'a~)
**skiing** 스키 sŭ·k'i
**skin** n 피부 p'i·bu
**skirt** 치마 ch'i·ma
**skull** 두개골 tu·gae·gol
**sky** 하늘 ha·nŭl
**sledding** 썰매타기 ssŏl·mae·t'a·gi
**sleep** n 잠 cham
**sleep** v 자요 (자~) cha·yo (cha~)
**sleeping bag** 침낭 ch'im·nang
**sleeping car** 침대차 ch'im·dae·cha
**sleeping pills** 수면제 su·myŏn·jé
**sleepy** 졸린 chol·lin
**slice** n 조각 cho·gak
**slide film** 슬라이드 필름 sŭl·la·i·dŭ
p'il·lŭm
**slow** a 느린 nŭ·rin
**slowly** 느리게 nŭ·ri·gé
**small** 작은 cha·gŭn
**smaller** 더 작은 tŏ ja·gŭn
**smallest** 제일 작은 che·il cha·gŭn
**smell** n 냄새 naem·sae
**smile** v 웃어요 (웃~) u·sŏ·yo (us~)
**smoke** v 담배 피워요 (담배 피우~)
tam·bae p'i·wŏ·yo (tam·bae p'i·u~)
**smoking area** 흡연 구역 hŭ·byŏn
ku·yŏk
**snack** n 간식 kan·shik
**snail** 달팽이 tal·p'aeng·i
**snake** 뱀 paem
**snow** n 눈 nun
**snowstorm** 눈보라 nun·bo·ra
**soap** 비누 pi·nu
**soap opera** 연속극 yŏn·sok·kŭk
**soccer** 축구 ch'uk·ku
**socialist** n 사회주의자 sa·hoé·ju·i·ja
**social welfare** 사회 복지 sa·hoé
pok·chi
**socks** 양말 yang·mal
**soft drink** 탄산 음료 t'an·san ŭm·nyo
**soldier** 군인 ku·nin
**some** a 어떤 ŏt·tŏn
**some (a little)** 약간 yak·kan
**someone** 어떤 사람 ŏt·tŏn sa·ram
**something** 어떤 것 ŏt·tŏn·gŏt
**sometimes** 가끔 kak·kŭm

son 아들 a·dŭl
song 노래 no·rae
soon 곧 kot
sore 아픈 a·p'ŭn
sound n 소리 so·ri
soup 수프 su·p'ŭ
south 남쪽 nam·tchok
South Korea 남한 nam·han
souvenir 기념품 ki·nyŏm·p'um
souvenir shop 기념품 가게
ki·nyŏm·p'um ka·gé
soy milk 두유 tu·yu
soy sauce 간장 kan·jang
spa 스파 sŭ·p'a
space (room) n 공간 kong·gan
Spain 스페인 sŭ·p'e·in
speak 말해요 (말하~) mal·hae·yo
(mal·ha~)
special a 특별한 t'ŭk·p'yŏl·han
specialist n 전문가 chŏn·mun·ga
speed (travel) n 속도 sok·to
speed limit 제한 속도
che·han·sok·to
speedometer 속도계 sok·to·gyé
spicy (hot) 매운 mae·un
spider 거미 kŏ·mi
spinach 시금치 shi·gŭm·ch'i
spoilt (food) 썩은 ssŏ·gŭn
spoke n 스포크 sŭ·p'o·k'ŭ
spoon n 숟가락 suk·ka·rak
sport 운동 un·dong
sportsperson 운동선수
un·dong·sŏn·su
sports store 운동용품 가게
un·dong·yong·p'um ka·gé
sprain n 염좌 yŏm·jwa
spring (coil) 용수철 yong·su·ch'ŏl
spring (season) 봄 pom
spring onion 파 p'a
square (town) 광장 kwang·jang
squid 오징어 o·jing·ŏ
stadium 경기장 kyŏng·gi·jang
stairway 계단 kye·dan
stale 싱싱하지 못한 shing·shing·ha·ji
mo·t'an
stamp (postage) n 우표 u·p'yo
stand-by ticket 대기표 dae·gi·p'yo

star n 별 pyŏl
(four-)star (사)성 (sa)·sŏng
start n 시작 shi·jak
start v 시작해요 (시작하~)
shi·ja·k'ae·yo (shi·ja·k'a~)
station 역 yŏk
stationer 문방구 mun·bang·gu
statue 조각상 cho·gak·sang
stay (at a hotel) v 묵어요 (묵~)
mu·gŏ·yo (mug~)
stay (in one place) v 머물러요
(머무르~) mŏ·mul·lŏ·yo (mŏ·mu·rŭ~)
steal v 훔쳐요 (훔치~) hum·chŏ·yo
(hum·ch'i~)
steamed 찐 jjin
steep 가파른 ka·p'a·rŭn
step n 걸음 kŏ·rŭm
stew n 찌개 jji·gae
stock (food) 육수 yuk·su
stockings 스타킹 sŭ·t'a·k'ing
stolen 훔친 hum·ch'in
stomach 위 wi
stomachache 복통 pok·t'ong
stone n 돌 tol
stoned (drugged) 취한 ch'wi·han
stop (bus, tram) n 정류장
chŏng·nyu·jang
stop (cease) 그만해요 (그만하~)
kŭ·man·hae·yo (kŭ·man·ha~)
stop (prevent) 막아요 (막~)
ma·ga·yo (mag~)
storm n 폭풍 pok·p'ung
story 이야기 i·ya·gi
stove 난로 nal·lo
strange 이상한 i·sang·han
stranger 낯선 사람 nas·sŏn sa·ram
strawberry 딸기 ddal·gi
stream n 개울 kae·ul
street 길 kil
street market 노점 시장 no·jŏm
shi·jang
strike (labour) n 파업 p'a·ŏp
string n 끈 ggŭn
stroke (health) n 뇌졸중
noé·jol·chung
stroller 유모차 yu·mo·ch'a
strong 힘센 him·sen

**T**

stubborn 완고한 wan·go·han
student n 학생 hak·saeng
studio 스튜디오 sŭ·t'yu·di·o
studio apartment 원룸 wŏn·num
stuffed 속을 채운 so·gŭl ch'ae·un
stupid 바보 같은 pa·bo ka·t'ŭn
style n 스타일 sŭ·t'a·il
subtitles 자막 cha·mak
suburb 교외 kyo·oé
subway (train) 지하철 chi·ha·ch'ŏl
subway entrance 지하철 입구
chi·ha·ch'ŏl ip·ku
subway line 지하철 노선 chi·ha·ch'ŏl
no·sŏn
subway station 지하철 역
chi·ha·ch'ŏl·yŏk
sugar 설탕 sŏl·t'ang
suitcase 여행가방 yŏ·haeng·ga·bang
summer 여름 yŏ·rŭm
summit (peak) 정상 chŏng·sang
sun n 해 hae
sunblock 선크림 sŏn k'ŭ·rim
sunburn 햇빛에 탐 haep·pi·ch'é t'am
sunflower 해바라기 hae·ba·ra·gi
sunglasses 선글라스 sŏn·gŭl·la·sŭ
sunny 햇빛이 밝은 haep·pi·ch'i
bal·gŭn
sunrise 해돋이 hae·do·ji
sunset 해넘이 hae·nŏ·mi
sunstroke 일사병 il·sap·pyŏng
supermarket 슈퍼마켓 shu·p'ŏ
ma·k'et
superstition 미신 mi·shin
supporter (politics) 지지자 chi·ji·ja
supporter (sport) 서포터 sŏ·p'o·t'ŏ
surf n 파도 p'a·do
surf v 파도 타요 (파도 타~) p'a·do
t'a·yo (p'a·do t'a~)
surface mail (sea) 선편 우편
sŏn·p'yŏn u·p'yŏn
surfboard 서핑 보드 sŏ·p'ing·bo·dŭ
surfing 파도 타기 p'a·do t'a·gi
surname 성 sŏng
surprise n 놀람 nol·lam
sushi 생선 초밥 saeng·sŏn ch'o·bap
sweater 스웨터 sŭ·we·t'ŏ
sweet a 단 tan

sweets 사탕 sa·t'ang
swelling 팽창 p'aeng·ch'ang
swim v 수영해요 (수영하~)
su·yŏng·hae·yo (su·yŏng·ha~)
swimming 수영 su·yŏng
swimming pool 수영장 su·yŏng·jang
swimsuit 수영복 su·yŏng·bok
Switzerland 스위스 sŭ·wi·sŭ
synthetic a 합성의 hap·sŏng·é
syringe 주사기 chu·sa·gi

**T**

table 탁자 t'ak·cha
tablecloth 식탁보 shik·t'ak·po
table tennis 탁구 t'ak·ku
taekwondo 태권도 t'aek·kwŏn·do
t'ai chi 태극권 t'ae·gŭk·kwŏn
tail n 꼬리 ggo·ri
tailor n 양복 재단사 yang·bok
chae·dan·sa
take v 가져가요 (가져가~)
ka·jŏ·ga·yo (ka·jŏ·ga~)
take a photo 사진 찍어요 (사진 찍~)
sa·jin·tchi·gŏ·yo (sa·jin·tchig~)
talk v 이야기해요 (이야기하~)
i·ya·gi·hae·yo (i·ya·gi·ha~)
tall 큰 k'ŭn
tampon 탐폰 t'am·p'on
tanning lotion 선탠 로션 sŏn·t'aen
ro·shŏn
tap n 수도꼭지 su·dok·kok·chi
tap water 수돗물 su·don·mul
tasty 맛있는 ma·shin·nŭn
tax n 세금 se·gŭm
taxi 택시 t'aek·shi
taxi stand 택시 정류장 t'aek·shi
jŏng·nyu·jang
tea 차 ch'a
teacher 선생님 sŏn·saeng·nim
teahouse 찻집 ch'at·chip
team 팀 t'im
teaspoon 찻숟가락
ch'as·suk·ka·rak
technique 기술 ki·sul
teeth 이 i
telegram 전보 chŏn·bo
telephone n 전화 chŏn·hwa

T

telephone v 전화해요 (전화하~)
chŏn·hwa·hae·yo (chŏn·hwa·ha~)
telescope 망원경 mang·won·gyŏng
television 텔레비전 t el·le·bi·jŏn
tell 이야기해요 (이야기하~)
i·ya·gi·hae·yo (i·ya·gi·ha~)
temperature (fever) 열 yŏl
temperature (weather) 기온 ki·on
temple (body) 관자놀이 kwan·ja·no·ri
temple (building) 절 chŏl
tennis 테니스 t'e·ni·sŭ
tennis court 테니스 경기장 t'e·ni·sŭ
kyŏng·gi·jang
tent 텐트 t'en·t'ŭ
tent peg 텐트용 말뚝 t'en·t'ŭ·yong
malt·tuk
terrible 형편없는 hyŏng·p'yŏ·nŏm·nŭn
test n 시험 shi·hŏm
thank 감사드려요 (감사드리~)
kam·sa·dŭ·ryŏ·yo (kam·sa·dŭ·ri~)
that (away from listener) a 저 chŏ
that (near listener) a 그 kŭ
that one (away from listener) pron
저것 chŏ·gŏt
that one (near listener) pron 그것
kŭ·gŏt
theatre (cinema) 영화관
yŏng·hwa·gwan
theatre (plays) 극장 kŭk·chang
their 그들의 kŭ·dŭ·rё
there (away from listener) 저기
chŏ·gi
there (near listener) 거기 kŏ·gi
thermometer 체온계 ch'e·on·gyё
they 그들 kŭ·dŭl
thick 두꺼운 tuk·kŏ·un
thief 도둑 to·duk
thin 얇은 yal·bŭn
think 생각해요 (생각하~)
saeng·gak·hae·yo (saeng·gak·ha~)
third a 셋째 set·tchae
thirsty 목마른 mong·ma·rŭn
this a 이 i
this (one) pron 이것 i·gŏt
thought 생각 saeng·gak
thread n 실 shil
throat 목 mok

thrush (health) 아구창 a·gu·ch'ang
ticket 표 p'yo
ticket booth 표 파는 곳 p'yo
p'a·nŭn·got
ticket machine 표 자판기 p'yo
cha·pan·gi
ticket office 매표소 mae·p'yo·so
tide n 조수 cho·su
tiger 호랑이 ho·rang·i
time n 시간 shi·gan
time difference 시차 shi·ch'a
timetable 시간표 shi·gan·p'yo
tin (can) 캔 k'aen
tin opener 캔 오프너 k'ae·no·p'ŭ·nŏ
tip (gratuity) n 팁 t'ip
tire n 타이어 t'a·i·ŏ
tired 피곤한 p'i·gon·han
tissues 티슈 t'i·shyu
to ... ...으로/로 ...ŭ·ro/·ro
tobacco 담배 tam·bae
today 오늘 o·nŭl
toe 발가락 pal·ga·rak
tofu 두부 tu·bu
together 같이 ka·ch'i
toilet 화장실 hwa·jang·shil
toilet paper 두루마리 휴지
tu·ru·ma·ri hyu·ji
tollbooth 요금 내는 곳 yo·gŭm
nae·nŭn·got
tomb 무덤 mu·dŏm
tomorrow 내일 nae·il
tongue 혀 hyŏ
tonight 오늘 밤 o·nŭl·bam
too (also) 또한 ddo·han
too (expensive) 너무 (비싸요)
nŏ·mu (piss·a·yo)
tooth 이 i
toothache 치통 ch'i·t'ong
toothbrush 칫솔 ch'is·sol
toothpaste 치약 ch'i·yak
toothpick 이쑤시개 iss·u·shi·gae
torch (flashlight) 손전등
son·jŏn·dŭng
touch v 건드려요 (건드리~)
kŏn·dŭ·ryŏ·yo (kŏn·dŭ·ri~)
tour n 여행 yŏ·haeng
tourist n 여행자 yŏ·haeng·ja

**tourist office** 관광안내소 kwan·gwang an·nae·so

**towards ... ...** 쪽으로 ...tcho·gŭ·ro

**towel** 수건 su·gŏn

**tower** 타워 t'a·wŏ

**town** 마을 ma·ŭl

**toxic waste** 유독성 폐기물 yu·dok·sŏng p'ye·gi·mul

**toy shop** 장난감 가게 chang·nan·gam ka·gé

**track (path)** 길 kil

**track (sport)** 트랙 t'ŭ·raek

**trade** n 무역 mu·yŏk

**tradesperson** 상인 sang·in

**traffic** n 교통 kyo·t'ong

**traffic light** 신호등 shin·ho·dŭng

**trail** n 길 kil

**train** n 기차 ki·ch'a

**train station** 기차역 ki·ch'a·yŏk

**transit lounge** 환승 라운지 hwan·sŭng ra·un·ji

**translate** 번역해요 (번역하~) pŏ·nyŏ·k'ae·yo (pŏ·nyŏ·k'a~)

**translator** 통역 t'ong·yŏk

**transport** n 수송 su·song

**travel** v 여행해요 (여행하~) yŏ·haeng·hae·yo (yŏ·haeng·ha~)

**travel agency** 여행사 yŏ·haeng·sa

**travellers cheque** 여행자 수표 yŏ·haeng·ja su·p'yo

**travel sickness** 멀미 mŏl·mi

**tree** 나무 na·mu

**trend** 유행 yu·haeng

**trip (journey)** 여행 yŏ·haeng

**trolley** 카트 k'a·t'ŭ

**trousers** 바지 pa·ji

**truck** 트럭 t'ŭ·rŏk

**trust** v 믿어요 (믿~) mi·dŏ·yo (mid~)

**truth** 진실 chin·shil

**try (sample/test)** v 시도해요 (시도하~) shi·do·hae·yo (shi·do·ha~)

**try (attempt)** v 노력해요 (노력하~) no·ryŏ·k'ae·yo (no·ryŏ·k'a~)

**tube (tyre)** 튜브 t'yu·bŭ

**tumour** 종양 chong·yang

**tuna** 참치 ch'am·ch'i

**tune** n 선율 sŏ·nyul

**turkey** 칠면조 ch'il·myŏn·jo

**turn** v 돌아요 (돌~) to·ra·yo (tol~)

**TV** 티브이 t'i·bŭ·i

**tweezers** 족집게 chok·chip·ké

**twice** 두 번 tu·bŏn

**twin beds** 트윈 베드 t'ŭ·win·be·dŭ

**twins** 쌍둥이 ssang·dung·i

**type** n 유형 yu·hyŏng

**typhoon** 태풍 t'ae·p'ung

**typical** 전형적인 chŏn·hyŏng·jŏ·gin

**tyre** 타이어 t'a·i·ŏ

**ultrasound** 초음파 ch'o·ŭm·p'a

**umbrella** 우산 u·san

**uncomfortable** 불편한 pul·p'yŏn·han

**underground walkway** 지하도 chi·ha·do

**understand** 이해해요 (이해하~) i·hae·hae·yo (i·hae·ha~)

**underwear** 속옷 so·got

**unemployed** 직업이 없는 chi·gŏ·bi ŏm·nŭn

**unfair** 불공평한 pul·gong·p'yŏng·han

**uniform** n 유니폼 yu·ni·p'om

**universe** 우주 u·ju

**university** 대학교 tae·hak·kyo

**unleaded petrol** 무연 휘발유 mu·yŏn hwi·bal·yu

**unmarried** 미혼 mi·hon

**unsafe** 안전하지 않은 an·jŏn·ha·ji a·nŭn

**until ... ...** 까지 ...kka·ji

**unusual** 특이한 t'ŭ·gi·han

**up** 위로 wi·ro

**uphill** 오르막 o·rŭ·mak

**urgent** 급한 kŭ·p'an

**urinary infection** 요도염 yo·do·yŏm

**USA** 미국 mi·guk

**useful** 유용한 yu·yong·han

**vacant** 빈 pin

**vacation** 휴가 hyu·ga

**vaccination** 예방주사 ye·bang·ju·sa

**W**

**validate** 확인해요 (확인하~)
hwa·gin·hae·yo (hwa·gin·ha~)
**valley** 계곡 kye·gok
**valuable** 귀중한 kwi·jung·han
**value (price)** n 가격 ka·gyŏk
**van** 미니밴 mi·ni·baen
**veal** 송아지 고기 song·a·ji go·gi
**vegan** 완전 채식주의자 wan·jŏn
ch'ae·shik·chu·i·ja
**vegetable** n 야채 ya·ch'ae
**vegetarian** n 채식주의자
ch'ae·shik·chu·i·ja
**vein** 정맥 chŏng·maek
**venereal disease** 성병 sŏng·byŏng
**very** 아주 a·ju
**video camera** 캠코더 k'aem·k'o·dŏ
**video recorder** 비디오 녹화기 pi·di·o
no·k'wa·gi
**video tape** 비디오 테이프 pi·di·o
t'e·i·p'ŭ
**view** n 전망 chŏn·mang
**village** 마을 ma·ŭl
**vine** 포도나무 p'o·do·na·mu
**vinegar** 식초 shik·ch'o
**virus** 바이러스 pa·i·rŏ·sŭ
**visa** 비자 pi·ja
**visit** v 방문해요 (방문하~)
pang·mun·hae·yo (pang·mun·ha~)
**visually impaired** 시각 장애의
shi·gak chang·ae·ŭi
**vitamins** 비타민 pi·t'a·min
**voice** 목소리 mok·so·ri
**volcano** 화산 hwa·san
**volleyball (sport)** 배구 pae·gu
**volume** 볼륨 pol·lyum
**vote** v 투표해요 (투표하~)
t'u·p'yo·hae·yo (t'u·p'yo·ha~)

**W**

**wage** n 임금 im·gŭm
**wait** v 기다려요 (기다리~)
ki·da·ryŏ·yo (ki·da·ri~)
**waiter** 웨이터 we·i·t'ŏ
**waiting room** 대기실 tae·gi·shil
**wake (someone) up** 깨워요 (깨우~)
ggae·wŏ·yo (ggae·u~)
**walk** n 산책 san·ch'aek

**walk** v 걸어요 (걷~) kŏ·rŏ·yo (kŏt~)
**wall (building)** 벽 pyŏk
**walnut** 호두 ho·du
**want (an object)** 원해요 (원하~)
wŏn·hae·yo (wŏn·ha~)
**war** n 전쟁 chŏn·jaeng
**wardrobe** 옷장 ot·chang
**warm** a 따뜻한 ddat·ttŭt·han
**warn** 경고해요 (경고하~)
kyŏng·go·hae·yo (kyŏng·go·ha~)
**wash** v 씻어요 (씻~) shi·sŏ·yo (shis~)
**wash cloth (flannel)** 행주 haeng·ju
**washing machine** 세탁기 se·t'ak·ki
**wasp** 말벌 mal·bŏl
**watch** n 손목시계 son·mok·shi·gyé
**watch** v 봐요 (보~) pwa·yo (po~)
**water** n 물 mul
**water bottle** 물병 mul·byŏng
**(hot) water bottle** 보온병
po·on·byŏng
**waterfall** 폭포 p'ok·p'o
**watermelon** 수박 su·bak
**waterproof** 방수 pang·su
**water-skiing** 수상 스키 su·sang sŭ·k'i
**wave (beach)** n 파도 p'a·do
**way** 길 kil
**we** 우리 u·ri
**weak** 힘이 없는 hi·mi ŏm·nŭn
**wealthy** 부유한 pu·yu·han
**wear** a 입어요 (입~) i·bŏ·yo (ib~)
**weather** n 날씨 nal·shi
**wedding** 결혼 kyŏl·hon
**week** 주 chu
**weekend** 주말 chu·mal
**weigh** 무게가 나가요 (무게가 나가~)
mu·ge·ga·na·ga·yo (mu·ge·ga·na·ga~)
**weight** 무게 mu·ge
**weights** 역기 yŏk·ki
**welcome** v 환영해요 (환영하~)
hwa·nyŏng·hae·yo (hwa·nyŏng·ha~)
**well (healthy)** 건강한 kŏn·gang·han
**well** adv 잘 chal
**west** 서쪽 sŏ·tchok
**Western** 서양의 sŏ·yang·é
**wet** a 젖은 chŏ·jŭn
**whale** 고래 ko·rae
**what** 무엇 mu·ŏt

**Y**

wheat 밀 mil
wheel n 바퀴 pa·k'wi
wheelchair 휠체어 hwil·ch'ë·ö
when 언제 ön·jé
where 어디 ö·di
which 어느 ö·nŭ
white 흰 hin
white-water rafting 급류 래프팅
küm·nyu rae·p'ŭ·t'ing
who 누구 nu·gu
whole 전부 chön·bu
why 왜 wae
wide 폭이 넓은 p'o·gi nöl·bŭn
wife 아내 a·nae
win v 이겨요 (이기~) i·gyö·yo (i·gi~)
wind n 바람 pa·ram
window 창문 ch'ang·mun
windscreen 앞유리 am·nyu·ri
windy 바람이 많이 부는 pa·ra·mi
ma·ni pu·nŭn
wine 와인 wa·in
wings 날개 nal·gae
winner 우승자 u·sŭng·ja
winter 겨울 kyö·ul
wire n 철사 chöl·sa
wish v 희망해요 (희망하~)
hi·mang·hae·yo (hi·mang·ha~)
with ... (someone) ...과/와 함께
...gwa/·wa hamk·ké
without ... (someone) ... 없이
... öp·shi
wok 중국 냄비 chung·gung·naem·bi
woman 여자 yö·ja
wonderful 훌륭한 hul·lyung·han
wood n 나무 na·mu
wool n 모직물 mo·jing·mul
word n 단어 ta·nö
work n 일 il
work v 일해요 (일하~) il·hae·yo
(il·ha~)
workout n 운동 un·dong
work permit 취업 허가증 ch'wi·öp
hö·ga·jŭng
workshop n 워크숍 wö·k'ŭ·shop
world n 세계 se·gyé
worms (intestinal) 기생충
ki·saeng·ch'ung

worship n 찬양 ch'a·nyang
wrist 손목 son·mok
write 써요 (쓰~) ssö·yo (ssŭ~)
writer 작가 chak·ka
wrong a 틀린 t'ŭl·lin

**Y**

yacht 요트 yo·t'ŭ
year 해 hae
yellow 노랑 no·ran
yes 네 né
yesterday 어제 ö·jé
(not) yet 아직 (아니에요) a·jik
(a·ni·e·yo)
yogurt 요구르트 yo·gu·rŭ·t'ŭ
you inf sg 너 nö
you pol sg 당신 tang·shin
you inf pl 너희 들 nö·hi·dŭl
you pol pl 여러분 yö·rö·bun
young a 젊은 chöl·mŭn
your inf sg 너의 nö·é
your pol sg 당신의 tang·shi·né
your inf pl 너희 들의 nö·hi·dŭ·ré
your pol pl 여러분의 yö·rö·bu·né
youth hostel 유스호스텔
yu·sŭ·ho·sŭ·t'el

**Z**

zip/zipper 지퍼 chi·p'ö
zoo 동물원 tong·mur·wön
zoom lens 줌렌즈 chum·nen·jŭ
zucchini 애호박 ae·ho·bak

# Dictionary

### KOREAN *to* ENGLISH
한국어 – 영어

This dictionary has been ordered according to the consonants in the Korean alphabet (see **pronunciation**, p12). Words are marked as nouns n, verbs v, adjectives a, adverbs adv, pronouns pron or prepositions prep for clarity where required. The abbreviations sg (singular), pl (plural), inf (informal) and pol (polite) are also used where applicable. Korean verbs are given in their polite form (ending in ~yo ~요). The verb stem is repeated between brackets after the verb. For more information, see **grammar**. For any food items, refer to the **menu decoder**.

## ㄱ

가게 ka·gé shop n

가게 좀도둑 ka·gé chom·do·duk shoplifter

가격 ka·gyŏk price

가구 ka·gu furniture

가까운 kak·ka·un close a

가까워요 (가깝~) kak·ka·wŏ·yo (kak·kap~) be close v

가득 찬 ka·dŭk·ch'an full

가려운 ka·ryŏ·un itchy

가리켜요 (가리키~) ka·ri·k'yŏ·yo (ka·ri·k'i~) point v

가방 ka·bang bag

가까운 ka·byŏ·un light (weight) a

가스 ka·sŭ gas (for cooking)

가요 (가~) ka·yo (ka~) go

가위 ka·wi scissors

가이드 ka·i·dŭ guide (person)

가이드 책자 ka·i·dŭ ch'aek·cha guidebook

가이드 투어 ka·i·dŭ t'u·ŏ guided tour

가져요 (갖~) ka·jŏ·yo (kaj~) have

가족 ka·jok family

가죽 ka·juk leather n

각각의 kak·ka·gé each

간식 kan·shik snack n

간호사 kan·ho·sa nurse n

갈색의 kal·sae·gé brown a

감기 kam·gi cold n • flu

감사해요 (감사하~) kam·sa·hae·yo (kam·sa·ha~) grateful

감염 ka·myŏm infection

강 kang river

강사 kang·sa lecturer

같이 ka·ch'i together

개 kae dog

거기 kŏ·gi there (near listener)

거울 kŏ·ul mirror n

건강한 kŏn·gang·han well (healthy)

건강해요 (건강하~) kŏn·gang·hae·yo (kŏn·gang·ha~) be well v

건초열 kŏn·ch'o·yŏl hay fever

건축 kŏn·ch'uk architecture
건축가 kŏn·ch'uk·ka architect
걸어요 (걷~) kŏ·rŏ·yo (kŏt~) walk v
검은 kŏ·mŭn black
겨울 kyŏ·ul winter
결혼한 kyŏl·hon·han married
경찰 kyŏng·ch'al police
경찰관 kyŏng·ch'al·gwan police officer
경찰서 kyŏng·ch'al·sŏ police station
계단 kye·dan stairway
계산기 kye·san·gi calculator
계산서 kye·san·sŏ bill/check n
계절 kye·jŏl season n
고객 ko·gaek client
고속 버스 ko·sok bŏ·sŭ express intercity bus
고속도로 ko·sok·to·ro highway • motorway • tollway
고용해요 (고용하~) ko·yong·hae·yo (ko·yong·ha~) hire v
고장 난 ko·jang·nan broken down • out of order
고전 ko·jŏn classical
고통 ko·t'ong pain n
곧 kot soon
골동품 kol·dong·p'um antique n
골프 kol·p'ŭ golf
골프장 kol·p'ŭ·jang golf course
공산주의 kong·san·ju·i communism
공연장 kyong·yŏn·jang gig
공예품 kong·ye·p'um crafts
공원 kong·wŏn park n
공중전화 kong·jung·jŏn·hwa public phone
공중 화장실 kong·jung hwa·jang·shil public toilet
공짜의 kong·tcha·é free (gratis)
공책 kong·ch'aek notebook
공항 kong·hang airport
공항세 kong·hang·sé airport tax
과학 kwa·hak science
과학자 kwa·hak·cha scientist
관광 버스 kwan·gwang bŏ·sŭ tourist bus
관광안내소 kwan·gwang an·nae·so tourist office

광장 kwang·jang square (town) n
괜찮은 kwaen·cha·nŭn OK
괴로운 koé·ro·un painful
교통 위반 kyo·t'ong wi·ban traffic violation
교통카드 kyo·t'ong k'a·dŭ prepaid transit pass
교환 kyo·hwan exchange n
교환해요 (교환하~) kyo·hwan·hae·yo (kyo·hwan·ha~) exchange v
구급 상자 ku·gŭp·sang·ja first-aid kit
구급차 ku·gŭp·ch'a ambulance
구명 조끼 ku·myŏng·jok·ki life jacket
국경 kuk·kyŏng border (national) n
귀 kwi ear
귀고리 kwi·go·ri earrings
귀중한 kwi·jung·han valuable
그 kŭ he inf • that (near listener) a
그것 kŭ·gŏt it • that one (near listener) pron
그녀 kŭ·nyŏ she inf
그녀의 kŭ·nyŏ·é her (possessive)
그늘 kŭ·nŭl shade n
그램 kŭ·raem gram
그리고 kŭ·ri·go and
그분 kŭ·bun he pol • she pol
그의 kŭ·é his
그저께 kŭ·jŏk·ké day before yesterday
극장 kŭk·chang theatre (for plays)
금 kŭm gold n
금연 구역 kŭ·myŏn gu·yŏk nonsmoking area
금전 등록기 kŭm·jŏn dŭng·nok·ki cash register
급수대 kŭp·su·dae drinking fountain
급한 kŭp'·an urgent
급해요 (급하~) kŭ·p'ae·yo (kŭ·p'a~) be in a hurry v
기념품 ki·nyŏm·p'um souvenir
기념품 가게 ki·nyŏm·p'um ka·gé souvenir shop
기다려요 (기다리~) ki·da·ryŏ·yo (ki·da·ri~) wait v
기름 ki·rŭm oil (cooking)
기억해요 (기억하~) ki·ŏ·k'ae·yo (ki·ŏ·k'a~) remember

기온 ki·on temperature (weather)
기저귀 ki·jŏ·gwi diaper • nappy
기차 ki·ch'a train n
기차역 ki·ch'a·yŏk railway station
기침 해요 (기침 하~) ki·ch'im hae·yo (ki·ch'im ha~) cough v
기침약 ki·ch'im·nyak cough medicine
긴 kin long
길 kil path • street
길어요 (길~) ki·rŏ·yo (kil~) be long v

## ㄲ

깨끗한 ggaek·kŭt'an clean a
깨워요 (깨우~) ggae·wŏ·yo (ggae·u~) wake (someone) up
깨지기 쉬운 ggae·ji·gi shi·un fragile
깨진 ggae·jin broken
꽃집 ggot·chip florist
꾸러미 ggu·rŏ·mi packet (general)
끝 ggŭt end n

## ㄴ

나 na I inf
나가요 (나가~) na·ga·yo (na·ga~) go out
나눠요 (나누~) na·nwŏ·yo (na·nu~) share (with) v
나쁜 nap·pŭn bad
나의 na·é my inf
나이트 클럽 na·i·t'ŭ k'ŭl·lŏp nightclub
낚시 nakk·shi fishing
날아요 (날~) na·ra·yo (nal~) fly v
날짜 nal·tcha date (day) n
남자 nam·ja man n
남자 아이 nam·ja·a·i boy
남자 친구 nam·ja ch'in·gu boyfriend
남쪽 nam·tchok south n
남편 nam·p'yŏn husband
남한 nam·han South Korea
낭만적인 nang·man·jŏ·gin romantic a
낮 nat daytime
내려요 (내리~) nae·ryŏ·yo (nae·ri~) get off (bus, train)
내일 nae·il tomorrow
냄비 naem·bi pot (cooking) • saucepan
냄새 naem·sae smell n

냅킨 naep·k'in napkin • serviette
냉동 식품 naeng·dong shik·p'um frozen food
냉방 중 naeng·hang·jŭng air-conditioned
냉장고 naeng·jang·go refrigerator
너 nŏ you inf sg
너무 (비싸요) nŏ·mu (piss·a·yo) too (expensive)
너무 많은 nŏ·mu ma·nŭn too many
너무 많이 nŏ·mu ma·ni too much
너의 nŏ·é your inf sg
너희 들 nŏ·hi·dŭl you inf pl
너희 들의 nŏ·hi·dŭ·ré your inf pl
네 né yes
년 nyŏn year (as a classifier)
노란 no·ran yellow
노력해요 (노력하~) no·ryŏ·k'ae·yo (no·ryŏ·k'a~) try (make an effort) v
노리개 젖꼭지 no·ri·gae chŏk·kok·chi dummy/pacifier
노점 시장 no·jŏm shi·jang street market
노트북 no·t'ŭ·buk laptop
놓쳐요 (놓치~) no·ch'ŏ·yo (no·ch'i~) miss (not catch train, etc)
누구 nu·gu who
누나 nu·na older sister (male speaker)
눈 nun eye • snow n
뉴스 nyu·sŭ news
느껴요 (느끼~) nŭk·kyŏ·yo (nŭk·ki~) feel (touch) v
느리게 nŭ·ri·gé slowly
늙은 nŭl·gŭn old (people)
늦게 nŭk·ké late adv

## ㄷ

다른 ta·rŭn different • other
다리 ta·ri bridge n • leg (body)
다리미질 ta·ri·mi·jil iron (for clothes) n
다시 ta·shi again
다음 ta·ŭm next (following)
다음에 ta·ŭ·mé later
다친 ta·ch'in injured
단 tan sweet a
단단한 tan·dan·han hard (not soft)
단추 tan·ch'u button n

## ㄷㄷ

닫긴 tak·kin shut a
닫아요 (닫~) ta·da·yo (tad~) close v
달 tal month
달러 tal·lŏ dollar
닭 tak chicken (animal)
담배 tam·bae cigarette
담배 피워요 (담배 피우~) tam·bae p'i·wŏ·yo (tam·bae p'i·u~) smoke v
담요 tam·nyo blanket
(하루)당 (ha·ru)·dang per (day)
당뇨병 tang·nyo·byŏng diabetes
당신 tang·shin you pol sg
당신의 tang·shi·né your pol sg
대기실 tae·gi·shil waiting room
대기표 tae·gi·p'yo stand-by ticket
대사관 tae·sa·gwan embassy
대학교 tae·hak·kyo university
대한민국 tae·han min·guk Republic of Korea
대형 할인점 tae·hyŏng ha·rin·jŏm market (indoor) n
더 나은 tŏ·na·ŭn better
더 많은 tŏ·ma·nŭn more
더 작은 tŏ ja·gŭn smaller
더 큰 tŏ·k'ŭn bigger
더러운 tŏ·rŏ·un dirty
더블 룸 tŏ·bŭl·lum double room
더블 베드 tŏ·bŭl be·dŭ double bed
더운 tŏ·un hot (weather)
더워요 (덥~) tŏ·wŏ·yo (tŏp~) be hot v
데오드란트 te·o·dŭ·ran·t'ŭ deodorant
데운 te·un heated
데이트 de·i·t'ŭ date (romantic) n
도로 to·ro road
도서관 to·sŏ·gwan library
도시 to·shi city
도와줘요 (도와주~) to·wa·jwŏ·yo (to·wa·ju~) help v
도움 to·um help n
도착 to·ch'ak arrivals
독감 tok·kam flu • influenza
돈 ton money
돌려줘요 (돌려주~) tol·lyŏ·jwŏ·yo (tol·lyŏ·ju~) return (give back) v
돌아가요 (돌아가~) to·ra·ga·yo (to·ra·ga~) return (go back) v

동네 tong·né neighbourhood
동료 tong·nyo colleague • companion
동물원 tong·mur·wŏn zoo
동생 tong·saeng younger sibling
동전 tong·jŏn coins
동쪽 tong·tchok east n
두 개의 tu·gae·é two
두루마리 휴지 tu·ru·ma·ri hyu·ji toilet paper
두통 tu·t'ong headache
둘 다 tul·da both
뒤쪽의 twi·tcho·gé rear (location)
드레스 tŭ·re·sŭ dress n
들어가요 (들어가~) tŭ·rŏ·ga·yo (tŭ·rŏ·ga~) enter
들어요 (듣~) tŭ·rŏ·yo (tŭt~) listen
들어요 (들~) tŭ·rŏ·yo (tŭl~) cost v
등기우편 tŭng·gi·u·p'yŏn registered mail
등산 tŭng·san hiking
등산로 tŭng·san·no hiking route
등산해요 (등산하~) tŭng·san·hae·yo (tŭng·san·ha~) hike v

## ㄸ

따뜻한 ddat·tŭt·han warm a
따뜻해요 (따뜻하~) ddat·tŭ·t'ae·yo (ddat·tŭ·t'a~) be warm v
딸 ddal daughter
떠나요 (떠나~) ddŏ·na·yo (ddŏ·na~) depart
또 하나의 ddo ha·na·é another
뚱뚱한 ddung·tung·han fat a
뜨거운 ddŭ·gŏ·un hot (to the touch)

## ㄹ

라디오 ra·di·o radio n
라이터 ra·i·t'ŏ cigarette lighter
렌즈 ren·jŭ lens (camera)
렌트카 ren·t'ŭ·k'a car hire
록 음악 ro·gŭ·mak rock (music)
리넨 ri·nen linen (material)
리넨천 ri·nen·ch'ŏn linen (sheets)
리모컨 ri·mo·k'ŏn remote control
리프트 ri·p'ŭ·t'ŭ chairlift (skiing)

마개 ma·gae plug (bath) n
마른 ma·rŭn dry a
마셔요 (마시~) ma·shŏ·yo (ma·shi~) drink v
마약 ma·yak dope (illicit drugs) n
마을 ma·ŭl town
마을 버스 ma·ŭl bŏ·sŭ neighbourhood bus
마지막 ma·ji·mak last (final)
막힌 ma·k'in blocked
말해요 (말하~) mal·hae·yo (mal·ha~) speak
맛있는 ma·shin·nŭn tasty
매니저 mae·ni·jŏ manager
매운 mae·un spicy (hot)
매워요 (맵~) mae·wŏ·yo (maep~) be spicy (hot) v
매일 mae·il daily adv
매트리스 mae·t'ŭ·ri·sŭ mattress
매표소 mae·p'yo·so ticket office
맥주 maek·chu beer
맥주집 maek·chu·jip pub
머리 mŏ·ri head n
먹어요 (먹~) mŏ·gŏ·yo (mŏg~) eat
멀리 mŏl·li far adv
멀미 mŏl·mi travel sickness
멀어요 (멀~) mŏ·rŏ·yo (mŏl~) be far v
메스꺼움 me·sŭk·kŏ·um nausea
메시지 me·shi·ji message
면 myŏn cotton (fabric) n
면도 크림 myŏn·do k'ŭ·rim shaving cream
면도기 myŏn·do·gi razor
면도날 myŏn·do·nal razor blade
면도해요 (면도하~) myŏn·do·hae·yo (myŏn·do·ha~) shave v
면세 myŏn·se duty-free n
모뎀 mo·dem modem
모두 mo·du everyone
모든 mo·dŭn all • every a
모래 mo·rae day after tomorrow
모범 택시 mo·bŏm t'aek·shi deluxe taxi
모자 mo·ja hat
모텔 mo·t'el motel

목 mok neck • throat
목걸이 mok·kŏ·ri necklace
목마른 mong·ma·rŭn thirsty
목말라요 (목마르~) mong·mal·la·yo (mong·ma·rŭ~) be thirsty v
목욕 mo·gyok bath n
목적지 mok·chŏk·chi destination
몰라요 (모르~) mol·la·yo (mo·rŭ~) not know
무거운 mu·gŏ·un heavy (weight)
무거워요 (무겁~) mu·gŏ·wŏ·yo (mu·gŏp~) be heavy v
무릎 mu·rŭp knee
문방구 mun·bang·gu stationer
문서 업무 mun·sŏ ŏm·mu paperwork
물 mul water n
물집 mul·chip blister n
미술 mi·sul art
미술관 mi·sul·gwan art gallery • art museum
미용실 mi·yong·shil beauty salon • hairdressing salon
미터 mi·t'ŏ metre
미혼 mi·hon unmarried
민박집 min·bak·chip guesthouse
민속 음악 min·sok ŭ·mak folk music
밀리미터 mil·li·mi·t'ŏ millimetre

바늘 pa·nŭl needle (sewing)
바다 pa·da ocean • sea
바람이 많이 부는 pa·ra·mi ma·ni pu·nŭn windy
바쁜 pap·pŭn busy (person)
바지 pa·ji pants • trousers
박물관 pang·mul·gwan museum
밖에서 pak·ke·sŏ outside adv
반 ban half n
반바지 pan·ba·ji shorts
반복해요 (반복하~) pan·bo·k'ae·yo (pan·bo·k'a~) repeat v
반지 pan·ji ring (jewellery) n
반창고 pan·ch'ang·go Band-Aid
받아들여요 (받아들이~) pa·da·dŭ·ryŏ·yo (pa·da·dŭ·ri~) accept
받아요 (받~) pa·da·yo (pad~) receive

ㅂ

발 pal foot (body)
발목 pal·mok ankle
발신음 pal·shi·nŭm dial tone
밝은 pal·gŭn light (colour) a
밤 pam night
밤새 pam·sae overnight adv
방 pang room n
방 같이 써요 (방 같이 쓰~) pang ka·ch'i ssŏ·yo (pang ka·ch'i ssŭ~) share (accommodation) v
방 번호 pang·bŏn·ho room number
방향 pang·hyang direction
배 pae boat • ship
배고파요 (배고프~) pae·go·p'a·yo (pae·go·p'ŭ~) be hungry v
배고픈 pae·go·p'ŭn hungry
배낭 pae·nang backpack • rucksack
배달해요 (배달하~) pae·dal·hae·yo (pae·dal·ha~) deliver
배변촉진제 pae·byŏn·ch'ok·chin·jé laxative n
배터리 bae·t'ŏ·ri battery
백 paek hundred
백만 paeng·man million
백화점 pae·k'wa·jŏm department store
밴드 paen·dŭ band (music)
버스 정류장 bŏ·su chŏng·nyu·jang bus stop
버스 터미널 bŏ·su t'ŏ·mi·nŏl bus station
번역해요 (번역하~) pŏ·nyŏ·k'ae·yo (pŏ·nyŏ·k'a~) translate
벌금 pŏl·gŭm fine n
법학 pŏ·p'ak law (profession/study)
베개 pe·gae pillow
베갯잇 pe·gaen·nit pillowcase
벼룩 시장 pyŏ·ruk shi·jang fleamarket
변비 pyŏn·bi constipation
변속 장치 pyŏn·sok chang·ch'i derailleur • gearbox
변호사 pyŏn·ho·sa lawyer
변화 pyŏn·hwa change n
병 pyŏng bottle
병따개 pyŏngt·ta·gae bottle opener
병원 pyŏng·won hospital
보다 적은 po·da chŏ·gŭn less

보도 po·do footpath
보라색 po·ra·saek purple
보석 po·sŏk jewellery
보여줘요 (보여주~) po·yŏ·jwŏ·yo (po·yŏ·ju~) show v
보온병 po·on·byŏng hot water bottle
보증 po·jŭng guarantee n
보증금 po·jŭng·gŭm deposit n
보험 po·hŏm insurance
복통 pok·t'ong stomachache
볼펜 pol·p'en ballpoint pen
봄 pom spring (season)
봉투 pong·t'u envelope n
부모님 pu·mo·nim parents
부상 pu·sang injury
부유한 pu·yu·han rich
부채 pu·ch'ae fan (hand-held)
북쪽 puk·tchok north n
북한 pu·k'an North Korea
분 bun minute
분수 pun·su fountain
분실 수하물 pun·shil su·ha·mul left luggage
분실 수하물 보관소 pun·shil su·ha·mul po·gwan·so left-luggage office
분실물 센터 pun·shil·mul sen·t'ŏ lost-property office
분홍색 pun·hong·saek pink
불가능한 pul·ga·nŭng·han impossible
불량인 pul·lyang·in faulty
불편한 pul·p'yŏn·han uncomfortable
불평 pul·p'yŏng complaint
붕대 pung·dae bandage
브래지어 pŭ·rae·ji·ŏ bra
브레이크 pŭ·re·i·kŭ brakes
비 pi rain n
비누 pi·nu soap
비단 pi·dan silk n
비디오 녹화기 pi·di·o no·k'wa·gi video recorder
비디오 테이프 pi·di·o t'e·i·p'ŭ video tape
비무장지대 pi·mu·jang·ji·dae demilitarized zone (DMZ)
비상구 pi·sang·gu emergency exit
비싸요 (비싸~) piss·a·yo (piss·a~) be expensive v

DICTIONARY

비싼 piss·an expensive
비용 pi·yong cost n
비자 pi·ja visa
비즈니스 클래스 pi·jŭ·ni·sŭ k'ŭl·lae·sŭ business class
비행 pi·haeng flight
비행기 pi·haeng·gi airplane
빈 pin empty a • vacant
빌딩 pil·ding building
빌려요 (빌리~) pil·lyŏ·yo (pil·li~) rent v
빗 pit comb n
빛 pit light (brightness) n

## ㅃ

빠른 우편 bba·rŭn u·p'yŏn express mail
빨간 bbal·gan red
빨래 bbal·lae laundry (clothes)
빨래방 bbal·lae·bang launderette
빵 bbang bread
빵집 bbang·tchip bakery
빼고 ppae·go without

## ㅅ

사고 sa·go accident
사랑 sa·rang love n
사랑해요 (사랑하~) sa·rang·hae·yo (sa·rang·ha~) love v
사발 sa·bal bowl (for food) n
사업 sa·ŏp business n
사요 (사~) sa·yo (sa~) buy
사적인 sa·jŏ·gin private a
사전 sa·jŏn dictionary
사진 sa·jin photo
사진 찍어요 (사진 찍~) sa·jin tchi·gŏ·yo (sa·jin tchig~) take a photo
사진술 sa·jin·sul photography
사진작가 sa·jin chak·ka photographer
사치 sa·ch'i luxury
산 san mountain
산책 san·ch'aek walk n
상자 sang·ja box n
상한 sang·han off (spoilt)
새로운 sae·ro·un new
새벽 sae·byŏk dawn

색깔 saek·kal colour n
생년월일 saeng·nyŏn·wŏ·ril date of birth
생리대 saeng·ni·dae sanitary napkin
생선 가게 saeng·sŏn ka·ge fish shop
생수 saeng·su mineral water
생일 saeng·il birthday
샤워 sha·wŏ shower n
서류 sŏ·ryu papers (documents)
서류 가방 sŏ·ryu·ga·bang briefcase
서비스 sŏ·bi·sŭ service n
서양의 sŏ·yang·é Western
서점 sŏ·jŏm book shop
서쪽 sŏ·tchok west
선글라스 sŏn·gŭl·la·sŭ sunglasses
선물 sŏn·mul gift • present n
선생님 sŏn·saeng·nim teacher
선크림 sŏn·k'ŭ·rim sunblock
선탠 로션 sŏn·t'aen ro·shŏn tanning lotion
선편 우편 sŏn·p'yŏn u·p'yŏn surface mail (sea)
선풍기 sŏn·p'ung·gi fan (machine)
설사 sŏl·sa diarrhoea
설탕 sŏl·t'ang sugar
섬 sŏm island
성 sŏng family name • surname
성냥 sŏng·nyang matches (for lighting)
성당 sŏng·dang cathedral
성명 sŏng·myŏng name n pol
성별 sŏng·byŏl sex (gender)
세관 se·gwan customs
세탁기 se·t'ak·ki washing machine
섹스 sek·sŭ sex (intercourse)
센티미터 sen·t'i·mi·t'ŏ centimetre
셀프 서비스 sel·p'ŭ sŏ·bi·sŭ self-service a
셔츠 shŏ·ch'ŭ shirt
소금 so·gŭm salt n
소독약 so·dong·nyak antiseptic n
소리 so·ri sound n
소리가 큰 so·ri·ga k'ŭn loud
소책자 so·ch'aek·cha brochure
소포 so·p'o package • parcel
소풍 so·p'ung picnic n
소화불량 so·hwa bul·lyang indigestion
속옷 so·got underwear

ㅅ

속임수 so·gim·su cheat n
손 son hand
손가락 son·ga·rak finger
손녀 son·nyŏ granddaughter
손목시계 son·mok·shi·gyé watch n
손수건 son·su·gŏn handkerchief
손자 son·ja grandson
손전등 son·jŏn·dŭng flashlight • torch
손톱깎이 son·t'op·kkak·ki nail clippers
솔 sol brush n
쇼 show n
쇼핑 sho·p'ing shopping
쇼핑 센터 sho·p'ing sen·t'ŏ shopping
centre
쇼핑몰 sho·p'ing·mol shopping mall
쇼핑해요 (쇼핑하~) sho·p'ing·hae·yo
(sho·p'ing·ha~) go shopping
수건 su·gŏn towel
수공예품 su·gong·ye·p'um handicraft
수도꼭지 su·dok·kok·chi faucet • tap
수리해요 (수리하~) su·ri·hae·yo
(su·ri·ha~) repair v
수수료 su·su·ryo commission
수신자 부담 통화 su·shin·ja bu·dam
t'ong·hwa collect call
수영장 su·yŏng·jang swimming pool
수영해요 (수영하~) su·yŏng·hae·yo
(su·yŏng·ha~) swim v
수저와 포크 su·jŏ·wa p'o·k'ŭ cutlery
수제 su·jé handmade
수표 su·p'yo cheque (banking)
수하물 su·ha·mul baggage • luggage
수하물 수취대 su·ha·mul su·ch'wi·dae
baggage claim
수하물 허용량 su·ha·mul
hŏ·yong·nyang baggage allowance
수화 su·hwa sign language
숙박 suk·pak accommodation
숟가락 sut·ka·rak spoon n
술 sul alcohol • alcoholic drink
술 취한 sul·ch'wi·han drunk a
술 취해요 (술 취하~) sul·ch'wi·hae·yo
(sul·ch'wi·ha~) be drunk v
술집 sul·chip bar n
숫자 sut·cha number n
숲 sup forest

슈퍼 shu·p'ŏ food shop • grocery
슈퍼마켓 shu·p'ŏ ma·k'et supermarket
스웨터 sŭ·we·t'ŏ jumper • sweater
스카프 sŭ·k'a·p'ŭ scarf
스키 sŭ·k'i ski n • skiing
스타킹 sŭ·t'a·k'ing stockings
스파 sŭ·p'a spa
슬라이드 필름 sŭl·la·i·dŭ p'il·lŭm
slide film
승강장 sŭng·gang·jang platform
승객 sŭng·gaek passenger
승마 sŭng·ma horse riding
시가 shi·ga cigar
시간 shi·gan hour • time n
시간표 shi·gan·p'yo timetable
시골 shi·gol countryside
시끄러운 shik·kŭ·rŏ·un noisy
시끄러워요 (시끄럽~) shik·kŭ·rŏ·wŏ·yo
(shik·kŭ·rŏp~) be noisy v
시내 shi·nae city centre
시내 버스 shi·nae bŏ·sŭ intracity bus
시도해요 (시도하~) shi·do·hae·yo
(shi·do·ha~) try (sample/test) v
시아버지 shi·a·bŏ·ji father-in-law
(husband's father)
시어머니 shi·ŏ·mŏ·ni mother-in-law
(husband's mother)
시작해요 (시작하~) shi·ja·k'ae·yo
(shi·ja·k'a~) begin
시장 shi·jang market (outdoor) n
시차 shi·ch'a time difference
시차증 shi·ch'a·jŭng jet lag
시트 shi·t'ŭ sheet (bed)
식당 shik·tang restaurant
식량 shing·nyang provisions
식사 shik·sa meal
식중독 shik·chung·dok food poisoning
식품점 shik·p'um·jŏm delicatessen
신경 써요 (신경 쓰~) shin·gyŏng
ssŏ·yo (shin·gyŏng ssŭ~) care (about
something)
신문 shin·mun newspaper
신문 가판대 shin·mun ga·p'an·dae
kiosk • newsstand
신발 shin·bal shoes
신발 가게 shin·bal ka·gé shoe shop

신분증 shin·bun·tchŭng identification card (ID)
신선한 shin·sŏn·han fresh
신용카드 shi·nyong k'a dŭ credit card
신원 확인 shin·wŏn hwa·gin identification
신혼 여행 shin·hon yŏ·haeng honeymoon
실외 shi·loé outdoor a
심장 shim·jang heart
심장 상태 shim·jang sang·t'ae heart condition
싱글 shing·gŭl single (person) a
싱글 룸 shing·gŭl·lum single room

## ㅆ

싼 ssan cheap
써요 (쓰~) ssŏ·yo (ssŭ~) write
쓰레기통 ssŭ·re·gi·t'ong garbage can
쓴 ssŭn bitter
씻어요 (씻~) shi·sŏ·yo (shis~) wash v

## ㅇ

아기 a·gi baby
아내 a·nae wife
아들 a·dŭl son
아래로 a·rae·ro down
아름다운 a·rŭm·da·un beautiful
아름다워요 (아름답~) a·rŭm·da·wŏ·yo (a·rŭm·dap~) be beautiful v
아버지 a·bŏ·ji father
아스피린 a·sŭ·p'i·rin aspirin
아이 돌보기 a·i·dol·bo·gi child-minding service
아이스크림 a·i·sŭ·k'ŭ·rim ice cream
아저씨 a·jŏ·shi older man
아주머니 a·ju·mŏ·ni older woman
아침 a·ch'im breakfast • morning
아파트 a·p'a·t'ŭ apartment
아픈 a·p'ŭn ill • sick
안 an not
안경 an·gyŏng glasses (spectacles)
안내 an·nae information
안녕히 가세요 an·nyŏng·hi ka·se·yo goodbye (when staying) pol

안녕히 계세요 an·nyŏng·hi kye·se·yo goodbye (when leaving) pol
안마 an·ma massage n
안마사 an·ma·sa masseur/masseuse
안전 an·jŏn safe n
안전벨트 an·jŏn·bel·t'ŭ seatbelt
알람 시계 al·lam shi·gyé alarm clock
알레르기 al·le·rŭ·gi allergy
알약 al·lyak pill (medicine)
애프터쉐이브 ae·p'ŭ·t'ŏ·she·i·bŭ aftershave
야영해요 (야영하~) ya·yŏng·hae·yo (ya·yŏng·ha~) camp v
야채 ya·ch'ae vegetable n
약 yak drug • medication • medicine
약간 yak·kan some (a little)
약국 yak·kuk chemist • pharmacy
약도 yak·to map (of neighbourhood)
약사 yak·sa chemist • pharmacist
약속 yak·sok appointment
약해요 (약하~) ya·k'ae·yo (ya·k'a~) be weak v
약혼 ya·k'on engagement (to marry)
약혼녀 ya·k'on·nyŏ fiancée
약혼자 ya·k'on·ja fiancé
약혼한 ya·k'on·han engaged (to be married)
양말 yang·mal socks
양복 재단사 yang·bok chae·dan·sa tailor n
어깨 ŏk·kae shoulder
어느 ŏ·nŭ which
어댑터 ŏ·daep·t'ŏ adaptor
어두운 ŏ·du·un dark
어두워요 (어둡~) ŏ·du·wŏ·yo (ŏ·dup~) be dark v
어디 ŏ·di where
어떤 ŏt·tŏn some a
어린이 ŏ·ri·ni child • children (general)
어린이용 좌석 ŏ·ri·ni·yong chwa·sŏk child seat
어머니 ŏ·mŏ·ni mother
어제 ŏ·jé yesterday
언니 ŏn·ni older sister (female speaker)
언어 ŏ·nŏ language

언제 ŏn·jé when
얼굴 ŏl·gul face n
얼음 ŏ·rŭm ice
없어요 (없~) ŏp·sŏ·yo (ŏps~) not be present • not exist
에스컬레이터 e·sŭ·k'ŏl·le·i·t'ŏ escalator
엔지니어 en·ji·n·i·ŏ engineer n
엔진 en·jin engine
엘리베이터 el·li·be·i·t'ŏ elevator • lift
여관 yŏ·gwan motel
여권 yŏk·kwŏn passport
여권번호 yŏk·kwŏn·bŏn·ho passport number
여기 yŏ·gi here
여러분 yŏ·rŏ·bun you pol pl
여러분의 yŏ·rŏ·bu·né your pol pl
여름 yŏ·rŭm summer
여성의 yŏ·sŏng·é female a
여자 yŏ·ja woman
여자 아이 yŏ·ja·a·i girl
여자 친구 yŏ·ja ch'in·gu girlfriend
여행 yŏ·haeng journey n • tour n
여행 복대 yŏ·haeng·bok·tae bumbag
여행 일정 yŏ·haeng il·chŏng itinerary
여행가방 yŏ·haeng·ga·bang suitcase
여행사 yŏ·haeng·sa travel agency
여행자 수표 yŏ·haeng·ja su·p'yo travellers cheque
역 yŏk station
연극 yŏn·gŭk play (theatre) n
연금 생활 자 yŏn·gŭm saeng·hwal·cha pensioner
연필 yŏn·p'il pencil
열 yŏl fever • heat n
열쇠 yŏl·soé key (door, etc)
염좌 yŏm·jwa sprain
엽서 yŏp·sŏ postcard
영사관 yŏng·sa·gwan consulate
영수증 yŏng·su·jŭng receipt n
영어 yŏng·ŏ English (language)
영업 시간 yŏng·ŏp shi·gan opening hours
영화 yŏng·hwa film • movie
영화관 yŏng·hwa·gwan cinema/theatre
예를 들면 ye·rŭl·dŭl·myŏn for example
예방주사 ye·bang·ju·sa vaccination
예산 ye·san budget n
예약 ye·yak reservation (booking)
예약해요 (예약하~) ye·ya·k'ae·yo (ye·ya·k'a~) make a booking
옛것 yet·t'ŏ ruins
오늘 o·nŭl today
오늘 밤 o·nŭl·bam tonight
오래된 o·rae·doén old (things)
오른쪽 o·rŭn·tchok right (direction)
오빠 op·pa older brother (female speaker)
오후 o·hu afternoon
온천 on·ch'ŏn hot spring
옷 ot clothing
옷가게 ok·ka·gé clothing store
와인 wa·in wine
완전 채식주의자 wan·jŏn ch'ae·shik·chu·i·ja vegan n
왕복 표 wang·bok p'yo return ticket
왜 wae why
외국의 oé·gu·gé foreign
외국인 oé·gu·gin foreigner
왼쪽 oén·tchok left (direction)
요금 yo·gŭm fare n
요금 내는 곳 yo·gŭm nae·nŭn·got tollbooth
요리사 yo·ri·sa chef • cook n
요리해요 (요리하~) yo·ri·hae·yo (yo·ri·ha~) cook v
욕실 yok·shil bathroom
우리의 u·ri·é our
우비 u·bi raincoat
우산 u·san umbrella
우스운 u·sŭ·un funny
우유 u·yu milk n
우체국 u·ch'e·guk post office
우체통 u·ch'e·t'ong mailbox
우편 u·p'yŏn mail (postal system) n
우편번호 u·p'yŏn·bŏn·ho postcode
우표 u·p'yo postage stamp
운동용품 가게 un·dong·yong·p'um ka·gé sports store
운전면허증 un·jŏn myŏn·hŏ·jŭng drivers licence
운전해요 (운전하~) un·jŏn·hae·yo (un·jŏn·ha~) drive v

웨이터 we·i·t'ŏ waiter
위 wi stomach
위로 wi·ro up
위에 wi·é on
위장염 wi·jang·nyŏm gastroenteritis
위치 wi·ch'i location
위험한 wi·hŏm·han dangerous
유기농 식품 yu·gi·nong shik·p'um organic food
유로 yu·ro euro
유료 주차 yu·ryo chu·ch'a paid parking
유모차 yu·mo·ch'a stroller (for child)
유스호스텔 yu·sŭ·ho·sŭ·t'el youth hostel
유아식 yu·a·shik baby food
유제품 yu·je·p'um dairy products
육수 yuk·su stock (food)
육아 도우미 yu·ga do·u·mi babysitter
윤활제 yun·hwal·ché lubricant
은 ŭn silver n
은행 ŭn·haeng bank n
은행 계좌 ŭn·haeng kye·jwa bank account
음료수 ŭm·nyo·su drink n
음반 매장 ŭm·ban mae·jang music shop
음식 ŭm·shik food
음악 ŭ·mak music
응급 상황 ŭng·gŭp sang·hwang emergency
의류 매장 ŭi·ryu mae·jang boutique (fashion)
의사 ŭi·sa doctor (medical)
의자 ŭi·ja chair n
의학 ŭi·hak medicine (profession)
이 주일 i·ju·il fortnight
이등 i·dŭng second class n
이른 i·rŭn early adv
이름 i·rŭm first name • name inf
이메일 i·me·il email n
이코노미석 i·k'o·no·mi·sŏk economy class
이혼한 i·hon·han divorced
인터넷 in·t'ŏ·net internet
일 il job
일 인당 i·rin·dang per person

일기 il·gi diary
일반 택시 il·ban t'aek·shi regular taxi
일방통행 il·bang t'ong·haeng one-way
잃어버린 i·rŏ·bŏ·rin lost
임신 중인 im·shin jung·in pregnant
입 ip mouth
입구 ip·ku entrance
입장 ip·chang entry n
입장료 ip·jang·nyo admission (price)
있어요 (있~) iss·ŏ·yo (iss~) be present • exist

## ㅈ

자녀 cha·nyŏ children (offspring)
자동차 등록증 cha·dong·ch'a dŭng·nok·chŭng car registration
자리 cha·ri seat (place) n
자막 cha·mak subtitles
자매 cha·mae sister
자물쇠 cha·mul·soé padlock
자요 (자~) cha·yo (cha~) sleep v
자전거 cha·jŏn·gŏ bicycle
자정 cha·jŏng midnight
작아요 (작~) cha·ga·yo (chak~) be small v
작은 cha·gŭn short (height) • small
잔 chan glass (drinking)
잔돈 chan·don change (coins) n
잘라요 (자르~) chal·la·yo (cha·rŭ~) cut v
잘생긴 chal saeng·gin handsome
잠궈요 (잠그~) cham·gwŏ·yo (cham·gŭ~) lock v
잠긴 cham·gin locked
장갑 chang·gap gloves (clothing)
장마 chang·ma monsoon • rainy season
장모님 chang·mo·nim mother-in-law (wife's mother)
장애인 chang·ae·in disabled person
장인어른 chang·i·nŏ·rŭn father-in-law (wife's father)
재떨이 chaet·tŏ·ri ashtray
재미없는 chae·mi·ŏm·nŭn boring
재미없어요 (재미없~) chae·mi·ŏpsŏ·yo (chae·mi·ŏp~) be boring v

ㅈ

재킷 chae·k'it jacket

저 chŏ I pol • that (away from listener) a

저것 chŏ·gŏt that one (away from listener) pron

저기 chŏ·gi there (away from listener)

저기에 chŏ·gi·é over there

저녁 chŏ·nyŏk dinner • evening

저의 chŏ·é my pol

전기 chŏn·gi electricity

전류 chŏl·lyu current (electricity) n

전망 chŏn·mang view n

전보 chŏn·bo telegram

전부 chŏn·bu everything • whole

전자레인지 chŏn·ja·re·in·ji microwave oven

전자제품 chŏn·ja·je·p'um electronics

전파사 chŏn·p'a·sa electrical store

전화 chŏn·hwa telephone n

전화박스 chŏn·hwa bak·sŭ phone box

전화번호부 chŏn·hwa·bŏn·ho·bu phone book

전화카드 chŏn·hwa k'a·dŭ phonecard

전화해요 (전화하~) chŏn·hwa·hae·yo (chŏn·hwa·ha~) telephone v

점심 chŏm·shim lunch n

접시 chŏp·shi dish n • plate

정각에 chŏng·ga·gé on time

정오 chŏng·o midday • noon

정원 chŏng·wŏn garden n

정육점 chŏng·yuk·chŏm butcher's shop

정확히 chŏng·hwa·k'i exactly

제일 가까운 che·il kak·ka·un nearest

제일 작은 che·il cha·gŭn smallest

제일 큰 che·il·k'ŭn biggest

제한 속도 che·han·sok·to speed limit

조명 측정기 cho·myŏng ch'ŭk·jŏng·gi light meter

조선인민공화국 cho·sŏn in·min kong·hwa·guk Democratic People's Republic of Korea

조용한 cho·yong·han quiet

족집게 chok·chip·ké tweezers

종이 chong·i paper n

좋아요 (좋~) cho·a·yo (cho~) be good v

좋아해요 (좋아하~) cho·a·hae·yo (cho·a·ha~) like v

좋은 cho·ŭn good • great

좌석 버스 chwa·sŏk bŏ·sŭ deluxe metropolitan bus

주 chu week

주류 판매점 chu·ryu p'an·mae·jŏm liquor store

주말 chu·mal weekend

주방 chu·bang kitchen

주사 chu·sa injection

주사바늘 chu·sa·ba·nŭl needle (syringe)

주소 chu·so address n

주유소 chu·yu·so petrol/gas station

주차 빌딩 chu·ch'a bil·ding parking structure

주차 위반 chu·ch'a wi·ban parking violation

주차해요 (주차하~) chu·ch'a·hae·yo (chu·ch'a·ha~) park (a car) v

주황색 chu·hwang·saek orange a

죽여요 (죽이~) chu·gyŏ·yo (chu·gi~) kill

중앙 chung·ang centre n

중요한 chung·yo·han important

중요해요 (중요하~) chung·yo·hae·yo (chung·yo·ha~) be important v

지금 chi·gŭm now

지난 chi·nan last (previous)

지도 chi·do map (of country)

지방에 chi·bang·é local a

지불 chi·bul payment

지연 chi·yŏn delay n

지퍼 chi·p'ŏ zip/zipper

지폐 chi·p'yé banknote

지프차 chi·p'ŭ·ch'a jeep

지하철 chi·ha·ch'ŏl metro (train)

지하철 역 chi·ha·ch'ŏl·yŏk metro station

직업 chi·gŏp profession

직접적인 chik·chŏp·chŏ·gin direct a

직통 전화 chik·t'ong jŏn·hwa direct-dial

진동 chin·dong concussion
진실 chin·shil truth
진통제 chin·t'ong·jé painkiller
짐 보관함 chim po·gwan·ham luggage locker
짐 chim baggage • luggage
집 chip home • house
집세 chip·sé rent n

### ㅉ

짠 jjan salty

### ㅊ

차 ch'a car • tea
차가운 ch'a·ga·un cold (to senses) a
찻숟가락 ch'as·suk·ka·rak teaspoon
찻집 ch'at·chip teahouse
창문 ch'ang·mun window
채식주의자 ch'ae·shik·chu·i·ja vegetarian n
책 ch'aek book n
처방전 ch'ŏ·bang·jŏn prescription
처음으로 ch'ŏ·ŭ·mŭ·ro first adv
철도 ch'ŏl·do railway
첫 ch'ŏt first a
청바지 ch'ŏng·ba·ji jeans
청소 ch'ŏng·so cleaning
청소해요 (청소하~) ch'ŏng·so·hae·yo (ch'ŏng·so·ha~) clean v
체육관 ch'e·yuk·kwan gym (gymnasium)
체조 ch'e·jo gymnastics
체크 인 ch'e·k'ŭ·in check-in (desk)
초과 수하물 ch'o·gwa su·ha·mul excess baggage
초록색 ch'o·rok·saek green a
초콜릿 ch'o·k'ol·lit chocolate
최고의 ch'oé·go·é best
추운 ch'u·un cold (weather) a
추워요 (춥~) ch'u·wŏ·yo (ch'up~) be cold (weather) v
추천해요 (추천하~) ch'u·ch'ŏn·hae·yo (ch'u·ch'ŏn·ha~) recommend
축구 ch'uk·ku football • soccer
출구 ch'ul·gu exit n

출국장 ch'ul·guk·chang departure hall
출발 ch'ul·bal departure
출장 ch'ul·chang business trip
춤 ch'um dance n
춤 춰요 (춤 추~) ch'um·ch'wŏ·yo (ch'um·ch'u~) dance v
충분한 ch'ung·bun·han enough
충치 ch'ung·ch'i dental cavity
취소해요 (취소하~) ch'wi·so·hae·yo (ch'wi·so·ha~) cancel
층 ch'ŭng floor (storey)
치과의사 ch'ik·kwa ŭi·sa dentist
치마 ch'i·ma skirt
치수 ch'i·su size (clothes, shoes) n
치실 ch'i·shil dental floss
치약 ch'i·yak toothpaste
치통 ch'i·t'ong toothache
친구 ch'in·gu friend
친절한 ch'in·jŏl·han kind (nice)
침낭 ch'im·nang sleeping bag
침대 ch'im·dae bed
침대 시트 ch'im·dae shi·t'ŭ bed sheet
침대차 ch'im·dae·ch'a sleeping car
침실 ch'im·shil bedroom
칫솔 ch'is·sol toothbrush

### ㅋ

카메라 k'a·me·ra camera
카세트 k'a·se·t'ŭ cassette
카트 k'a·t'ŭ trolley
카페 k'a·pé cafe
칼 k'al knife n
캔 k'aen can • tin
캔 오프너 k'aen·o·p'ŭ·nŏ can opener • tin opener
캠코더 k'aem·k'o·dŏ video camera
커요 (크~) k'ŏ·yo (k'ŭ~) be big v
커피 k'ŏ·p'i coffee
컬러 필름 k'ŏl·lŏ p'il·lŭm colour film
컴퓨터 k'ŏm·p'yu·t'ŏ computer
컵 k'ŏp cup
코 k'o nose
코르크 따개 k'o·rŭ·k'ŭ tta·gae corkscrew
코트 k'o·t'ŭ coat n • tennis court
콘돔 k'on·dom condom

**DICTIONARY**

콘돔 사용하는 섹스 k'on·dom sa·yong·ha·nŭn sek·sŭ safe sex
콘서트 k'on·sŏ·t'ŭ concert
콘택트 렌즈 k'on·t'aek·t'ŭ ren·jŭ contact lenses
크기 k'ŭ·gi size (general)
큰 k'ŭn big
킬로그램 k'il·lo·gŭ·raem kilogram
킬로미터 k'il·lo·mi·t'ŏ kilometre

**ㅌ**

타고 t'a·go aboard
타요 (타~) t'a·yo (t'a~) board (plane, ship) v
타이어 t'a·i·ŏ tire • tyre
탈 것 t'al·gŏt ride n
탈의실 t'a·ri·shil changing room
탐폰 t'am·p'on tampon
탑승권 t'ap·sŭng·kwŏn boarding pass
태풍 t'ae·p'ung typhoon
택시 정류장 t'aek·shi jŏng·nyu·jang taxi stand
테니스 t'e·ni·sŭ tennis
테니스 경기장 t'e·ni·sŭ kyŏng·gi·jang tennis court
텔레비전 t'el·le·bi·jŏn television
토스터 t'o·sŭ·t'o toaster
통로 t'ong·no aisle (on plane)
통신사 t'ong·shin·sa newsagency
통역사 t'ong·yŏk·sa interpreter
통화 중 t'ong·hwa·jung busy (phone)
튀겨요 (튀기~) t'wi·gyŏ·yo (t'wi·gi~) fry
트윈 베드 t'ŭ·win·be·dŭ twin beds
티브이 t'i·bŭ·i TV
티셔츠 t'i·shŏ·ch'ŭ T-shirt
티슈 t'i·shyu tissues
팁 t'ip cover charge • service charge • tip (gratuity) n

**ㅍ**

파란 p'a·ran blue
파업 p'a·ŏp strike (labour) n
파티 p'a·t'i party (night out) n
팔 p'al arm (body)
패션 p'ae·shŏn fashion n

팩스 p'aek·sŭ fax machine
팬티라이너 p'aen·t'i·ra·i·nŏ panty liners
팬티스타킹 p'aen·t'i·sŭ·t'a·k'ing pantyhose
퍼스트 클래스 p'ŏ·sŭ·t'ŭ k'ŭl·lae·sŭ first class
페리 p'e·ri ferry n
편도 표 p'yŏn·do p'yo one-way ticket
편안한 p'yŏ·nan·han comfortable
편의점 p'yŏ·ni·jŏm convenience store
편지 p'yŏn·ji letter • mail n
편지 부쳐요 (편지 부치~) p'yŏn·ji bu·ch'ŏ·yo (p'yŏn·ji bu·ch'i~) post (letter) v
평평한 p'yŏng·p'yŏng·han flat a
포크 p'o·k'ŭ fork
포함된 p'o·ham·doen included
표 p'yo ticket
표 자판기 p'yo cha·p'an·gi ticket machine
표 파는 곳 p'yo p'a·nŭn·got ticket booth
푸드 코트 p'u·dŭ k'o·t'ŭ food court
푹푹 쪄요 (푹푹 찌~) p'uk·p'uk tchŏ·yo (p'uk·p'uk tchi~) be hot and humid v
풍습 p'ung·sŭp custom
프라이팬 p'ŭ·ra·i·p'aen frying pan
프리마 p'ŭ·ri·ma creamer (for coffee)
프린터 p'ŭ·rin·t'ŏ printer (computer)
플러그 p'ŭl·lŏ·gŭ plug (electricity) n
피곤한 p'i·gon·han tired
피곤해요 (피곤하~) p'i·gon hae·yo (p'i·gon ha~) be tired v
피시방 p'i·shi·bang internet café
필름 p'il·lŭm film (for camera)
필름 감도 p'il·lŭm kam·do film speed

**ㅎ**

하루 ha·ru day
하숙집 ha·suk·chip boarding house
학생 hak·saeng student n
한가한 han·ga·han free (available) a
한국 han·guk Korea
한국어 han·gu·gŏ Korean (language) n
한국의 han·gu·gé Korean a

할머니 hal·mŏ·ni elderly woman •
grandmother
할아버지 ha·ra·bŏ·ji elderly man •
grandfather
할인 ha·rin discount n
항공 우편 hang·gong u·p'yŏn airmail
항공사 hang·gong·sa airline
항생제 hang·saeng·jé antibiotics
해 hae sun • year
해넘이 hae·nŏ·mi sunset
해돋이 hae·do·ji sunrise
해변 hae·byŏn beach (seaside)
해수욕장 hae·su·yok·chang beach
(for swimming)
해외 hae·oé overseas n
핸드백 haen·dŭ·baek handbag • purse
햇빛에 탐 haep·pi·ch'é t'am sunburn
행복한 haeng·bo·k'an happy
행복해요 (행복하~) haeng·bo·k'ae·yo
(haeng·bo·k'a~) be happy v
향수 hyang·su perfume n
허리 hŏ·ri back (body)
헤드라이트 he·dŭ·ra·i·t'ŭ headlights
헤어 커트 he·ŏ·k'ŏ·t'ŭ haircut
헬스장 hel·sŭ·jang gym (health club)
혀 hyŏ tongue
현금 hyŏn·gŭm cash n
현금으로 바꿔요 (현금으로 바꾸~)
hyŏn·gŭ·mŭ·ro pak·kwŏ·yo
(hyŏn·gŭ·mŭ·ro pak·ku~) cash (a
cheque) v
현금인출기 hyŏn·gŭ·min·ch'ul·gi ATM
현대의 hyŏn·dae·é modern
혈액 hyŏ·raek blood
혈액형 hyŏ·rae·k'yŏng blood group
형 hyŏng older brother (male speaker)
형제 hyŏng·jé brother
형편 없는 hyŏng·p'yŏn ŏm·nŭn awful
호수 ho·su lake
호스텔 ho·sŭ·t'el hostel
호텔 ho·t'el hotel
홀로 hol·lo alone
후에 ... hu·é after ...
화상 hwa·sang burn n
화장 hwa·jang make-up n
화장실 hwa·jang·shil toilet

확인해요 (확인하~) hwa·gin·hae·yo
(hwa·gin·ha~) confirm (a booking) •
validate
환불 hwan·bul refund n
환승 라운지 hwan·sŭng ra·un·ji
transit lounge
환율 hwa·nyul exchange rate
환자 hwan·ja patient n
환전해요 (환전하~) hwan·jŏn·hae·yo
(hwan·jŏn·ha~) change (money) v
회사 hoé·sa company (firm)
회색의 hoé·sae·gé grey
회의 hoé·i conference
회화책 hoé·hwa·ch'aek phrasebook
훔친 hum·ch'in stolen
휘발유 hwi·bal·yu gas • petrol
휠체어 hwil·ch'é·ŏ wheelchair
휴가 hyu·ga vacation
휴대폰 hyu·dae·p'on cell/mobile phone
휴대품 보관소 hyu·dae·p'um
bo·gwan·so cloakroom
휴무 hyu·mu closed
휴식 시간 hyu·shik shi·gan intermission
휴양지 hyu·yang·ji resort n
흑백 필름 hŭk·paek·p'il·lŭm B&W film
흡연 구역 hŭ·byŏn ku·yŏk smoking area
희귀한 hi·gwi·han rare (uncommon)
흰 hin white
히치하이크해요 (히치하이크하~)
hi·ch'i·ha·i·k'ŭ·hae·yo
(hi·ch'i·ha·i·k'ŭ·ha~) hitchhike v
히터 hi·t'ŏ heater

ㅎ

**KOREAN** *to* **ENGLISH**

# Index

For topics that are covered in several sections of this book, we've indicated the most relevant page number in bold.

INDEX

# **10 Ways** to Start a Sentence

| | | |
|---|---|---|
| **When's (the next bus)?** | (다음 버스) 언제 있나요? | (ta·ŭm bŏ·sŭ) ŏn·jé in·na·yo |
| **Where's (the train/ subway station)?** | (역) 어디예요? | (yŏk) ŏ·di·ye·yo |
| **Where do I (buy a ticket)?** | 어디에서 (표 사나요)? | ŏ·di·e·sŏ (p'yo sa·na·yo) |
| **I'm looking for (a hotel).** | (호텔) 찾고 있어요. | (ho·t'el) ch'ak·ko iss·ŏ·yo |
| **Do you have (a map)?** | (지도) 가지고 계신가요? | (chi·do) ka·ji·go kye·shin·ga·yo |
| **Is there (a toilet)?** | (화장실) 있나요? | (hwa·jang·shil) in·na·yo |
| **I'd like (the menu).** | (메뉴) 주세요. | (me·nyu) ju·se·yo |
| **I'd like to (hire a car).** | (차 빌리고) 싶어요. | (ch'a pil·li·go) shi·p'ŏ·yo |
| **Do I need (a visa)?** | (비자) 필요 한가요? | (pi·ja) p'i·ryo·han·ga·yo |
| **I have (a passport).** | (여권) 있어요. | (yŏk·kwŏn) iss·ŏ·yo |